I0464745

CYBARIS®
AN INTELLECTUAL PROPERTY
LAW REVIEW

Volume 7        2016        Issue 2

EDITOR-IN-CHIEF
Molly R. Littman

EXECUTIVE EDITORS
Joseph Dubis
Kelly Fermoyle

NOTES & COMMENTS EDITORS

Bryan Jarvis        Caitlin Kowalke        Jaime Sekenski

STAFF

| | | |
|---|---|---|
| Karen Beckman | Jacob Crawford | Reed Grimwood |
| Lars Gunnerson | Trevor Haney | Alissa Harrington |
| Wojciech Jankiewicz | John Kuehl | Landon Larivee |
| Chad Reverman | Elizabeth Scheibel | Christopher Tebow |

FACULTY ADVISOR
Ken Port

2016

Cybaris®, an Intellectual Property Law Review, is published two times per year by the students of the Intellectual Property Institute of Mitchell Hamline School of Law at 875 Summit Avenue, Saint Paul, Minnesota, 55105. Telephone: 651-290-6425. E-mail: eic.cybaris@mitchellhamline.edu

Manuscripts: Cybaris®, an Intellectual Property Law Review, welcomes unsolicited manuscripts. All manuscripts submitted for consideration should be double spaced, with citations placed in footnotes that conform to THE BLUEBOOK: A UNIFORM SYSTEM OF CITATION (20th ed. 2015). Please forward all submissions to the Cybaris® Editorial Office at the address listed above.

CYBARIS®
AN INTELLECTUAL PROPERTY
LAW REVIEW

Volume 7                    2016                    Issue 2

*Articles*

# COPYRIGHT'S NOT SO LITTLE SECRET: THE ORPHAN WORKS PROBLEM AND PROPOSED ORPHAN WORKS LEGISLATION
### AARON C. YOUNG, JD, LLM[1]

> "Whenever a copyright law is to be made or altered, then the idiots assemble"[2]

---

[1] Aaron C. Young is a 2001 graduate of Marquette University Law School in Milwaukee, WI, and a 2003 graduate of the Entertainment & Media Law Master of Laws program at Southwestern Law School, Los Angeles, CA. Aaron is a former Adjunct Professor of Law at Hamline University School of Law teaching Sports Law, Adjunct Professor of Law at William Mitchell College of Law teaching Client Representation, and Adjunct Professor at McNally Smith College of Music teaching Legal Aspects of Music & Entertainment. Special thanks to my proofreaders: my mother, Juanita Young, and my part-time paralegal and full-time friend, Katherine Finn.

I.          INTRODUCTION

What is an orphan work? When you hear the term "orphan work," do you immediately think of a copyright dressed in rags and holding a bowl saying, "Please, sir, I want some more?" à la Mark Lester as the orphan Oliver in the movie of the same name?[3] Have you ever interacted with, viewed, read, heard, or used an orphan work? Are you an author of an orphan work? These are all important questions regarding the issues of orphan works in the United States and, more broadly, the entire world. The answer to at least one of these questions is almost certainly "yes" for the vast majority of the United States population, even though most people probably do not realize it.

The majority of twentieth and twenty-first century original works of authorship probably fall within a general definition of orphan works.[4] It has been estimated that up to ninety percent of all works presently under copyright fall within a definition of orphan works.[5] These numbers and the severity of the orphan works problem, however, are by no means universally accepted. Certain national trade groups and unions have disputed the severity or actual existence of an orphan works problem.[6] The Copyright Office, however, refutes these views as outliers from the general consensus that a substantial orphan works problem is at hand.[7]

The explosion in the number of photographs taken since the year 2000 is a prime example of the increase in the number of copyrighted works created and the potential for exasperation from the orphan works problem. Kodak estimated that 80 billion photographs

---

[2] *Copyright*, TWAINQUOTES.COM, http://www.twainquotes.com/Copyright.html (last visited May 14, 2016) (collecting quotes by Mark Twain by subject).

[3] OLIVER! (Columbia Pictures 1968).

[4] CENTER FOR THE STUDY OF THE PUB. DOMAIN. DUKE LAW SCH., ORPHAN WORKS ANALYSIS AND PROPOSAL 2 (Mar. 2005), https://web.law.duke.edu/cspd/pdf/cspdproposal.pdf [hereinafter ORPHAN WORKS ANALYSIS AND PROPOSAL]; *Orphan Works*, CENTER FOR THE STUDY OF THE PUB. DOMAIN, https://web.law.duke.edu/cspd/orphanworks.html (last visited May 14, 2016).

[5] Helen Sedwick, *The Problem of Orphan Works*, HELEN SEDWICK (Nov. 22, 2015), http://helensedwick.com/the-problem-of-orphan-works/.

[6] U.S. COPYRIGHT OFFICE, ORPHAN WORKS AND MASS DIGITIZATION: A REPORT OF THE REGISTER OF COPYRIGHTS 37 (June 2015), http://copyright.gov/orphan/reports/orphan-works2015.pdf [hereinafter ORPHAN WORKS AND MASS DIGITIZATION] (referencing statements by the Authors Guild, Inc. and the National Writers Union).

[7] *Id.* at 37–38.

were taken worldwide in the year 2000, which set a new record for photos taken in a year.[8] It is estimated that more than 1 trillion photographs were taken worldwide in 2015.[9] Of those one trillion photos taken, an estimated 748 billion were taken using cameras in phones.[10] Now imagine how those billions and billions of photographs are made public through sharing in social media and mobile applications.

Facebook, at the close of 2015, had over 1.5 billion monthly active users worldwide who posted 300 million photos per day.[11] According to Snapchat, a photo sharing application, in mid-2015 there were 8,796 photos shared every second. That equates to 759,974,400 photos shared per day by users on the application.[12] These statistics do not take into account other photo sharing sites such as Whatsapp, Flickr, Pinterest, or Tapiture, among many others, that also account for millions of photo postings each day.[13] The sharing and re-sharing of billions of photographs each year will likely lead to a loss of the identity of the original owner of photographs and an explosion in the number of works that fall within a general definition of orphan works.

This proliferation of authorship, in part due to technological advancements like the camera phone, has created a vast ocean of works whose authorship is often difficult to ascertain at best and absolutely indeterminable at worst . These orphan works are then left to live in the orphanage of copyright limbo, neither able to further the advancement of culture through their use nor able to benefit their authors through licensing and monetization. Due to this, the issue of orphan works

---

[8] Stephen Heyman, *Photos, Photos Everywhere*, N.Y. TIMES (July 29, 2015), http://www.nytimes.com/2015/07/23/arts/international/photos-photos-everywhere.html?_r=0.

[9] *Id.*; Jaron Schneider, *Infographics: There Will Be One Trillion Photos Taken in 2015*, RESOURCE MAG. (Dec. 12, 2014), http://resourcemagonline.com/2014/12/infographic-there-will-be-one-trillion-photos-taken-in-2015/45332/.

[10] *Id.*

[11] *The Top 20 Valuable Facebook Statistics – Updated December* 2015, ZEPHORIA DIGITAL MARKETING, https://zephoria.com/top-15-valuable-facebook-statistics/ (last visited May 14, 2016).

[12] *If you were to view all the photos shared on Snapchat in the last hour how long would it take?*, CEWE-PHOTOWORLD.COM, https://cewe-photoworld.com/how-big-is-snapchat/ (last visited May 14, 2016); Kimberlee Morrison, *How Many Photos Are Uploaded to Snapchat Every Second?*, SOCI. TIMES (Jun. 9, 2015, 10:00 AM), http://www.adweek.com/socialtimes/how-many-photos-are-uploaded-to-snapchat-every-second/621488.

[13] Morrison, *supra* note 12.

legislation has been a growing topic of interest for inclusion into the United States Copyright Act.

The issue of orphan works legislation has been kicked around, debated, lamented, and generally stressed over for more than a decade in the United States. This handwringing over orphan works legislation has not been, and is not, a one-sided affair. Both the creators of original works of authorship and potential users of those works have had, and continue to have, serious reservations concerning the potential passage of orphan works legislation and the potential impact thereof.

On June 4, 2015, the United States Copyright Office issued *Orphaned Works and Mass Digitalization: A Report of the Register of Copyright*[14] ("2015 Report"). The 2015 Report, in part, outlines the Copyright Office's proposal for orphan works legislation and the reasoning behind the recommendations. The 2015 Report was lauded by many as the best-yet proposed solution to the orphan works issue in the United States. At the same time, it also brought a firestorm of anger and dread that the solutions proposed by the 2015 Report would strip authors of their basic right and ability to control their own works.

There can be little argument that the orphan works issue has become divisive and hyperbolic in the United States. A basic Internet search of "orphan works" finds thousands search results on the subject.[15] In general, the spectrum of many of the search results range from "the sky is falling" alarmism that the government is going to take away copyrights from authors and make works available for use by anyone without regard for the author to even-minded, thoughtful analysis of proposed orphan works legislation to cheerleaders for addressing the orphan works issue with very little regard for authors.[16]

This paper will examine the issue of orphan works in general, issues that orphan works legislation brings into question, and the legislation proposed by the Copyright Office in the 2015 Report. This paper will then offer analysis and recommendations regarding the handling of orphan works in the United States. As there is presently no statutory law regarding orphan works in the United States, this paper

---

[14] ORPHAN WORKS AND MASS DIGITIZATION, *supra* note 6.

[15] *Orphan Works – Google Search*, GOOGLE, https://www.google.com/search?sourceid=chrome-psyapi2&ion=1&espv=2&ie=UTF-8&q=Orphan%20Works&oq=Orphan%20Works&aqs=chrome.0.69i59j0l5.1906j0j7 (last visited May 14, 2016).

[16] *See e.g., A Little More Orphan Works*, RICHMOND ILLUSTRATION, INC., (JULY 21, 2015), http://www.tomrichmond.com/2015/07/21/a-little-more-orphan-works/ (spanning all three categories).

will focus on the perspectives of numerous groups, including: artists, non-profit institutions, for-profit companies, and the Copyright Office. Finally, this paper will endeavor to provide observations and analyses that are applicable to academic readers, practitioners, and laypersons.

## II.      ORPHAN WORKS IN THEORY

Prior to delving into an analysis of the 2015 Report and considering recommendations for future legislation, it is important to get a perspective of the state of orphan works today. This understanding includes: how orphan works are defined in the legal profession; , what falls within the definition of orphan works; and what, if anything, could possibly be excluded from orphan works.

### A.   Orphan Works Generally Defined

What is the definition of orphan works? It depends upon whom you ask. There is no official, codified definition of orphan works. The Copyright Act of 1976 does not address or define orphan works. The "Report on Orphaned Works" issued by the Copyright Office in 2006 ("2006 Report") defines orphan works as: "a term used to describe the situation where the owner of a copyrighted work cannot be identified and located by someone who wishes to make use of the work in a manner that requires permission of the copyright owner."[17]

This definition, however, was never codified or officially adopted. The 2015 Report discusses orphan works in depth but never provides a standalone definition of orphan works. However, the 2015 Report does include a Federal Register entry for notice of inquiry regarding the 2015 Report that notes and expands on the 2006 Report definition: "An 'orphan work' is an original work of authorship for which a good faith, prospective user cannot readily identify and/or locate the copyright owner(s) in a situation where permission from the copyright owner(s) is necessary as a matter of law."[18]

By researching beyond the Copyright Office, a number of differing definitions of orphan works can be found. The *NOLO Plain-Language Dictionary* takes a more simplistic approach, defining orphan works as: "Works protected under copyright whose owners are difficult

---

[17] U.S. COPYRIGHT OFFICE, REPORT ON ORPHAN WORKS: A REPORT OF THE REGISTER OF COPYRIGHTS 1 (Jan. 2006), http://copyright.gov/orphan/orphan-report.pdf.
[18] ORPHAN WORKS AND MASS DIGITIZATION, *supra* note 6, app. B.

to locate -- for example, a photograph taken of Elvis Presley as a teenager, or a newspaper column from a 1950s newspaper."[19]

The Cornell University Law School's Legal Information Institute has also adopted the NOLO definition.[20] USLegal.com defines an orphan work as:

> Orphan works are works which are under copyright, but whose owner or the estate either cannot be found or cannot be identified. Sometimes the name of the creator or copyright owner may be known but other than the name no information can be established. Other reasons for a work to be orphan include that the copyright owner is unaware of their ownership or that the copyright owner has died and it is not possible to establish to whom ownership of the copyright has passed.[21]

Legal standards such as Black's Law Dictionary[22] and the FindLaw Legal Dictionary[23] have no listings for or definitions of "orphan works" at all.

An examination of the varying definitions brings to light a number of general similarities but also a glaring lack of specific similarities. The overarching issue in all definitions of orphan works is: who is the owner of the copyright in question?, and, can that copyright owner be contacted? There are other substantive issues to be considered when defining orphan works that are not expressly covered in any of the definitions above.

*B.   Is a Work Truly an Orphan or Only Anti-Social?*

When professionals and scholars in the legal profession cannot make a determination of what constitutes orphan works, it is unlikely

---

[19] *Orphan Works*, NOLO'S PLAIN-ENGLISH DICTIONARY, http://www.nolo.com/dictionary/orphan-works-term.html (last visited May 14, 2016).
[20] *Orphan works*, CORNELL UNIV. L. SCH.: LEGAL INFO. INST., https://www.law.cornell.edu/wex/orphan_works (last visited May 14, 2016).
[21] *Orphan Work Law & Legal Definition*, USLEGAL.COM, http://definitions.uslegal.com/o/orphan-work/ (last visited May 14, 2016).
[22] THE LAW DICTIONARY, http://thelawdictionary.org (last visited May 14, 2016) ("[f]eaturing" *Black's Law Dictionary*).
[23] *FindLaw Legal Dictionary*, FINDLAW, http://dictionary.findlaw.com (last visited May 14, 2016).

that a non-legal professional or copyright owner will have much luck doing so or even be familiar with the term "orphan works." A comparison of the language of the differing definitions of orphan works illustrates a significant issue in addressing the orphan works problem; what, exactly, constitutes an orphan work?

For the moment, let us accept the basic premise, for argument's sake, that an orphan work is a work of authorship whose owner cannot be readily identified and/or located by a prospective user of the work in question and for which a license would more likely than not be required from the copyright owner for the proposed use. Now consider a situation in which an owner of a copyrighted work can be identified and can be located but simply refuses to reply or have any contact with the proposed licensor of the copyrighted work. If the artist is a recluse, à la J.D. Salinger, or living off the grid, and affirmatively chooses to ignore all requests for a license, does this make the work an orphan?

According to the 2015 Report, these types of situations may or may not create an orphan work situation. In the 2015 Report, the act of locating the owner of a copyright is consistently equated with a response from the copyright owner in order to avoid the work being designated as an orphan work. The issue of an intentionally non-responsive copyright owner is never addressed. However, it is addressed in the proposed orphan works legislation, which states that if a copyright owner fails to respond to "any inquiry or other communication," the non-response by the copyright owner is not enough to qualify as a diligent search.[24] This could be read to mean non-responses to multiple requests in conjunction with other searches would be enough to qualify as a diligent search for the purpose of an orphan works limitation of liability. A potential user could make a reasonable argument that multiple non-responses to license requests submitted to a copyright owner's last known address indicate that the copyright owner cannot be "located." If the copyright owner cannot be "located" and other diligent searches have been performed, the work could then be designated an orphan work because the copyright owner chose not to respond to the license requests. This situation could create an affirmative duty on the part of the copyright owner to respond to all

---

[24] Orphan Works and Mass Digitization, *supra* note 6, app. A at 3–4 (giving proposed language for amended 17 U.S.C. § 514(b)(2)(A)(iv)(II)).

copyright license requests in order to avoid an orphan work designation for the work requested.

The establishment of an affirmative duty on the part of all copyright owners to reply to all licensing requests creates a consequential new burden upon copyright owners. This situation would be a significant departure from the general premise that copyright owners have the right to control their copyrights as they see fit with the affirmative duty of obtaining a license on the prospective user. This scenario, although potentially in the minority of licensing requests, is nonetheless important to consider, as this could be the creation of a new affirmative duty on the part of the copyright owner, which would be a significant departure from the present requirements of copyright owners. The examination of a situation similar to this one leads to the consideration of what other tenets of copyright might be affected if orphan works legislation is enacted.

## C.  The Inclusion of Unpublished Works in Orphan Works

The question of whether both published and unpublished works should be included within the definition of orphan works is controversial and sharply contested. As a matter of practicality, the issue of what constitutes a published work is itself sharply debated. While this paper does not fully discuss what constitutes published and unpublished works,[25] it is important to address the published and unpublished works issue as it pertains to the orphan works discussion.

The inclusion of unpublished works into the orphan works discussion must bring about the recognition that a copyright owner generally has the right to control the first publication of a work.[26] The right to first publication, although not expressly set forth within 17 U.S.C. § 106, is addressed in several other sections of the 1976 Copyright Act, including sections 108 and 115.[27] Furthermore, the United States Supreme Court in *Harper & Row Publishers, Inc. v.*

---

[25] For more information on the issue of what constitutes a published work, see generally RayMing Chang, *Publication Does Not Really Mean Publication: The Need to Amend the Definition of Publication in the Copyright Act*, 33 AIPLA Q.J. 225 (2005), and Deborah R. Gerhardt, *Copyright Publication: An Empirical Study*, 87 NOTRE DAME L. REV. 135 (2011). *See also* Thomas F. Cotter, *Toward a Functional Definition of Publication in Copyright Law*, 92 MINN. L. REV. 1724, 1770 (2008).
[26] ORPHAN WORKS AND MASS DIGITIZATION, *supra* note 6, at 85 n.346 (citing Harper & Row Publishers, Inc. v. Nation Enters., 471 U.S. 539, 553 (1985)).
[27] *Id.*

*Nation Enterprises* stated that "[t]he fact that a work is unpublished is a critical element of its 'nature.'"[28] Although *Harper & Row* was a case dealing with fair use, the Court did not qualify that statement as only applying to the fair use analysis.

The acknowledgement by the Court of the importance of whether a work is published or unpublished should cause pause when considering if orphan works should include unpublished works. If being unpublished is a "critical element" to the "nature" of the work's copyright, then the next question must be: What constitutes publication? Again, this is not an easy question to answer. The Copyright Act of 1976 defines publication as:

> "Publication" is the distribution of copies or phonorecords of a work to the public by sale or other transfer of ownership, or by rental, lease, or lending. The offering to distribute copies or phonorecords to a group of persons for purposes of further distribution, public performance, or public display, constitutes publication. A public performance or display of a work does not of itself constitute publication.
>
> To perform or display a work "publicly" means—
>
> (1) to perform or display it at a place open to the public or at any place where a substantial number of persons outside of a normal circle of a family and its social acquaintances is gathered; or
> (2) to transmit or otherwise communicate a performance or display of the work to a place specified by clause (1) or to the public, by means of any device or process, whether the members of the public capable of receiving the performance or display receive it in the same place or in separate places and at the same time or at different times.[29]

This definition, however, is not as straightforward as it may first appear. Because this definition of publication was created prior to the

---

[28] *Harper & Row Publishers*, 471 U.S. at 564 (citing 3 NIMMER 13.05[A]; Joseph R. Re, Comment, *Stage of Publication as a 'Fair Use' Factor:* Harper & Row, Publishers Inc. v. Nation Enterprises, 58 ST. JOHN'S L. REV. 597, 613 (1984)).
[29] 17 U.S.C. § 101 (2012).

advent of the Internet and digital distribution, it has not been able to keep pace with the rapid development of technology. The Copyright Office stated in a Circular that the 17 U.S.C. § 101 definition of "publication" does not address online transmission of works and that it is up to the person filing for a copyright to make the determination whether a work had been published or not at the time of copyright application.[30]

The courts have made numerous rulings since the adoption of the "publication" definition in 17 U.S.C. § 101 that have created significant confusion in determining when publication has actually occurred. Three rulings out of the Southern District of New York highlight this confusion. The court in *Getaped.com, Inc. v. Cangemi* ruled that the posting of a webpage was enough to constitute publication.[31] The court in *Einhorn v. Mergatroyd Productions* found that a posting of an off Broadway play performance on the Internet did not constitute publication, even if it did constitute distribution, due to a lack of commercial exploitation, which the court said was required for publication.[32] The court in *McLaren v. Chico's FAS, Inc.* found that the mere posting of images onto a website did not rise to the level of publication.[33]

Cases from a variety of other courts further illustrate the inconsistencies in this area. A court in the Northern District of California commented that the act of posting a website online and making it open to the public was enough to constitute publication.[34] Another court in the Southern District of Florida ruled that the posting of a music file to the Internet was enough to constitute publication, if the music file was available to be downloaded by the public.[35] But, a court in the Southern District of Texas ruled that the posting of webpages online was not enough to constitute distribution of the webpages and therefore did not rise to the level of publication.[36]

---

[30] U.S. COPYRIGHT OFFICE, CIRCULAR 66, COPYRIGHT REGISTRATION FOR ONLINE WORKS 3 (2009), http://www.copyright.gov/circs/circ66.pdf [hereinafter CIRCULAR 66].
[31] Getaped.com, Inc. v. Cangemi, 188 F. Supp. 2d 398, 402 (S.D.N.Y. 2002). This decision has been significantly criticized. *See e.g.* RayMing Chang, *supra* note 25, at 239.
[32] Einhorn v. Mergatroyd Prods., 426 F. Supp. 2d 189, 197 (S.D.N.Y. 2006).
[33] McLaren v. Chico's FAS, Inc., No. 10 Civ. 2481(JSR), 2010 WL 4615772, at *4 (S.D.N.Y. Nov. 9, 2010).
[34] Sleep Sci. Partners v. Lieberman, No. 09-04200 CW, 2010 WL 1881770, at *6 (N.D. Cal. May 10, 2010).
[35] Kernal Records Oy v. Mosley, 794 F. Supp. 2d 1355, 1364 (S.D. Fla. 2011).
[36] Rogers v. Better Bus. Bureau of Metro. Houston, Inc., No. H-10-3741 (Aug. 15, 2011).

Adding to the confusion of what constitutes publication for the purpose of copyright is the consideration of when a particular copyrighted work was potentially published. The applicable definition for what constitutes publication depends on when the publication supposedly took place.[37] If the purported publication of a work took place prior to January 1, 1978, then the present statutory definition, set forth above, would not be applied. The copyright holder or the court would be required to determine what constituted publication under the law at the time the work was claimed to be published.

Taking into consideration the above issues of defining what constitutes publication, when and if publication occurred, and the Copyright Office's admission that technology issues have out-stretched the pre-Internet Copyright Act, it is not difficult to imagine an untenable situation arising if unpublished works were excluded from orphan works legislation. The exclusion of unpublished works from any orphan works legislation would potentially create more of a quagmire within the United States copyright system than presently exists with no orphan works legislation. Each potential designation of a work as an orphan work could be challenged on the grounds of publication, potentially clogging the courts with thousands of cases over publication or lack thereof.

While copyright owners' rights to control first publication are important, they are by no means sacrosanct. The Copyright Office acknowledges that the definition of "publication" in 17 U.S.C. § 101 is out of date and in need of revision.[38] The courts, as set forth above, have provided very little continuity in determining what constitutes publication and how the statutory definition should be interpreted and applied. Some courts appear to have broadened the definition of publication in some circumstances in an attempt to address new issues in on-line publication that were not foreseeable by the drafters of the 1976 Copyright Act. As distasteful as it might be for copyright owners, the inclusion of unpublished works must necessarily be included in any orphan works legislation in order to create a semi-functional orphan works solution.

---

[37] Cotter *supra* note 25, at 1726; Gerhardt *supra* note 25, at 6.
[38] CIRCULAR 66, *supra* note 30.

III.     PROPOSED ORPHAN WORKS LEGISLATION

The Copyright Office states in the 2015 Report, "[t]he goal of any orphan works provision should be to unite owners and users."[39] To this end, the Copyright Office proposed a general "limited liability" model of orphan works legislation that it believes will be the best fit for the United States copyright system.[40] This model would apply to both commercial and noncommercial actors and have an eye on global copyright developments.[41] The 2015 Report also set forth a number of specific recommendations for the application of future orphan works legislation.

A.   Case-By-Case v. Systematic Analysis

Following the release of the 2015 Report, one of the many concerns reported throughout the blogosphere was concern over a mass taking of copyright owners' rights.[42] The perception by some was that the new orphan works recommendations were set to broadly designate huge groups of works as orphan works for anyone to use and profit from with no concern for the copyright owner. This could not be further from the truth.

This confusion may have arisen due to the 2015 Report's dual purpose: addressing both orphan works and mass digitalization. The 2015 Report takes drastically different approaches to each issue, addressing orphan works on a case-by-case basis and mass

---

[39] ORPHAN WORKS AND MASS DIGITIZATION, *supra* note 6, at 60.

[40] *Id.* at 3.

[41] *Id.*

[42] *See generally* Brad Holland, *The Return of Orphan Works: "The Next Great Copyright Act,"* POOR BRADFORD'S ALMANAC (Jul. 2, 2015), http://www.drawger.com/holland/?article_id=15400; Brett, *Don't Believe the Hyperbole, There's No Orphan Works Law Before Congress (Updated)*, GRAPHIC POLICY: WHERE BOOKS AND POLITICS MEET... (Jul. 20, 2015), http://graphicpolicy.com/2015/07/20/dont-believe-the-hyperbole-theres-no-orphan-works-law-before-congress/; *Google Prevails in Copyright Lawsuit*, ILLUSTRATOR'S P'SHIP ORPHAN WORKS BLOG (Oct. 16, 2015), http://ipaorphanworks.blogspot.com; Katie Lane, *What's This "Orphan Works" Business About?*, WORK MADE FOR HIRE (Jul. 2015), http://www.workmadeforhire.net/the-rest/whats-this-orphan-works-business-about/; Sedwick, *supra* note 5; Michael Zhang, *Orphan Works Copyright Law Being Considered Again in the US*, PETAPIXEL (Jul. 21, 2015), http://petapixel.com/2015/07/21/orphan-works-copyright-law-being-considered-again-in-the-us/.

digitalization on a blanket systematic basis,[43] although this may not
always be clear to the casual reader. One of the other areas that may
have exacerbated copyright owners' concerns was that the 2015 Report
focused heavily on nonprofit institutions, such as archives, educational
institutions, libraries, museums, and public broadcasters, and the
problems that these institutions faced regarding orphan works in their
collections.[44] Nevertheless, the 2015 Report specifically set forth that
the entire recommendation on the orphan works problem was based
upon a case-by-case application.[45] This recommendation of a case-by-
case application, however, is not universally applauded.

     There are factions within the groups of archives, libraries, and
museums that contend that a case-by-case system is overly burdensome
and completely unworkable for institutions that may hold hundreds or
thousands of works that could be orphaned.[46] These groups are
concerned that the steps that would be required to be taken in order to
reach the orphan works limitation on liability would be so time
consuming and expensive as to make their execution untenable.[47]

     The Copyright Office recognized the concerns of nonprofit
institutions and formulated an extended safe harbor for nonprofit
educational institutions, museums, libraries, archives, and public
broadcasting entities.[48] The extended safe harbor for these nonprofit
institutions would provide for further limited liability for qualifying
uses. If a qualifying nonprofit could show that it had: 1) complied with
the other orphan works safe harbor requirements; 2) performed the
infringement without any intent of direct or indirect commercial
advantage; 3) used the orphan work primarily for educational, religious,
or charitable purposes; and 4) promptly ceased use of the orphan work
upon notification of copyright infringement from the copyright owner,
then a court would be barred from ordering the nonprofit institution to
pay even reasonable compensation for the use of the work.[49] However,
this extended safe harbor would not be applicable to qualifying

---

[43] ORPHAN WORKS AND MASS DIGITIZATION *supra* note 6, at 72.
[44] *Id.* at 38, 64.
[45] *Id.* at 2, 34, 72.
[46] *Id.* at 52, 60, 61.
[47] *Id.*
[48] ORPHAN WORKS AND MASS DIGITIZATION, *supra* note 6, at 64–65.
[49] *Id.*.

nonprofit institutions that did not comply with all of the requirements set forth above.[50]

The Copyright Office noted in the 2015 Report that nonprofit educational institutions, museums, libraries, archives, and public broadcasting entities use of works for educational, religious, or charitable purposes may tangentially touch on commercial use as well.[51] The inclusion of the qualifier "primarily" in step 3 of the nonprofit extended safe harbor is intentional. The 2015 Report acknowledges that nonprofit educational, religious, or charitable purposes may at times generate minor commercial revenue. The Copyright Office makes clear that potential for minor commercial revenue is not an automatic disqualifier from the nonprofit extended safe harbor. As long as the purpose is primarily for nonprofit educational, religious, or charitable purposes, that is enough to qualify for the orphan works nonprofit extended safe harbor.

The Copyright Office also noted in the 2015 Report that a case-by-case application instead of blanket systematic uses would provide greater protection for copyright owners.[52] This would be achieved through the prerequisite that each potential user of a work be required to take the appropriate steps to reach the orphan works limitation on liability. No potential user of a work would be allowed to free ride on the prior research and filing of a previous user.[53] By each potential user being required to do the appropriate research and file the required forms, it is presumed to be more likely that a copyright owner may be identified and contacted before a future use of the owner's copyrighted work.[54] Through these required steps, it is then more likely to put the copyright owner on notice that the work in question may be considered an orphan work by other potential users, as well as providing the copyright owner with possible licensing fees for the work.

The result is that a case-by-case system is friendlier to copyright owners due to the requirement of individual research into each orphan work prior to the application of an orphan works limitation of liability, thus creating a greater chance of identifying the copyright

---

[50] *Id.* at 65–66 (noting that not all nonprofit organizations are non-commercial in their business activities and discussing the effect of those activities on the market).
[51] *Id.*
[52] *Id.* at 72.
[53] *Id.* at 64.
[54] ORPHAN WORKS AND MASS DIGITIZATION, *supra* note 6, at 2–4.

owner and removing that work from an orphan work designation. At the same time, the case-by-case system also takes into consideration the importance of protecting nonprofit institutions and the work that they do in the preservation of works.

## B.   Reaching the Orphan Works Limitation on Liability

The 2015 Report proposes a two-step process for inclusion in the proposed orphan works legislation.[55] These steps, as part of the limited liability scheme proposal, would be requirements for any orphan work user before receiving the orphan works limitation of liability protection.

### 1.   Good Faith Diligent Search

Anyone that has ever done any type of copyright clearance is familiar with the research that goes into making sure that all of the proper rights are acquired and that nothing is missed. The research can be time intensive and involves searching broad and diverse realms. This is precisely what the Copyright Office proposes to be Step One in order to reach the orphan works limitation on liability: a "good faith diligent search."[56]

#### a.   Domestic Searches

The 2015 Report proposes to "[d]efine a diligent search as, at a minimum, searching Copyright Office records; searching sources of copyright authorship, ownership, and licensing; using technology tools; and using databases, all as reasonable and appropriate under the circumstances."[57] However, the 2015 Report goes on to specify that a search is only diligent if a user searches and utilizes, "(1) Copyright Office online records; (2) reasonably available sources of copyright authorship and ownership information, including licensor information where appropriate; (3) technology tools and, where reasonable, expert assistance (such as a professional researcher or attorney); and (4) appropriate databases, including online databases."[58]

---

[55] *Id.* at 3–4.
[56] *Id.* at 56.
[57] *Id.* at 3 (emphasis added).
[58] *Id.* at 57 (emphasis added).

As discussed previously, each use is evaluated on a case-by-case basis, and each search must be reasonable for the individual case and circumstances. A good faith diligent search for the copyright owner of a book or a play may require a user to search Copyright Office online records, perform an extensive online search through an internet search engine, and contact and search various libraries and/or archives. A good faith diligent search for the copyright owner of a musical composition may include a search of the Copyright Office's online records, contacting ASCAP, BMI, Harry Fox, or one of the other musical rights organizations, and an extensive Internet search engine search. A good faith diligent search for the copyright owner of a piece of urban art (think the art of the artist Banksy[59] or other graffiti artists) may be very different; a search for this type of work may include a search of the Copyright Office online records, a search of various webpages dedicated to urban art,[60] contacting various art galleries and art schools near the location of the piece of art, possibly contacting local police to inquire if they know the artist's name and location, and possibly even asking people near the location of the art piece if they can identify the artist.

This last example may seem extreme, but the recommendations are clear that each case is unique and that in some cases more "out of the box" methods may be required. A lack of identifying information for the copyright owner might be persuasive in limiting a user's search, but it is not determinative. The 2015 Report notes that:

> [A] search of Copyright Office records is only necessary if sufficient identifying information already exists on which to base the search. Users, however, cannot rely solely on a lack of identifying information; instead the user must undertake the most comprehensive search possible in light of limited information, because a lack of identifying

---

[59] BANKSY, http://banksy.co.uk (last visited May 14, 2016); *Banksy – 209 Artworks, Prints for Sale, Bio & More*, ARTSY, https://www.artsy.net/artist/banksy (last visited May 14, 2016).

[60] *Art Crimes: The Writing on the Wall*, GRAFFITI ART WORLDWIDE, http://www.graffiti.org (last visited May 14, 2016); Vitaly Friedman, *Tribute To Graffiti: 50 Beautiful Graffiti Artworks*, SMASHING MAG. (Sep. 14, 2008), https://www.smashingmagazine.com/2008/09/tribute-to-graffiti-50-beautiful-graffiti-artworks.

information does not excuse a user from conducting
any searches.[61]

Therefore, as urban artists often use a nom de guerre when signing their
works, a user might be required to turn to unconventional sources to
identify the copyright owner, as discussed above.

The "reasonableness" of a search is extremely important, and
each search is a case unto itself. The Copyright Office went further in
emphasizing the important nature of searches by stating that the
proposed legislation includes the requirement that users take "any other
actions that are reasonably likely to be useful in identifying and
locating the copyright owner."[62] The Report goes on to state that a
search depends upon the facts that the user possesses and that the
search could be required to adapt, change, and expand during the
course of the search.[63] A user also cannot assume that a search will be
without charge. The 2015 Report specifically notes that good faith
diligent searches may require the use of paid search websites or other
types of paid searches.[64]

To further clarify what constitutes a good faith diligent search,
the 2015 Report recommends that legislation include language that
would "[r]equire the Copyright Office to maintain and update
Recommended Practices for diligent searches for various categories of
works, through public consultation with interested stakeholders."[65]
Furthermore, a search would only qualify as a good faith diligent
search if the user makes the diligent search to locate the copyright
owner prior to the use of the work and "at a time reasonably proximate
to" the beginning of the use.[66] These qualifications, however, also
require definition. Does prior to the beginning of the use mean prior to
publication or prior to completing a derivative work that encompasses
the orphan work, or does it mean prior to any use whatsoever? By
extension, how close does "reasonably proximate" have to be prior to
use? The 2015 Report does not address these questions.

A user may reasonably conclude that because of the nature of
the orphan works case-by-case approach, each instance of "prior to

---

[61] ORPHAN WORKS AND MASS DIGITIZATION, *supra* note 6, at 57.
[62] *Id.*
[63] *Id.* at 58.
[64] *Id.*
[65] *Id.* at 4.
[66] *Id.* at 56.

use" and "reasonably proximate" could be different. But if this is the case, then the user is provided no direction by the Copyright Office as to what steps must be taken, and when, in order to qualify for the orphan works limitation on liability. A user may perform an extensive good faith diligent search before making any use of an orphan work but the search may or may not be "reasonably proximate" to the use depending upon the interpretation of "reasonably proximate" by a court. Providing a definition of when use begins for orphan works purposes and setting a definitive time period as being "reasonably proximate" to use would provide both the copyright owner and user important information for determining if a use would fall under an orphan works limitation on liability.

### b.    Foreign Searches

The global nature of copyright issues did not escape the Copyright Office when preparing the 2015 Report and proposed orphan work legislation. In the 2015 Report, two questions arose regarding foreign searches: 1) what if a work is determined to be an orphan work in a foreign jurisdiction and the user from the foreign jurisdiction wants to use the work in the U.S.; and 2) what weight, if any, should a foreign diligent search be given by U.S. courts when determining if a search was diligent?[67] In recognition of the global nature of copyright and the expansion of orphan works legislation around the world, the Copyright Office included specific provisions for addressing diligent searches made under foreign copyright law. The Copyright Office proposes that a U.S. court be given leeway to review and accept a qualifying diligent search conducted under the orphan works legislation of a foreign jurisdiction as part of a diligent search in the United States, on the condition that the foreign jurisdiction also accepts qualifying U.S. diligent searches.[68]

The answer to question number one was relatively straightforward. The Copyright Office proposes that a user, whether the same foreign jurisdiction user or a different user, would still be required to perform a diligent search in the U.S., just like any other user. This is a new approach for the Copyright Office. In previous reports, the Copyright Office had not recommended the acceptance of

---

[67] ORPHAN WORKS AND MASS DIGITIZATION, *supra* note 6, at 58.
[68] *Id.* at 59.

foreign jurisdiction diligent searches. However, the Copyright Office made a 180° turn in the most recent report. The 2015 Report cites the orphan works laws of Canada, Hungary, and the United Kingdom as examples of foreign jurisdictions that require diligent searches of orphan works.[69] The Copyright Office contends that diligent searches from these foreign jurisdictions should be accepted because the orphan works laws in each country require government approval of a search for it to be deemed diligent and government approval to be given to use the work as an orphan work.[70] The Copyright Office posits that allowing U.S. courts to accept diligent searches from foreign jurisdictions as probative of a diligent search in the United States will open the door to foreign jurisdictions allowing United States diligent searches the same evidentiary weight in their jurisdictions.[71] The Copyright Office, however, is clear that a diligent search in a foreign jurisdiction is not a replacement for a diligent search in the U.S. but is a potentially important supplement to a diligent search in the United States. A diligent search in the United States would still require a search of Copyright Office records as well as other qualifying searches, but a qualified foreign search could be presented as part of the diligent search in the United States if a copyright owner were to challenge a user on the basis of an insufficient diligent search.

c.   *Searches for Visual Works*

The issue of searches for visual works is of particular concern for copyright owners due to the present technological limitations on searching images compared to searching text. A text search is able to be performed on numerous Internet search engines simply by entering a portion of the text of the work into the search bar. However, at this point in time, there is no such search available to the average person for visual works. There is no way to do an Internet search by dropping a JPEG of a photograph or a MP4 of a video into an internet search engine, which puts potential users of orphan visual works at a disadvantage compared to users of text works when performing diligent searches.

---

[69] *Id.* at 58.
[70] *Id.* at 58.
[71] *Id.* at 59.

The issue of searches for visual works was acknowledged and addressed in the 2015 Report.[72] The Copyright Office contends in the Report that the use of third-party registries for visual works alleviates the search concern for users of visual orphan works by providing cataloged sites on which copyright owners can register their works.[73] The Report makes particular note of the Picture Licensing Universal System (PLUS)[74] as an important third-party registry where copyright owners may register their works and where users may perform searches.[75] The Copyright Office acknowledges that searching PLUS alone would not be a diligent search, but a search of PLUS in conjunction with other searches could constitute a diligent search.[76]

The problem with the Copyright Office's third-party registry suggestion is that it makes a number of assumptions that do not hold up under closer inspection. The Report makes the assumption that copyright owners will register their works with third-party registries.[77] However, the Copyright Office acknowledges that third-party registries, such as PLUS, are geared towards professional artists and not all photographers.[78] Therefore, this immediately excludes a large portion of photographs and copyright owners.[79] The exclusion of this large segment of copyright owners seems to be counter to the Copyright Office's stated purpose of bringing users and copyright owners together.[80]

The Copyright Office also puts forth that third-party registries will proliferate as more artists register their works.[81] The Copyright Office, however, provides little proof of this claim beyond the wording "We believe . . . ."[82] This is an important assumption because if it is incorrect that third-party registries do not proliferate and that visual artists do not register their works with third-party registries, then what

[72] Id. at 51–54.
[73] ORPHAN WORKS AND MASS DIGITIZATION, supra note 6, at 52.
[74] Id. at 48–49; see also PLUS REGISTRY, www.plusregistry.org (last visited May 14, 2016).
[75] ORPHAN WORKS AND MASS DIGITIZATION, supra note 6, at 49, 52–53, 60.
[76] Id. at 53, 60.
[77] Id. at 53.
[78] See id. at 52.
[79] See id.
[80] Id. at 1.
[81] ORPHAN WORKS AND MASS DIGITIZATION, supra note 6, at 53.
[82] Id.

diligent search options are available to users? The Report provides no clear alternative to where users may search.

For the sake of argument, assume arguendo that at least professional artists will register their works at increased rates. Then, the questions become about cost and accessibility. Will third-party registries be free to copyright owners and users, or will there be charges involved for copyright owners to upload visual works and for users to perform searches? The more charges involved in the deposit of works or in the search of works, the less likely copyright owners and users will participate in third-party registries. At this point, PLUS does not charge for basic membership and searches, which is a benefit to expanded use by both copyright owners and users.

PLUS, like most other third-party registries, as of this writing, does not have a search engine for images.[83] Searches are restricted to textual search terms, which raises the issue of a user's ability to search through thousands, millions, or potentially billions of images. As discussed above, there was an estimated one trillion photographs taken worldwide in 2015.[84] If one percent of those photographs was posted to PLUS or another third party registry, they would constitute ten billion photos for just 2015, let alone all of the photographs taken since the invention of photography.[85] It is extremely unlikely that with only a text-based search that a user will be able to diligently search through the 2015 photographs, let alone the billions of photos taken in previous years.

The problem with the assumptions by the Copyright Office regarding third-party registries is just that: they are assumptions. The Copyright Office is assuming that a searchable database for visual works that will allow copyright owners and users to connect and that is simple, user-friendly, and inexpensive will be available sooner rather than later. While this assumption might be reasonable based on the rate at which technology advances, it is by no means guaranteed.[86] Without

---

[83] See PLUS REGISTRY, www.plusregistry.org (last visited May 14, 2016).

[84] See Schneider, supra note 9.

[85] See Philip Greenspun, History of Photography Timeline, PHOTO.NET (Jan. 2007), http://photo.net/history/timeline; Vsauce, How Many Photos Have Been Taken?, YOUTUBE (Nov. 10, 2012), https://www.youtube.com/watch?v=4e_kz79tjb8&feature=youtu.be. The first permanent photographic image was taken in 1826, and the first photograph uploaded to the worldwide web was in 1992. Id.

[86] The author is still waiting for consumer-friendly flying cars, jetpacks, and real hoverboards.

sufficient technology to adequately sift through the billions of photographs produced each year, a user of a visual work would be at a significant disadvantage conducting a diligent search as opposed to users of written material using basic text internet search engines or even users of sound recordings using relatively new sound recording identification software through free third-party search services such as Shazam[87] and SoundHound.[88] Therefore, the Copyright Office should not assume a technological solution will be developed to address the area of copyright that has seen the greatest increase in content creation. Reasonable diligent search parameters should be set forth by the Copyright Office for each type of copyrightable work. These search parameters should take into consideration the technological hurtles confronting the average user when performing a good faith diligent search.

### d.  How "Diligent" Should A Diligent Search Be?

The good faith diligent search requirements set forth by the Copyright Office are not universally endorsed. The matter of what constitutes a diligent search and how a diligent search should be defined has been addressed and pondered by many individuals and groups.[89] The diligent search issue boils down to how far will and should a user go in his search for the copyright owner of a work and how comprehensive should a diligent search be required to be?

As discussed above, the Copyright Office's standard for a diligent search fluctuates on a case-by-case basis[90], but overall, the recommended diligent search standards are to be set at a relatively high level.[91] Under the Copyright Office's proposed legislation, the time and cost to a user may not be insignificant in order to reach the level of a diligent search for purposes of orphan works limitation on liability.[92] The Center for the Study of the Public Domain at Duke University Law School (Duke) argues that a diligent search should not be as exhaustive

---

[87] SHAZAM, http://www.shazam.com (last visited May 14, 2016).
[88] SOUNDHOUND, http://www.soundhound.com/soundhound (last visited May 14, 2016).
[89] *See generally* ORPHAN WORKS ANALYSIS AND PROPOSAL, *supra* note 4; Jane C. Ginsburg, *Recent Developments in US Copyright Law: Part I - 'Orphan' Works* (Columbia Pub. Law Research Paper No. 08-183, (Oct. 2008), http://ssrn.com/abstract=1263361.
[90] ORPHAN WORKS AND MASS DIGITIZATION, *supra* note 6, at 72.
[91] *Id.* at 57–58.
[92] *See id.*

as the Copyright Office proposes.[93] In its proposal on orphan works submitted to the Copyright Office, Duke takes the position that search requirements for orphan works should be less stringent due to an increased difficulty of performing a reasonable search.[94] Duke postulates that modern technology is actually making the search process more difficult instead of easier.[95] The thought is that because of worldwide distribution channels, the ever increasing number of distribution formats, both physical and digital, and the ever increasing amount of content created, locating a specific copyright owner of a specific work is not tantamount to finding a needle in a haystack but rather more like finding a particular needle in a needle stack.[96] Basically, Duke proposes that it is often a near impossibility to identify and locate a copyright owner, especially if the search is done in an economical fashion.[97]

Duke then addresses the economic reality of the cost of doing a reasonable search. Search costs are addressed on a dual front. First, Duke argues that the economic reality of an orphan works search is that if the search costs are too high, or just perceived to be too high prior to attempting a search, the user will choose to abandon the search instead of spending the money.[98] The key, in this situation, is finding the economic tipping point. Duke reasons that lower search requirements will effectuate lower search costs, which would encourage more searches to occur and more copyright owners to be united with users.[99]

Duke also proposes that searches should be tiered depending upon the use of the orphan work as opposed to uniform search requirements.[100] The proposition is that since not all licensing fees are the same and fluctuate greatly depending upon the use, likewise, so should the extent and cost of a qualifying search.[101] Duke proposes that uses should be divided into different categories requiring different levels of searches.[102] A higher level of search would be required for higher level commercial enterprises, while a lower level search would

---

[93] Orphan Works Analysis and Proposal, *supra* note 4, at 4–5.
[94] *Id.* at 3.
[95] *Id.* at 3, 5.
[96] *See id.* at 4.
[97] *Id.* at 4 -5.
[98] *Id.* at 4–5.
[99] Orphan Works Analysis and Proposal, *supra* note 4, at 4.
[100] *Id.* at 4–5.
[101] *Id.*
[102] *Id.* at 5

be required for economically minor uses, and virtually no search would be required of a nonprofit entity such as a library, the provision of notice being the primary requirement for nonprofits.[103]

The Duke proposal, while important to take into consideration, may not afford copyright owners a sufficient level of protection. A copyright owner's rights must be balanced with the desire to afford users greater latitude in the use of works whose owners are not readily identifiable and/or locatable. The Duke proposal, however, also focuses on another important aspect of proposed orphan works legislation: notice of use.[104]

### 2. Notice

The second step in the orphan works limitation on liability pursuit is more straightforward than the good faith diligent search. The user must provide notice to the Copyright Office of the user's intention to use the orphan work.[105] This notice would be provided to a new Copyright Office registry that would maintain and archive orphan works Notice of Use filings.[106] These new filings would be required to include:

> (1) the type of work used (under 17 U.S.C. § 102(a)); (2) a description of the work; (3) a summary of the qualifying search conducted; (4) any other identifying indicia available to the user; (5) the source of the work (*e.g.*, library or website where work was located, publication where work originally appeared); (6) a certification that the user performed a qualifying search; and (7) the name of the user and a description of how the work will be used.[107]

Beyond these notice requirements, the user would also be required to provide attribution to the author and copyright owner of the work whenever possible.[108]

---

[103] *Id.*

[104] *Id.* at 6, 8.

[105] ORPHAN WORKS AND MASS DIGITIZATION, *supra* note 6, at 60.

[106] *Id.*

[107] *Id.* at 60–61.

[108] *Id.* at 4, 11.

It should be noted that the notice requirements only require a description of the work being used and do not require a submission of the work being used.[109] A submission of a copy of the actual work that the user is utilizing along with a description of the work might be more beneficial to a copyright owner searching the orphan works Notice of Use archive. This would allow copyright owners to make a quick determination whether or not the work that the user has provided notice for is that copyright owner's work. This would be an important search element to all manners of work. Written works could be easily searched for by copyright owners through a simple search of the database using a sentence or two of the copyright owner's work, much like is used by an Internet search engine. A submission of a copy of the work being utilized by the user may be even more important to the identification of visual works by copyright owners. A description of a work, as required in the proposed Notice of Use filing, is probably not sufficient for copyright owners to conclusively identify their visual works being used under a Notice of Use. This is due to the multitude of ways that a user may choose to describe a visual work of art.

As an example, let us hypothesize that the Mona Lisa[110] is still under copyright in the United States and is an orphan work of which a user wishes to make use. How may the user describe the work? A portrait of a woman dressed in dark colors. A painting of a woman set against a dark mountainous or hilly background. A portrait painting of a woman with dark hair, dressed in period clothing. A woman painted with a slight smile and wavy hair.

The Mona Lisa, arguably one of the most famous paintings in the world, could be described in a Notice of Use potentially hundreds of ways both brief and expansive. The problem is that any other number of paintings could be described in similar manners with those descriptions being just as accurate. Therefore, the work described in the Notice of Use could be numerous different paintings. Without the submission of a copy of the orphan work along with the description of the work, it would be unlikely or impossible that a copyright owner could identify a work by description alone. This would, more likely than not, be antithetical to the intent of the proposed orphan works legislation, which is to bring together users and copyright owners.

---

[109] See id. at 60–61.

[110] LEONARDO DA VINCI, Mona Lisa—Portrait of Lisa Gherardini, wife of Francesco del Giocondo, LOUVRE http://www.louvre.fr/en/oeuvre-notices/mona-lisa-portrait-lisa-gherardini-wife-francesco-del-giocondo (last visited May 14, 2016).

The 2015 Report emphasizes the importance of filing notice with the Copyright Office. The essential part of the notice is that the Notice of Use filings will be maintained and archived in a database that may be searched by copyright owners in order to bring users and copyright owners together.[111] However, nowhere in the 2015 Report does the Copyright Office indicate two essential parts to the Notice of Use filing and searchable orphan works archive: 1) what, if anything, will a Notice of Use cost to file with the Copyright Office?; and 2) what, if anything, will copyright owners be charged to access and search the orphan works notice of use archive?

These questions are potentially as important as any other question surrounding proposed orphan works legislation. Users will, more likely than not, think with their wallets first when considering moving forward with filing a Notice of Use. If the cost of filing a Notice of Use, or possibly multiple Notices of Use for multiple orphan works, is excessive or only slightly out of line with other copyright charges, a user may forgo the process and roll the dice on a fair use claim, or other defense, if the copyright owner ever happened upon the infringing use. A similar situation may also arise for copyright owners if there is a charge, large or small, for access to the orphan works archive. A copyright owner may choose to forgo spending the money on searching the orphan works archive on the outside chance that one of the copyright owner's works might show up in the archive, especially if the amount of the reasonable license fee that the copyright owner may receive from the user is not higher than the cost to access the archive.

If the Copyright Office does charge a fee to file the Notice of Use and also charges a fee to the copyright owner to search the orphan works archive, it should first do a cost-benefit analysis to determine the tipping point at which users and copyright owners will be willing to participate. The Copyright Office's goal in any orphan works legislation is to bring orphan works owners and user together.[112] This goal could potentially be frustrated if the price points associated with notice of use filings and copyright owner searches make it unappealing and/or not cost effective to the intended copyright owners and users.

---

[111] ORPHAN WORKS AND MASS DIGITIZATION, *supra* note 6.
[112] *Id.*

### 3.   Claim of Infringement

Once users have performed a good faith diligent search and filed a Notice of Use with the Copyright Office, their paths are not yet complete to reach the orphan works limitation on liability. The next step would come upon a receipt of a Notice of Claim of Infringement, which would bring about the requirement that the copyright owner and the user negotiate reasonable compensation for the use of the work.[113] The 2015 Report notes that "[w]here a user satisfies the eligibility requirements of the orphan works legislation, monetary relief is limited to 'reasonable compensation.'"[114] Reasonable compensation would not include actual damages, statutory damages, costs, and attorneys' fees.[115] The Copyright Office proposes that the exclusion of costs and attorneys' fees from orphan works settlements is justified due to the elimination of litigation.[116] However, this proposition might be an over-simplification.

### a.   Elimination of Damages, Costs, and Attorneys' Fees

Section 505 of the 1976 Copyright Act states:
> In any civil action under this title, the court in its discretion may allow the recovery of full costs by or against any party other than the United States or an officer thereof. Except as otherwise provided by this title, the court may also award a reasonable attorney's fee to the prevailing party as part of the costs.[117]

Presently, attorneys' fees are not available to plaintiffs in copyright infringement cases where the infringement occurs prior to the registration of the infringed work with the Copyright Office.[118] The elimination of attorneys' fees under the proposed orphan works legislation appears to presuppose that copyright owners will handle claims of infringement themselves and forgo hiring an attorney. The

---

[113] *Id.* at 63.
[114] *Id.*
[115] *Id.*
[116] *Id.*
[117] 17 U.S.C. § 505 (2012).
[118] 17 U.S.C. § 412 (2012).

Copyright Office postulates that the costs of litigation will be avoided due to the requirement to negotiate reasonable compensation under the proposed orphan works legislation.[119] This avoidance of litigation will therefore remove the need for costs and attorneys' fees.[120] However, this hypothesis does not take into account multiple instances, referenced in the 2015 Report, of courts addressing orphan works issues, including the determination of reasonable compensation. Copyright owners could realistically still end up in court paying attorneys' fees and costs, but the proceeding would be an orphan works proceeding, so no attorneys' fees or costs would be available.

The elimination of attorneys' fees and costs from orphan works cases could remove a key incentive for copyright owners to register their works with the Copyright Office upon creation, instead of after an infringement occurs. If the resulting reasonable compensation from claims of infringement under the orphan works designation is the same for registered and unregistered works, then this may de-incentivize copyright owners from spending the extra money to register their works.

The Copyright Office identified the potential for this situation, at least in part. The proposed orphan works legislation allows for "courts, when determining reasonable compensation, to take into account the value, if any, added to a work by virtue of its registration with the Copyright Office."[121] The reasoning behind this is that there may be instances in which certain types of registered works, such as instrumental sound recordings or works of visual art, are missed in a search of the Copyright Office records due to lack of textual search terms.[122] A court could then impose a portion of the otherwise applicable non-orphan works infringement damages on the user even if the search was properly performed and the work was not locatable.[123] The Copyright Office believes that this is an important exception in order to encourage copyright registration and to reward owners that register their copyrights.[124] However, the proposed orphan works legislation does not allow for the imposition of court costs or attorneys' fees.

---

[119] ORPHAN WORKS AND MASS DIGITIZATION, *supra* note 6, at 63.
[120] *Id.*
[121] *Id.* at 66.
[122] *Id.*
[123] *Id.*
[124] *Id.*

The continued exclusion of costs and attorneys' fees in this situation could be a significant barrier to the copyright owner seeking redress from a court. Alternatively, it could potentially cause a court to increase the added value to the work in order to offset the costs and attorneys' fees required to bring the action. The significant barrier to the copyright owner bringing a case in this situation is that potential costs and attorneys' fees may cost far more money than the copyright owner plaintiff could hope to recover, even with an added value increase in judgment from the court. A copyright owner plaintiff could roll the dice and bring an action, hoping that the court will provide added value to the work in an amount large enough to cover costs and attorneys' fees, but this is a significant gamble. This situation also creates uncertainty in the judicial system as to when and in what amount added value determinations should be made, which is not beneficial to the copyright owner, the user, or the courts. Therefore, costs and attorneys' fees should be allowed in infringement claims under the orphan works legislation dealing with registered works. The alternative is inequitable and unfair to registered copyright owners and has the potential of creating uncertainty for qualified users, which is what orphan works legislation is attempting to avoid.

### b.   Reasonable Compensation

The implementation of reasonable compensation under the proposed orphan works legislation would act as a replacement for traditional damages for infringement of both registered and unregistered works. The 2015 Report notes that in the majority of cases reasonable compensation will be the same or substantially similar to what a reasonable license fee would have been for the use of the work.[125] The Copyright Office cites the case of *Davis v. The Gap, Inc.,*[126] noting that this case specifically addresses the "reasonable license fee" formula as being "appropriate in situations where users have sought to find the owner through a good faith diligent search."[127] *Davis* also sets forth the principle that the burden of establishing a fair market value for the use of the work is to be borne by the copyright owner.[128]

---

[125] ORPHAN WORKS AND MASS DIGITIZATION, *supra* note 6, at 63.
[126] *Id.* at 63–64 (discussing Davis v. Gap, Inc., 246 F.3d 152 (2d Cir. 2001)).
[127] *Id.* at 63.
[128] *Id.* at 64.

The 2015 Report further notes that "reasonable compensation" is the fair market valuation of a work "immediately" prior to the infringement occurring.[129] This burden of establishing an ex ante fair market value for a work, based on the market immediately prior to the use of the work, is not necessarily a readily accomplishable goal. The establishment of a baseline fair market value for a specific work at a specific moment in time, possibly years prior, could present the copyright owner with a situation that is not tenable or cost effective. The court in *Davis* determined, as noted by the Copyright Office, that it fell to the copyright owner to prove that similarly situated copyright owners licensed similarly situated works for similar licensing fees.[130]

This presents the copyright owner with a significant hurdle to overcome when attempting to recover reasonable compensation from the user. The copyright owner may have no baseline for what other similarly situated works may have been licensed for at the time immediately prior to the use. The copyright owner could be required to pay fees to third-party experts to obtain a fair market analysis that would determine what constitutes reasonable compensation. The fees paid to third-party experts may exceed the determined amount of reasonable compensation. Thus, the payment of fees to third parties for valuation analysis could cause the copyright owner to take a financial loss when seeking redress for copyright infringement under orphan works legislation.

The potential for this scenario is acknowledged in the 2015 Report and alterations to strict fair market value evaluation are addressed. The Copyright Office states that reasonable compensation should include a percentage-based royalty as well as a one-time, fixed sum in order to avoid a user reaping an unfair windfall if the use of the work is a commercial success.[131] The Copyright Office, however, provides almost no guidance on how a percentage-based royalty might be applied or when it would be appropriate to be applied, with the exception of stating that a court may determine that a percentage-based royalty could constitute a form of reasonable compensation in the case of the ongoing use of the work in a user's derivative work.[132]

The problem with this scenario is two-fold: 1) it does not address the copyright owner's attorneys' fees, as discussed above, and

---

[129] *Id.*
[130] *Id.*
[131] ORPHAN WORKS AND MASS DIGITIZATION, *supra* note 6, at 64.
[132] *Id.* at 67.

the cost issues of determining the fair market value immediately prior to initial use and determining a royalty percentage basis; and 2) it creates a stronger bargaining position for the user.

This situation has the potential to shift significant costs onto the copyright owner. This is particularly true in the case of copyright owners with registered works, as discussed above regarding attorneys' fees. The Copyright Office does not address the costs to the copyright owner in providing proof of what reasonable compensation would be, let alone what the costs to the copyright owner to determine what a fair percentage-based royalty rate might be. Although, the Copyright Office does tip its hand slightly toward copyright owners who register their works when it made the assumption that "an owner who registers his or her works likely has more interest in its exploitation."[133] However, at no place in the 1976 Copyright Act is an interest in exploiting a work mentioned or cited as being determinative in a copyright owner being compensated for the use of a work. The Copyright Office simply cites *Davis* and then moves forward under the assumption that all costs of determining reasonable compensation for the use of a work are to be borne by the copyright owner.

The second issue in this matter, the stronger bargaining position of the user, is created when the user of a relatively or completely unknown work, which would probably include the majority of orphan works (otherwise they would not be orphaned), negotiates a relatively low reasonable compensation for the use of the work with the copyright owner based on the fair market value of the work immediately prior to the time of initial use. A relatively low reasonable compensation can be assumed by the fact that the work was little known or unknown at the time of initial use, as opposed to a work by a famous artist such as Roy Lichtenstein,[134] Bob Dylan,[135] or Dan Brown.[136]

---

[133] *Id.* at 66–67.

[134] *See Roy Lichtenstein: American Artist and Sculptor*, THE ART STORY.ORG, http://www.theartstory.org/artist-lichtenstein-roy.htm (last visited May 14, 2016); *Roy Lichtenstein*, MOMA.ORG, http://www.moma.org/collection/artists/3542 (last visited May 14, 2016).

[135] BOB DYLAN, http://bobdylan.com (last visited May 14, 2016); *Bob Dylan: biography*, BIO.COM, http://www.biography.com/people/bob-dylan-9283052 (last visited May 14, 2016).

[136] DAN BROWN, http://www.danbrown.com (last visited May 14, 2016); *Dan Brown*, IMDB.COM, http://www.imdb.com/name/nm1467010/ (last visited May 14, 2016).

The user then has the upper hand in negotiation of future uses of the work, if any. The user could simply cease using the work, pay the relatively low reasonable compensation, and make the argument that any royalty-based payments should be extremely low based on the perceived value and bargaining power of the copyright owner immediately prior to initial use. This argument could be expanded to include the exclusion of any type of royalty fee due to industry standards at the time immediately prior to initial use of the work and/or the existence of other non-royalty-based license agreements contemporaneous with the time immediately preceding the initial use. These situations would potentially allow the user to walk away having reaped the windfall of the use without bearing any of the costs required of the copyright holder to prove the value of the work immediately prior to use, while paying a small amount in reasonable compensation and possibly no royalty.

As noted previously, the professed intention of orphan works legislation is to bring copyright owners and users together. The Copyright Office also contends that orphan work legislation would economically benefit copyright owners and users through the streamlining of the system to provide more access to works to be used. However, the shouldering of the costs by the copyright owner to prove the worth of a work immediately prior to the work's use by the user, along with the potential for the reasonable compensation for the use of the work to be relatively low, could be a deterrent rather than an incentive.

If a copyright owner must bear the uncertainty of the costs required to make a determination of the value of his or her work with the possibility that he or she could end up out-of-pocket hundreds or thousands of dollars, then what is the incentive for the copyright owner to value or participate in the orphan works system? A savvy user could refuse to pay the copyright owner reasonable compensation without first being provided with at least three estimates of valuation from accredited experts in copyright valuation in the relevant subset works (books, painting, photographs, musical compositions, etc.). This stance of the user would be based on the proposition set forth by the Copyright Office that the cost of proving reasonable compensation is borne by the copyright owner.

The copyright owner would then be required to pay hundreds or thousands of dollars for expert copyright valuations in order to prove the value of the work immediately prior to the use. With no potential for cost shifting to the user, the copyright owner may determine that the cost of copyright valuation outweighs the benefit of reasonable compensation. This would then lead to the user receiving the "unfair windfall"[137] that the Copyright Office is seeking to avoid. Furthermore, the copyright owner, due to financial hardship, may not be able to hire experts to provide a copyright valuation to the user. In this situation, the user would again be receiving an "unfair windfall"[138] and disadvantaging a party already experiencing financial difficulties through being denied the reasonable compensation due to her for the use of the work.

A reasonable solution to the costs and attorneys' fees issues would be, at a minimum, to allow the recovery of costs and attorneys' fees for registered copyrights. This would maintain the status quo in providing incentives to copyright owners to register their works. A better solution for all works under the orphan works system would be to allow the court to award recovery of costs and attorneys' fees if no reasonable compensation is agreed upon through good faith negotiation within a set amount of time determined by the Copyright Office. This would incentivize the copyright owner and the user to work together to resolve the matter in a timely fashion. It would also encourage the copyright owner and the user to be economical and reasonable in their respective demands for reasonable compensation and proof of valuation, as the costs of unreasonable demands and/or requirements could end up being borne by the demanding party. The potential for both the copyright owner and the user to bear the costs and attorneys' fees of the other is a possibly strong incentive to come to a mutually agreeable, reasonable compensation.

### c.   Injunctive Relief

Injunctive relief is a mainstay of copyright remedies.[139] It allows copyright owners to control their copyrights and affords them a form of relief when monetary damages are curtailed or unavailable. However, injunctive relief under the proposed orphan works legislation, while technically still available, could be curtailed for most copyright owners and unavailable to other copyright owners when the

---

[137] ORPHAN WORKS AND MASS DIGITIZATION, *supra* note 6, at 64.
[138] *Id.*
[139] 17 U.S.C. § 502 (2012).

user has complied with the proposed search and notice of use requirements.

The 2015 Report proposes that courts restrain the use of injunctive relief in cases where the user has gone through the proper search and notice of use requirements proscribed in the orphan works legislation.[140] The Copyright Office proposes that a court "should account for the harm caused by users' reliance on the orphan works provision."[141] Essentially, it is proposed that if a user establishes the minimum steps to be in compliance with the search and notice requirements of the orphan works legislation, the court should provide certain leeway for the user. An example of this is that a court may enjoin a user from "further printing or publication of copies of an orphan work, but permit the retail sale of existing copies."[142] Thus, the user would reap the benefit of following the orphan works search and notice of use requirements and be able to profit from the orphan work, while the copyright owner would be able to stop any further use of the work in the creation of new products and receive reasonable compensation, as discussed above, for the use of the work in the existing products. On the surface this arrangement appears to be relatively fair and equitable to both the copyright owner and the user. However, it is when one begins to dig down and take deeper considerations into account that this injunctive relief proposal becomes concerning to copyright owners.

The two main areas of concern addressed in the 2015 Report and provided for specifically in the proposed orphan works legislation are the role of injunctive relief in cases involving derivative works and in cases of derivative works involving an author's honor and reputation. These two areas for potential injunctive relief are addressed very differently in the 2015 Report than in the legislation.

In the matter of derivative works, the Copyright Office endorses a position favorable to the user. The Copyright Office proposes that "a user may, upon paying a reasonable compensation to the owner of the work in a reasonably timely manner and providing attribution (where requested), avoid an injunction and continue to prepare and use the new work."[143] The reasoning behind this position is that the user, having fulfilled the search and notice requirements, would

---

[140] ORPHAN WORKS AND MASS DIGITIZATION, *supra* note 6, at 67.
[141] *Id.*
[142] *Id.*
[143] *Id.*

have a good faith basis for moving forward to create a new derivative work that would effectively entangle the orphan work with the user's new creative content in a manner that would mean irreparable damage to the user's new derivative work if injunctive relief were allowed.[144] The Copyright Office further notes that the restriction on injunctive relief for derivative works runs for the life of the orphan works copyright, which would allow the user to use the derivative work without restriction, regardless of objections from the orphan work's owner. This would also allow for full copyright protection for the derivative work.[145]

This proposal for limitations on injunctive relief did not go uncontested. The Copyright Office noted that these limitations were concerning to some and that this was a substantial exit from a traditional tenant of copyright law: the copyright owner's exclusive right to control.[146] In the matter of injunctive relief for derivative works, the 2015 Report specifically noted a differentiation between a concern for copyright owners and authors. The Copyright Office sets forth the proposition that when the copyright owner is also the author of the work, a higher risk of damage to the author is present through potential harm to honor and/or reputation.[147] Therefore, the Copyright Office created a special proviso in the proposed orphan works legislation specifically for author-owners of copyrights. This provision allows for injunctive relief for an orphan work derivative work "only if the continued preparation or use of the new work would be prejudicial to the author-owner's honor or reputation, and a Court finds that such harm cannot be cured through reasonable compensation."[148] This means that in order to take advantage of injunctive relief in a derivative work situation, the court must determine that: 1) the copyright owner is also an author of the orphan work; 2) the copyright owner-author has suffered some form of harm to his/her honor and/or reputation; and 3) the harm suffered by the copyright owner-author cannot be reasonably compensated monetarily.

This provision for injunctive relief is an important exception to the proposed limitations on injunctive relief for derivatives works in

---

[144] Id.

[145] Id. at 67–68.

[146] ORPHAN WORKS AND MASS DIGITIZATION, supra note 6, at 68 n.281. See also Ginsburg, supra note 89. http://ssrn.com/abstract=1263361.

[147] ORPHAN WORKS AND MASS DIGITIZATION, supra note 6, at 68.

[148] Id.

orphan works. Unfortunately, this exception is also too narrowly drafted. The requirement that this exception only apply to copyright owner-authors puts non-author copyright owners at a distinct disadvantage in the control of their works, especially when considering the potential damage to a copyright owner through forced association with an unsavory or damaging user. As an example, what if an author gifted or willed her copyrights to the Simon Wiesenthal Center[149] or her synagogue and one of the works was then used as an orphan work to create a derivative work glorifying the holocaust or advocating for the American Nazi Party?[150] Or, what if the Gordon Parks Foundation[151] found that a photograph taken by Mr. Parks and the copyright held by the Gordon Parks Foundation was listed in the orphan works archive by a user who had satisfied the search and notice requirements and was using the photo in a derivative work that advocated for the Ku Klux Klan?[152] Should these non-author copyright owners not be entitled to injunctive relief? Are the associations created by the derivative uses not potentially harmful to the name and reputation of the non-author copyright owners in a manner not rectifiable through monetary compensation?

Limitations on injunctive relief under the proposed orphan works legislation are an important piece to furthering the purpose of the proposed legislation. Injunctive relief, however, should be addressed on a case-by-case basis, just as qualification as an orphan work is addressed on a case-by-case basis. The near blanket exclusion of injunctive relief for derivative works of orphan works puts copyright owners at a distinct disadvantage and takes the right to control one's copyright out of the hands of the copyright owner. Furthermore, copyright owner-authors are not the only parties that may suffer irreparable harms from damage to honor and/or reputation due to association with a user and/or a derivative work that are not compensable with monetary damages. As set forth in the hypotheticals above, non-author copyright owners could suffer the same or substantially similar harms to honor and/or reputation through these unwanted and forced associations. Because of this, non-author

---

[149] SIMON WIESENTHAL CENTER, http://www.wiesenthal.com (last visited May 14, 2016).
[150] AMERICAN NAZI PARTY, http://www.americannaziparty.com (last visited May 14, 2016).
[151] THE GORDON PARKS FOUND., http://www.gordonparksfoundation.org (last visited May 14, 2016).
[152] See ORPHAN WORKS AND MASS DIGITIZATION, supra note 6, at 64.

copyright owners should also be eligible for injunctive relief in these exceptional cases. Orphan works legislation should address injunctive relief and seek to encourage amicable resolution between owners of orphan works and users. It should not, however, restrict the use of injunctive relief by the courts to the point that it forces copyright owners to accept associations with users regardless of how offensive or distasteful those uses might be to the copyright owner or how unconscionable the use might be in a non-orphan works setting. The balance of copyright owners' rights with orphan works users' rights under any orphan works legislation should, when in doubt, always carefully lean in favor of the copyright owner, because a copyright owner's rights in the orphan work are senior to a user's right to use.

### 4. Fair Use

The issue of fair use is discussed extensively in the 2015 Report. The Copyright Office acknowledges that its approach to fair use in regards to orphan works legislation has changed significantly since the 2006 Report.[153] The 2006 Report generally dismissed fair use as inapplicable because orphan works uses would be beyond the application of fair use.[154] The 2015 Report, however, reverses this view. The Copyright Office now takes the stance that fair use continues to be an important mechanism that can both co-exist with orphan works legislation and benefit users whether or not users choose to avail themselves of an orphan works limitation of liability. The 2015 Report specifically notes that, "The application of fair use to new fact patterns, such as uses of orphan works, is an essential aspect of copyright law jurisprudence, and should not be foreclosed by the introduction of a limitation on liability."[155]

The importance of fair use is not overlooked by the Copyright Office as an important affirmative defense available to users.[156] Fair use is also not overlooked by opponents of orphan works legislation. The Library Copyright Alliance (LCA) argued that the recent advances in fair use law sufficiently address LCA needs and that orphan works

---

[153] *Id.* at 41.
[154] *Id.*
[155] *Id.* at 70.
[156] *Id.* at 40.

legislation would be overly complex and restrictive and any benefits would be offset by diligent search requirements.[157]

The arguments against orphan works legislation in favor of fair use are not without merit. The diligent search and notice requirements proposed in the orphan works legislation have the potential to be cumbersome, time consuming, and expensive. However, there is no requirement in the proposed orphan works legislation that requires users to first avail themselves of orphan works protections or that forestalls users from taking advantage of fair use prior to a potential orphan works analysis. LCA members could continue to avail themselves of fair use exclusively and completely forego any options afforded them under an orphan works limitation of liability.

The Copyright Office acknowledged the possibility that some users may prefer the fair use route as opposed to the orphan works limitation on liability. The 2015 Report notes that, "less risk-averse entities may prefer testing the limits of fair use instead of undertaking good faith diligent searches, and they should not be precluded from making that choice."[158] The inclusion of this language in the 2015 Report appears to be a direct response to concerns with of a potential limitation of fair use due to the implementation of orphan works legislation. In order to assure that there was no implication of restraining the use of fair use, a provision was included in the draft legislation that specifically states that fair use, along with all other rights and defenses under copyright law, are preserved.[159]

## IV.     RECOMMENDATIONS

The proposed orphan works legislation in the 2015 Report, as with most proposed legislation, has strong points and points that may require clarification, reconsideration, and revision. The draft legislation is an improvement over the past proposed orphan works legislation, but it is not sufficiently drafted to the point that it should be considered for enactment.

The first change that should be applied to any orphan works legislation is that it should provide a definition of what constitutes an orphan work. A proposed definition may appear similar to:

---

[157] *Id.* at 42.
[158] ORPHAN WORKS AND MASS DIGITIZATION, *supra* note 6, at 71.
[159] *Id.* at 70, app. A § 514(d).

> An Orphan Work is any original work of authorship, whether published or unpublished, registered or unregistered, which is not in the public domain and whose owner(s) cannot be identified, located, and/or contacted by a prospective user of the work following a reasonably diligent, good faith search for the copyright owner(s) identity and location.

While perhaps a bit drawn out, this definition provides a more substantive description of what constitutes an orphan work than the definitions provided above.[160] This definition also puts all copyright owners and users on notice that any work not in the public domain could potentially fall into the orphan works realm.

Orphaned works legislation should also make clear that a new affirmative action is possibly required of all copyright owners. In certain circumstances ,copyright owners could now be required to actively engage all requests for licenses or potentially suffer the fate of being deemed un-locatable and having a work classified as an orphan work. However, to alleviate some of the imposition this potential new affirmative response requirement lays upon copyright owners, a searchable affirmative notice from copyright owners archive should be established, much like the proposed Notice of Use archive for users.

This affirmative notice archive would be a location where copyright owners could file their names, contact information, and lists of works that are not available for license. One key provision to this recommendation is that the filing fee for copyright owners should be very low or nonexistent. If a copyright owner took advantage of this affirmative step to file with this archive, this would satisfy the copyright owner's requirement to respond to all licensing requests. This archive would be searchable by users and would be a mandatory portion of any good faith diligent search. Any unauthorized use of any work listed on this archive would not be subject to protection under the orphan works limitation on liability. The copyright owner could then proceed with an infringement case against the unauthorized user unfettered by orphan works restrictions on remedies. This archive would also further the Copyright Office's desire of alleviating the orphan works problem by providing a location where copyright owners

---

[160] *See supra* Part II.

can provide notice to users without having to deal with users on an individual basis.

The limitation on liability model proposed by the Copyright Office generally appears to be the best option for the United States copyright system. The case-by-case approach of the orphan works legislation is a fair balance to the blanket approach supported by the Copyright Office for mass digitalization legislation. A case-by-case approach provides copyright owners with reasonable assurance that their works cannot be widely used by any user that wishes to exploit the copyright user's work. At the same time, a case-by-case approach also provides users a fair chance at using works, while limiting potential liability, which may otherwise be unusable due to the inability of the user to identify and locate the copyright owner of the work.

The requirements for a good faith diligent search under the case-by-case limited liability model, however, are an area of contention that is not so easily solved. The Copyright Office's requirements in the 2015 Report for a good faith diligent search are awkward and burdensome on the user. Search requirements are not well defined; searches must be extensive; and searches may possibly be expensive if paid searches must be performed. All of this would be required without providing the user assurance that the search will be deemed diligent for purposes of orphan works limitation on liability. The lack of definitive search requirements leaves the user open to liability if the user's search is determined, for whatever reason a court may find, not to be diligent. The combination of time, money, and doubt are detrimental factors that tend to suggest that users may forego the orphan works process in favor of rolling the dice that no copyright owner will step forward or, in the alternative, mounting a fair use defense.

The Duke proposal for search requirements is the yang to the Copyright Office's yin. The Duke proposal imposes very few requirements on the user to perform a diligent search and focuses more heavily on the provision of notice. Herein lies the rub: a search should be diligent and performed with the intent of discovering the copyright owner of a work, but it also should not be overly expensive and time consuming. A middling of the Copyright Office's proposed requirements and those proposed by Duke appears to be optimal. The problem with this is how to define it.

A search of the Copyright Office's archives, including copyright registration archives, orphan works notice archives, and copyright owner affirmative response archives, as proposed above, should be mandatory for all searches. However, from that point forward, the defining of a reasonably diligent search becomes much more difficult. As discussed previously, the search for the copyright owner of a poem would probably be much different than a search for the copyright owner of a photograph. The difficulty in defining at what point a particular search becomes diligent without being overly burdensome on the user is the issue in the diligent search dilemma.

A reasonable solution to this dilemma is to install semi-rigid search requirement for orphan works searches that is annually or biannually reviewed and updated by the Copyright Office with input from copyright owners. Initial diligent search requirements could provide that users wishing to avail themselves of the orphan work limitation on liability would be required to perform searches of Copyright Office registration archives, Copyright Office Orphaned Works Notice of Use archives, Copyright Office Copyright Owner Affirmative Notice archives, a minimum of ten general Internet search engine searches, and searches of other databases and websites geared specifically toward the particular type of work being researched. All of these searches would be required to be documented either electronically through screen captures or through paper sources such as printing out screenshots. All documented searches would also be required to contain time and date stamps for verification that the search was performed prior to the use of the orphan work. Further, as provided for in the proposed orphan works legislation, each use of any work would require a separate search that comported with the required search requirements. A new user could not depend solely upon a search conducted by a previous user of the same work, but a previous user's search could be cited as part of the new user's diligent search. Certified diligent foreign searches may also qualify as part of a reasonably diligent search as determined on a case-by-case basis by a court.

The notice requirements proposed by the Copyright Office are substantial. However, the proposed Notice of Use requirements, while requiring the filing of the user's name, is silent on any requirement of the user to provide contact information in the event that the copyright owner should find the notice and want to contact the user. The provision of contact information for the user would be an important piece for bringing the copyright owner and user together. Imagine being a copyright owner and finding that a Notice of Use is filed with the Copyright Office for one of your works and the name of the user who filed the notice is James Smith, the most popular male name in the

United States,[161] but there is no contact information for Mr. Smith. With nearly 40,000[162] James Smiths in the United States, the task for the copyright owner to find James Smith the user would be daunting.[163] Common sense dictates that contact information for a user, in the form of an email address, telephone number, or physical address, would be required when a notice of use is filed with the Copyright Office. Users' contact information should also be required to be kept up to date by the user for the benefit of copyright owners. Without these features, the point of orphan works legislation, to bring copyright owners and users together, is stymied from the outset.

The other notice requirement recommendation, as discussed above, is the cost of filing a notice of use. The filing of a notice of use should be inexpensive or free, if done electronically. It can be reasonably concluded that a substantial filing cost would act as a barrier to filing a notice for many users. If the intended purpose of orphan works legislation is to foster access to works that would otherwise be inaccessible due to copyright restraints, then it would be logical to maintain the lowest price point possible to encourage maximum use.

The elimination of attorneys' fees for claims of infringement under orphan works legislation for registered works is troubling. As discussed previously, the elimination of attorneys' fees under an orphan works limitation on liability could negatively impact a copyright owner's willingness to register a work.[164] The intention of orphan works legislation, to open up access to works for qualified users by providing limitations on liability, should not overpower a copyright owner's rights to aggressively enforce his/her rights. The cost of pursuing an infringement claim can be substantial, and attorneys' fees are a significant factor in that cost. If a copyright owner is forced to shoulder the cost of attorneys' fees then that could act as a deterrent to the copyright owner to pursue reasonable compensation from a user.

Similarly, the elimination of costs is another significant deterrent to copyright owners seeking reasonable compensation under orphan works limitation on liability. The cost to the copyright owner of

---

[161] Lee Hartman, *Why Aren't There More John Smiths in the U.S.?*, SLATE (Nov. 3, 2013), http://www.slate.com/articles/life/slate_labs/2013/11/john_smith_why_don_t_more_amer icans_have_this_most_common_name.html

[162] *Id.*

[163] *Id.*

[164] *See supra* Part III.B.3.a.

providing valuations for a work immediately prior to the implementation of the use of the work by the user could be substantial. These substantial costs, like attorneys' fees, could dissuade a copyright owner from seeking reasonable compensation from a user if those costs and attorneys' fees are not potentially recoupable.

Reasonable compensation for the use of a work is not reasonable if the compensation does not take into consideration the expense that the copyright owner incurred to establish and retrieve said reasonable compensation. The limited liability purpose of orphan works legislation needs to be balanced against a copyright owner's costs in protecting her copyright. An equitable compromise in this situation would be the installation of a system for registered works that mimics the remedies for infringement that presently exist. If a registered work is legitimately registered as an orphan work, the copyright owner would then have the choice of seeking reasonable compensation from the user under a statutory damages scale, the scale for orphan works statutory damages being a significantly lower amount than the standard infringement range, or choose to do a valuation for the purpose of showing the likelihood of what a licensing fee would have been if entered into immediately prior to the use. Taking the statutory damages route could be a faster and less involved process for a copyright owner and user but less precise in valuation. Performing a valuation could be more precise in determining the actual value of the work immediately prior to the use but also more time consuming and expensive. When evaluating a reasonable compensation, a court could take these factors into account and apply none, part, or all of the cost of valuation on the user. This uncertainty would act as a motivator for both copyright owners and users to negotiate under the orphan works statutory damages range to avoid potentially higher and indeterminate costs. This would also eliminate the disincentive to registration that could occur if attorneys' fees and costs were eliminated for registered works under orphan works legislation.

At the same time, no provision for costs or attorneys' fees for unregistered works under orphan works legislation may provide a further incentive to copyright owners to register their works. The Copyright Office estimates that the majority of orphan works will be comprised of unregistered works. Registered works, which would comprise the minority of orphan works, would maintain the advantages of registration, while unregistered works, which would comprise the majority of orphan works, would have no such benefits and would provide significant limitations on liability to qualified orphan works users.

The potential curtailment or elimination of injunctive relief under orphan works legislation is a significant diversion from copyright procedures. As discussed above, injunctive relief is often the first remedy sought in an infringement suit and potentially the only remedy received. The proposed orphan works legislation does not eliminate injunctive relief completely, but it does restrain it significantly regarding derivative works and in the area of reputational harm. Furthermore, the 2015 Report makes clear that the Copyright Office's intention is to limit the application of injunctive relief by the courts in most orphan works cases.[165]

Injunctive relief is an important remedy in infringement cases that should be available to all copyright owners. That being said, the intention of the Copyright Office to strike a balance between copyright owners' rights and users' good faith use of orphan works is an important consideration. The Copyright Office's proposal to exempt derivative works from injunctive relief is logical when all orphan works requirements are met and the copyright owner and user agree to a reasonable compensation. A user that creates a derivative work after doing a good faith diligent search and filing notice of use should not have to fear that if the copyright owner of the original work comes forward that the derivative work would be enjoined from any further use. This limitation on injunctive relief would act as an encouragement to qualified users to utilize orphan works and invest in the creation of derivative works, as the Copyright Office contends. However, as discussed,[166] the 2015 Report does recognize that the unavailability of injunctive relief for derivative works is not appropriate in all situations.

The Copyright Office proposes that injunctive relief for derivative works be available only when reasonable compensation is insufficient to remedy the claimed harm to honor and/or reputation and the copyright owner is also the author of the original work.[167] In order for injunctive relief to be applied in this situation, a court would need to determine that the continued preparation or use of the derivative work would be so detrimental to a copyright owner-author's reputation and/or honor that the harm could not be curried by reasonable

---

[165] ORPHAN WORKS AND MASS DIGITIZATION, *supra* note 6, at 67.
[166] *See supra* Part III.B.3.c.
[167] ORPHAN WORKS AND MASS DIGITIZATION, *supra* note 6, at 68.

compensation alone.[168] This approach, while intended to address
copyright owner-authors' concerns and find a balance between good
faith users and copyright owner-authors, is too restrictive. Copyright
owner-authors are not the only parties that can suffer harm that would
be prejudicial to their reputation or honor. There are many situations
where a non-author copyright owner, whether individual or
organization, could suffer prejudicial and possibly irreparable harm to
her reputation and/or honor due to association with a derivative work
whose content or author is antithetical to the non-author copyright
owners moral stance and/or reputation in the community. It is for this
reason that orphan works legislation should not limit injunctive relief to
only copyright owner-authors in cases of derivative works. Courts
should have the ability to decide the application of injunctive relief on a
case-by-case basis for any copyright owner that claims prejudicial harm
to reputation and honor, regardless of authorship status.

The Copyright Office's new stance on fair use in the 2015
Report deserves recognition and endorsement. Fair use is arguably
more important to copyright at this moment in time than at any
previous time in its history. The importance of fair use is no longer a
consideration just for potential copyright users but also for copyright
owners.[169] The continued availability of fair use in conjunction with
orphan works legislation would provide users important protections and
peace of mind when entering the orphan works arena. Theoretically, a
user could do a good faith diligent search, as interpreted by the user,
with an eye on fair use as a back-up defense. If a copyright owner were
to sue for infringement in this situation and the court were to determine
that the user's search was not diligent or the notice of use was faulty,
the user would still be afforded the opportunity to present a fair use
defense. In the alternative, a user could choose to forego the orphan
works limitation on liability completely and move forward using a
work under a theory of fair use alone.[170] The Copyright Office's
decision to specifically address and maintain fair use in the proposed
orphan works legislation is an indication of the importance of fair use
to copyright users.

---

[168] *Id.*
[169] Lenz v. Universal Music Corp., 801 F.3d 1126 (9th Cir. 2015), *amended and superseded on denial of reh'g*, 815 F.3d 1145 (9th Cir. 2016).
[170] ORPHAN WORKS AND MASS DIGITIZATION, *supra* note 6, at 71.

V.     CONCLUSION

The discussion of orphan works, the analysis of the 2015 Report and the proposed orphan works legislation, and the recommendations for proposed orphan works legislation are not easily structured. Very few, if any, matters are black and white when dealing with orphan works. Opinions still differ as to whether there is an orphan works problem at all, or, if there is, whether the orphan works problem requires legislation or if existing legal principles are sufficient to address the issue.[171] The reality is that no one can say with certainty what benefit or detriment orphan works legislation may bring.

Copyright owners, copyright users, the Copyright Office, lawmakers, experts, practitioners, and lay people can speculate over the positive and negative results of orphan works legislation but none can know what impact, if any, it will have until it is enacted. However, there are two things that none of the people or groups involved in and concerned with the orphan works issue can deny: 1) technology is causing the proliferation of the number of original works of authorship, whether published or unpublished, that are entering the public view on a daily basis, which in turn have the potential to swell the orphan works ranks; and 2) any orphan works legislation enacted will be a twenty-first century addition to a twentieth century Act.

Orphaned works legislation, while well intentioned, is a stopgap approach to dealing with the issue of the proliferation of orphan works, especially in new technology. It is a digital patch added onto an 8-track tape[172] copyright statute. A standalone orphan works addition to the 1976 Copyright Act is not the solution to the orphan works issue. It is, more likely than not, another piece of legislation that will lead to unintended consequences, much like the dropping of copyright notice requirement for publication or the continuous extension of copyright terms.[173]

The consequences of eliminating the copyright notice requirement have had a direct impact upon the increase in orphan works. Prior to January 1, 1978, if a work was published without

---

[171] *Id.* at 70–71.
[172] *The History of the 8-Track Tape*, RECORDING HIST.: THE HIST. OF RECORDING TECH., http://www.recording-history.org/HTML/8track1.php (last visited May 14, 2016).
[173] DAVID R. HANSEN, ORPHAN WORKS: CAUSES OF THE PROBLEM (Berkeley Digital Library Copyright Project White Paper No. 3, Apr. 10, 2012), http://ssrn.com/abstract=2038068.

copyright notice, it went immediately into the public domain, and from January 1, 1978, until March 1, 1989, if a work was published without copyright notice and not subsequently registered with the Copyright Office within five years, the work fell to the public domain.[174] However, since March 1, 1989, there has been no copyright notice requirement, which has allowed people to publish millions and possibly billions of works, depending on how publication is interpreted, without the requirement for any identification of copyright ownership and still maintain copyright ownership. This plethora of works, which in the past would have flowed directly into the public domain, now often flows into the ocean of orphan works instead.

Similarly, the progressive extension of copyright terms has created a situation where virtually no new works are entering the public domain. The retention of copyrights in private hands for longer and longer periods, much like the changes in copyright formalities, is exacerbating the orphan works problem. Orphaned works legislation is then needed to attempt to alleviate the problem caused by the elimination of copyright formalities and the extension of copyright terms. Changes to the 1976 Copyright Act were held out as benefits when enacted by Congress.

Congress should look to institute a new copyright act instead of adding another patch to cover holes in the current copyright statute created by previous changes. A new copyright act could smoothly update and integrate changes to the United States copyright system.[175] A new copyright Act could also integrate the orphan works issue into the structure of the new act and account for issues such as notice, publication, and search requirements. A Band-Aid[176] is great for a scraped knee but not very effective for fixing a broken leg. Unfortunately, orphan works legislation is the equivalent of a Band-Aid, and the 1976 Copyright Act is the broken leg. Orphan works legislation might stop the bleeding for a while, but the leg is still broken. So is our current system of copyright.

---

[174] *Copyright Term and the Public Domain in the United States*, CORNELL, http://copyright.cornell.edu/resources/publicdomain.cfm (last updated Jan. 3, 2016).
[175] The author here is being an eternal optimist as opposed to a pragmatist.
[176] Band-Aid brand adhesive bandages is a registered Trademark of Johnson & Johnson, 1 Johnson & Johnson Plaza, New Brunswick, New Jersey 08933-7001. BAND-AID, Registration No. 4182885.

# MAKE AMERICA INNOVATE AGAIN: CONSTRUING PATENT BOX PROPOSALS IN VIEW OF A POLICY MIX APPROACH
ADAM E. SZYMANSKI[1]

---

[1] Adam Szymanski is a graduate of William Mitchell College of Law. He is a practicing attorney at Kinney & Lange PA in Minneapolis, Minnesota.

I.        INTRODUCTION

Recent Congressional proposals suggest budding bipartisan support for enacting a patent box.[2] A patent box[3] is a regulatory regime granting tax relief for commercial activity related to qualifying research and development (R&D), patents, or other intellectual property (IP).[4] Tax relief is often provided to firms[5] through a deduction, a reduced rate, or an exemption of IP income.[6] Congressmen Boustany's (R-LA) and Neal's (D-MA) patent box proposal allows corporations to deduct 71% of qualified profits, producing an effective 10% tax rate.[7] Meanwhile, Senator Feinstein's (D-CA) proposal seeks a 15% tax rate on income from patents developed and used for manufacture in the

---

[2] JANE G. GRAVELLE, CONG. RESEARCH SERV., IN10289, A U.S. PATENT BOX: ISSUES (2015), https://www.fas.org/sgp/crs/misc/IN10289.pdf ("Congressional proposals for the subsidy (known as a patent or innovation box) include a draft proposal by Representatives Boustany and Neal, the Innovation Promotion Act of 2015, proposed legislation by Senator Feinstein, and a bill introduced by Representative Schwartz in the 113th Congress (H.R. 2605)."); Evan Migdail & Bruce Thompson, *Patent box concept emerges on the tax reform agenda for U.S. Congress*, JDSUPRA BUS. ADVISOR (May 5, 2015), http://www.jdsupra.com/legalnews/patent-box-concept-emerges-on-the-tax-27232/ ("In recent weeks, a major concept has emerged in tax reform discussions: the establishment of a patent or innovation box.").
[3] Depending on the types of intellectual property covered, it is also known as an innovation box. See Bernard Knight & Goud Maragani, *It Is Time for the United States to Implement a Patent Box Tax Regime to Encourage Domestic Manufacturing*, 19 STAN. J.L. BUS. & FIN. 39, 52 (2013). Ireland implemented the first patent box in 1973, and the UK, France, and China, among others, have done so in recent years. GRAVELLE, *supra* note 2; ROBERT D. ATKINSON & SCOTT ANDES, THE INFO. TECH. & INNOVATION FOUND., PATENT BOXES: INNOVATION IN TAX POLICY AND TAX POLICY FOR INNOVATION 15 (2011), http://www.itif.org/files/2011-patent-box-final.pdf.
[4] Jim Shanahan, *Is it time for your Country to consider the "patent box"?*, PWC'S GLOBAL R&D TAX SYMPOSIUM ON DESIGNING A BLUEPRINT FOR REDUCING THE AFTER-TAX COST OF GLOBAL R&D 4 (2011), http://download.pwc.com/ie/pubs/2011_is_it_time_for_your_country_to_consider_the_patent_box.pdf; ATKINSON & ANDES, *supra* note 3.
[5] Per Bylund, *The Economic Theory of the Firm*, MISES DAILY (Sep. 20, 2011), https://mises.org/library/economic-theory-firm.
[6] Michael J. Graetz & Rachael Doud, *Technological Innovation, International Competition, and the Challenges of International Income Taxation*, 113 COLUM. L. REV. 347, 363 (2013).
[7] JASON J. FICHTNER & ADAM N. MICHEL, MERCATUS CENTER AT GEORGE MASON UNIV., DON'T PUT AMERICAN INNOVATION IN A PATENT BOX: TAX POLICY, INTELLECTUAL PROPERTY, AND THE FUTURE OF R&D, MERCATUS ON POLICY 2–3 (2015), http://mercatus.org/sites/default/files/Fichtner-Patent-Boxes-MOP.pdf; GRAVELLE, *supra* note 2.

US.[8] Although regimes vary,[9] nations typically deploy patent boxes to address certain market failures hindering innovation.[10] In particular, patent boxes have been adopted abroad as a back-end incentive to foster R&D commercialization and spending by domestic firms.[11]

Despite widespread adoption, patent boxes remain controversial.[12] Proponents cite potential domestic manufacturing gains and incentive effects.[13] Skeptics and opponents, on the other hand, raise redundancy and efficacy concerns.[14] Before expending political capital to adopt a patent box, its impact as a potential U.S. policy instrument should be considered.

Assessing the efficacy of a patent box elsewhere may inform the U.S. impact analysis. The U.K. recently enacted a patent box in 2013 and shares enough economic similarities to provide a useful comparison to the U.S.[15] A mere country-to-country comparison, however, fails to consider the broader, interactive factors that contribute to a country's innovation performance.[16] A policy mix approach offers a conceptual framework for understanding the

---

[8] GRAVELLE, *supra* note 2.

[9] *See* Shanahan, *supra* note 4, at 4. *See also* Knight & Maragani, *supra* note 3, at 48.

[10] Innovation refers to the "transformation of ideas into new products, services, or improvements in organization or process." RISING TO THE CHALLENGE: U.S. INNOVATION POLICY FOR THE GLOBAL ECONOMY 24 (Charles W. Wessner & Alan Wm. Wolff, eds., Nat'l Academies Press 2012), http://politiques-innovation.org/wp-content/uploads/2013/07/2012-Wessner-STEP-Rising-to-the-Challenge-U.S.-Innovation-Policy-for-Global-Economy.pdf. Accordingly, "[s]ome innovations are incremental; others are disruptive, displacing exiting technologies while creating new markets and value networks." *Id.* ATKINSON & ANDES, *supra* note 3, at 15–16; *see infra* Section III.

[11] ROBERT D. ATKINSON & STEPHEN J. EZELL, INNOVATION ECONOMICS: THE RACE FOR A GLOBAL ADVANTAGE 172 (2012); *see* GLOBAL TAX ACCOUNTING SERVICES, PRICEWATERHOUSECOOPERS, PATENT BOX AND TECHNOLOGY INCENTIVES: TAX AND FINANCIAL REPORTING CONSIDERATIONS 1–2 (2014), https://www.pwc.com/gx/en/tax/publications/assets/pwc-patent-box-and-technology-incentives-tax-and-financial-reporting-considerations.pdf; *see also* Graetz & Doud, *supra* note 6, at 362 ("A substantial number of European countries have recently implemented innovation tax incentives that focus on the income, rather than the development, side of IP by adopting 'patent boxes,' or 'innovation boxes.'").

[12] Simon Goodley, *George Osborne waters down flagship controversial tax break*, THE GUARDIAN (Nov. 11, 2014, 1:07 PM), http://www.theguardian.com/politics/2014/nov/11/george-osborne-patent-boxes-tax-break.

[13] *See, e.g.*, Knight & Margani, *supra* note 3, at 42–46.

[14] ATKINSON & ANDES, *supra* note 3, at 1, 9–14.

[15] ATKINSON & ANDES, *supra* note 3, at 15.

[16] *See infra* Section III.

interdependence of actors, ideas, structures, institutions, and policies integral to a country's innovation performance. Evaluating the impact of the U.K. patent box in this framework will overcome the pitfalls of a direct comparison.[17]

Therefore, to gauge the value of adopting a patent box, this paper first establishes the importance of innovation policy within the increasingly competitive nature of the global economy.[18] It then assesses the U.K. and U.S. policy instruments deployed to foster innovation: the patent box and the R&D tax credit, respectively.[19] With an understanding of these two exemplary policy instruments, a broader policy mix framework is then developed to provide a conceptual underpinning for evaluating the efficacy of the patent box and the innovation ecology of both countries.[20] This paper then, based on the comparison and policy mix framework, argues that the patent box provides little benefit beyond that of already implemented policy tools.[21] Finally, a more comprehensive and directed approach to innovation, rather than the incremental one used thus far, is recommended to ensure that the U.S. remains competitive in the global economy.[22]

II.     U.K. AND U.S. INNOVATION POLICY IN A COMPETITIVE
GLOBAL ECONOMY

A.   Global Competition to Foster Innovation

It is widely accepted by economists and nations alike that innovation drives economic prosperity.[23] It is also well established that private sector R&D is "crucial to ongoing technological advances," is

---

[17] See infra Section IV.
[18] See infra Section II.A.
[19] See infra Section II.B.
[20] See infra Section III.
[21] See infra Section IV.
[22] See infra Section IV.
[23] Graetz & Doud, supra note 6, at 348 ("Two things are clear and essentially uncontested among economists. First is the importance of technological innovations to economic growth."); ATKINSON & EZELL supra note 11, at 6 ("[M]ost nations recognize that they have to be intense competitors if they are to be successful . . . . And most nations also realize that high wage innovation and knowledge-based industries play a key role in driving prosperity."); RISING TO THE CHALLENGE, supra note 10, at 201 ("Virtually every important trading partner has declared innovation to be central to increasing productivity, economic growth, and living standards.").

capable of producing positive externalities, and "is underproduced in the absence of government support."[24] This, combined with the growing mobility of firms, has created an environment where countries look to reel in firms with beneficial policies.[25] Fierce competition has thus arisen between nations to develop innovation policies that attract firms willing to invest in R&D and increase commercialization by domestic firms:[26] "Nations around the world are establishing national innovation strategies, restructuring their tax and regulatory systems to become more competitive, expanding support for science and technology, improving their education systems, spurring investment in broadband and other IT areas, and taking a myriad of other pro-innovation steps."[27]

A nation hoping to compete in this environment must make innovation a focal point of its economic development.[28] Failure to acknowledge and adapt to the increasingly competitive international innovation arena could spell future economic trouble.[29]

The U.S. once stood at the forefront of innovation policy in the 1970s but has since fallen.[30] Although it now spends more on R&D than any other nation, "its relative position (measured by the share of such investment in national income) has been falling even as other countries increase their investments in research."[31] This decline will become increasingly problematic as the U.S. economy relies more and

---

[24] Graetz & Doud, *supra* note 6, at 349; *see* Laura Tyson & Greg Linden, *The Corporate R&D Tax Credit and U.S. Innovation and Competitiveness: Gauging the Economic and Fiscal Effectiveness of the Credit*, CTR. FOR AM. PROGRESS 1 (2012), http://www.americanprogress.org/wp-content/uploads/issues/2012/01/pdf/corporate_r_and_d.pdf

[25] *See* ATKINSON & ANDES, *supra* note 3, at 15.

[26] RISING TO THE CHALLENGE, *supra* note 10, at 201 ("The twenty-first century is witnessing a rapidly evolving, intensely competitive global landscape. Political and business leaders in both advanced and emerging economies see innovation-led development as central to growth. China, India, Russia, Germany, and Singapore are among the many nations that are formulating comprehensive national strategies for improving their innovation capacity."); *see* ATKINSON & ANDES, *supra* note 3, at 20 n.1 (quoting Rachel Griffith, Helen Miller & Martin O'Connell, "Corporate Taxes and the Location of Intellectual Property" (June 2011) (working paper) (Center for Economic Policy Research).

[27] 3 ATKINSON & EZELL, *supra* note 11, at 6.

[28] *Id.* at 8.

[29] *Cf. id.*, at 9–10 (arguing that rapid industrial decline is related to a lack of challenging the status quo thinking regarding innovation–supporting policies).

[30] *See id.*, at 6.

[31] TYSON & LINDEN, *supra* note 24, at 1.

more on innovation and IP.[32] To stem this decline, the U.S. must
reassess its innovation policy.[33]

### B.    Comparing U.K. and U.S. Innovation Policy

U.K. innovation policy and its effects serve as a useful
counterpoint to those of the U.S., providing the comparative utility of a
patent box and illustrative economic factors. Both, for example, are
world-leaders in research[34] and have top-notch universities, each an
important element in sustaining innovation. A key distinction, however,
lies in the U.K.'s comparatively low rate of business innovation.[35]
From 2000 to 2013, the U.K.'s business R&D intensity[36] ranked well
below the average of Organisation for Economic Co-operation and
Development (OECD) countries.[37] The U.S., on the other hand, ranked
above the OECD average during the period from 2000 to 2012.[38] These
distinctions will prove useful in assessing the potential efficacy of the
patent box in the U.S.[39]

---

[32] *See* ATKINSON & ANDES, *supra* note 3, at 17.

[33] *See id.*

[34] *See* OECD Science, *Technology and Industry Scoreboard* (2011), http://www.oecd-ilibrary.org/sites/sti_scoreboard-2011-
en/02/05/index.html?itemId=/content/chapter/sti_scoreboard-2011-16-en (last visited
May 14, 2016); Peter Coy, *The Bloomberg Innovation Index*, BLOOMBERG (2015),
http://www.bloomberg.com/graphics/2015-innovative-countries/.

[35] *See* THE ORG. FOR ECON. CO-OPERATION AND DEV., DIRECTORATE FOR SCI., TECH.
AND INNOVATION, R&D TAX INCENTIVE SUPPORT: UNITED KINGDOM (2016),
http://www.oecd.org/sti/OECD-STI-RDTaxIncentives-CountryProfile_GBR.pdf; THE
ORG. FOR ECON. CO-OPERATION AND DEV., DIRECTORATE FOR SCI., TECH. AND
INNOVATION, R&D TAX INCENTIVE SUPPORT: UNITED STATES (2016),
http://www.oecd.org/sti/OECD-STI-RDTaxIncentives-CountryProfile_USA.pdf.

[36] R&D intensity is a measure of an "economy's relative degree of investment in
generating new knowledge" and is calculated as the gross domestic expenditure on R&D
as a percentage of GDP. OECD, *OECD Science, Technology and Industry Scoreboard*
(2011), http://www.oecd-ilibrary.org/sites/sti_scoreboard-2011-
en/02/05/index.html?itemId=/content/chapter/sti_scoreboard-2011-16-en (last visited
May 14, 2016).

[37] *Id.*

[38] OECD, R&D TAX INCENTIVE SUPPORT: UNITED STATES,
http://www.oecd.org/sti/OECD-STI-RDTaxIncentives-CountryProfile_USA.pdf (last
visited May 14, 2016).

[39] *See infra* Section IV.

## 1. Innovation Policy in the UK

"The U.K. has made a conscientious decision to place innovation at the center of our nation's economic growth strategy"[40] by deploying, among other things, R&D tax incentives and tax advantaged venture capital schemes as innovation policy instruments.[41] Most relevant here, however, is its recent adoption of the patent box.

### a. History of the U.K. Patent Box

Responding to a growing number of companies moving patent holdings offshore, the government in 2010 announced its intent to introduce a patent box as part of a larger plan to develop a more competitive tax system for businesses.[42] In particular, the goal was to provide incentives for companies to retain and commercialize existing patents and to develop new patented products:[43] "The Patent Box will encourage companies to locate the high-value jobs and activity associated with the development, manufacture and exploitation of patents in the UK. It will also enhance the competitiveness of the UK tax system for high-tech companies that obtain profits from patents."[44]

The patent box was developed, in part, over the course of three consultations.[45] With each consultation, Her Majesty's Treasury (HM Treasury), the economic and finance ministry of the U.K.

---

[40] ATKINSON & EZELL, *supra* note 11, at 135.
[41] DEPARTMENT FOR BUSINESS INNOVATION & SKILLS, OUR PLAN FOR GROWTH: SCIENCE AND INNOVATION (2014), https://www.gov.uk/government/uploads/system/uploads/attachment_data/file/387780/P U1719_HMT_Science_.pdf.
[42] HM TREASURY, CONSULTATION ON THE PATENT BOX 3 (2011), https://www.gov.uk/government/uploads/system/uploads/attachment_data/file/81512/con sult_patent_box.pdf.
[43] CIRD200110 Patent Box: overview of the patent box regime: aim of the patent box, http://www.hmrc.gov.uk/Manuals/cirdmanual/CIRD200110.htm (last visited May 14, 2016).
[44] HM TREASURY, CORPORATE TAX REFORM: DELIVERING A MORE COMPETITIVE SYSTEM 47 (2010), https://www.gov.uk/government/uploads/system/uploads/attachment_data/file/81303/cor porate_tax_reform_complete_document.pdf.
[45] HM TREASURY, PATENT BOX: SUBSTANTIAL ACTIVITIES 3 (2015), https://www.gov.uk/government/uploads/system/uploads/attachment_data/file/469969/Pa tent_Box_substantial_activities.pdf.

government,[46] hoped to engage "businesses, representative bodies and others interested in the [sic] promoting the growth of innovative companies in the U.K. will play a full part in the consultation process."[47] Shortly after these consultations, the Finance Act of 2012 enacted the current patent box into law.[48]

Recent developments, however, promise forthcoming changes to the patent box.[49] On October 22, 2015, HM Treasury released a consultation discussing options for modifying the patent box in view of OECD recommendations predicated on curbing base erosion and profit shifting by multinational enterprises.[50] The U.K.'s new approach to the patent box will be that of a modified nexus approach.[51] Future legislation will likely "introduce a requirement that, in order to benefit from the regime, a business must conduct the substantial activities which generate the income benefiting from the regime."[52] The changes aligned with the OECD recommendations will apply to new entrants on July 1, 2016.[53]

b.   Design of the U.K. Patent Box

The current U.K. patent box, as yet unchanged by the OECD recommendations, applies a 10% lower rate of corporate tax to profits attributable to patents and equivalent forms of IP, whether received as a

---

[46] HM Treasury, *About us*, https://www.gov.uk/government/organisations/hm-treasury/about (last visited May 14, 2016) ("HM Treasury is the government's economic and finance ministry, maintaining control over public spending, setting the direction of the U.K.'s economic policy and working to achieve strong and sustainable economic growth.").

[47] CONSULTATION ON THE PATENT BOX, *supra* note 42.

[48] CIRD200120 Patent Box: overview of the patent box regime: history of the patent box, http://www.hmrc.gov.uk/Manuals/cirdmanual/CIRD200120.htm (last visited May 14, 2016); *see* Finance Act 2012, sch. 2, *available at* http://www.legislation.gov.uk/ukpga/2012/14/pdfs/ukpga_20120014_en.pdf (last visited May 14, 2016); *see also* PATENT BOX: SUBSTANTIAL ACTIVITIES, *supra* note 45, at 7.

[49] *See* PATENT BOX: SUBSTANTIAL ACTIVITIES, *supra* note 45, at 10.

[50] *See id.* at 1; Simmons & Simmons, *U.K. consultation on patent box changes*, ELIXICA (Oct. 30, 2015), http://www.elexica.com/en/legal-topics/tax/30-uk-consultation-on-patent-box-changes.

[51] Simmons & Simmons, *supra* note 50.

[52] *Id.*

[53] *Id.*

royalty or embedded in the sales price of a product.[54] The lower rate is achieved through an equivalent deduction based on relevant profits.[55] The deduction can be calculated according to the following formula:

$$RP \times FY\% \times ((MR - IPR) \div MR)$$

where RP is the profits of a company's trade relevant to patent box; FY% is the appropriate percentage for each financial year; MR is the main rate of Corporation Tax; and IPR is the reduced rate of 10%.[56] Qualifying companies can elect to receive this benefit.[57]

      In order to qualify, a company must satisfy one of three conditions: condition A, B, or C.[58] A company fulfills condition A if it holds qualifying IP rights or an exclusive license in qualifying IP rights.[59] Condition B is met if a company has held a 'qualifying IP right' or an exclusive license in respect of any qualifying IP rights, has received income in respect of an event or events occurring at times when it was a qualifying company and a patent box election had effect, and that income falls to be taxed in a later accounting period.[60] Lastly, condition C can be met only by members of a group and requires a company to have either developed or be actively managing its IP portfolio.[61] Qualifying IP includes patents granted under the U.K. Patents Act of 1977 and under the European Patent Convention.[62]

---

[54] HM REVENUE & CUSTOMS, CORPORATION TAX: THE PATENT BOX (Jan. 1, 2007) https://www.gov.uk/guidance/corporation-tax-the-patent-box; *see also* PATENT BOX: SUBSTANTIAL ACTIVITIES, *supra* note 45, at 7.; CIRD200120, *supra* note 48.
[55] PATENT BOX: SUBSTANTIAL ACTIVITIES, *supra* note 45, at 7.
[56] CORPORATION TAX: THE PATENT BOX, *supra* note 54.
[57] DLA Piper, *The UK Patent Box: Plan Now For 2013 and Beyond* 1 (2012), https://www.dlapiper.com/~/media/Files/Insights/Publications/2012/07/The%20UK%20p atent%20box/Files/UK_Patent_Box/FileAttachment/UK_Patent_Box.pdf (last visited May 14, 2016).
[58] CIRD210100 Patent Box: qualifying companies: meaning of 'qualifying company,' http://www.hmrc.gov.uk/manuals/cirdmanual/CIRD210100.htm (last visited May 14, 2016).
[59] *Id.*
[60] *Id.*
[61] *Id.*
[62] DLA Piper, *supra* note 57, at 2.

c.   *Efficacy of the U.K. Patent Box*

It may be too early to assess the true impact of the U.K. patent box.[63] One way to determine the effectiveness of the patent box would require data showing the extent to which it accomplished its aims.[64] A proper evaluation would thus require evidence showing the extent to which the tax regime incentivized companies to retain and commercialize existing patents or develop newly patented products at the margins.[65] It would also consider evidence tending to show the movement of high-value jobs into the U.K. to exploit the tax regime.[66] This, weighed against the loss of tax revenue resulting from these tax breaks would provide an idea of the measure's efficacy.[67]

Some emerging evidence may bear on this balance, but the overall outlook remains unclear. According to HM Treasury, "[t]he introduction of the Patent Box has encouraged investment and economic growth in the U.K. as well as limiting the movement of intellectual property offshore by innovative businesses that might otherwise have invested elsewhere."[68] As of October 22, 2015, 639 companies using the patent box had received a benefit having an aggregate total of £335 million.[69] Further dissection of this statistic, however, would be necessary to understand how it captures the commercialization of patents for companies that would not have otherwise done so. Additionally, GlaxoSmithKline, a pharmaceutical

---

[63] *See* CAMBRIDGE DESIGN PARTNERSHIP AND MARKS & CLERK, *An Industry Report on the Patent Box Initiative and its Impact on UK Innovation, Patent Box: Incentivizing UK Innovation* 6 (2013), http://www.marks-clerk.com/MarksClerk/media/MCMediaLib/PDF's/Reports/Marks-Clerk-Patent-Box-Report-2013.pdf?ext=.pdf (last visited May 14, 2016).

[64] ORGANISATION FOR ECONOMIC CO-OPERATION AND DEVELOPMENT, *Reducing the Risk of Policy Failure: Challenges for Regulatory Compliance* 7 (2000), https://www.oecd.org/gov/regulatory-policy/1910833.pdf ("A key determinant of government effectiveness is how well regulatory systems achieve their policy objectives."). *See also supra* Section II.B.a.

[65] *See* CHARLES LEVY & LAURA O'BRIEN, *Will the Patent Box Boost the U.K. Innovation Ecosystem?*, BIG INNOVATION CENTRE 7 (2013) https://fvstatic.s3.amazonaws.com/1425647105_0329808001425647105.pdf.

[66] *See supra* Section II.B.2.a.

[67] A similar balancing analysis would be needed to test the impact of the R&D tax credit. *See, e.g,.* GARY GUENTHER, CONG. RESEARCH SERV., RL31191, RESEARCH TAX CREDIT: CURRENT LAW AND POLICY ISSUES FOR THE 114TH CONGRESS 8 (2015), https://www.fas.org/sgp/crs/misc/RL31181.pdf; *see also supra* Section II.B.2.c.

[68] PATENT BOX: SUBSTANTIAL ACTIVITIES, *supra* note 45, at 24.

[69] *Id.* at 5.

company ranked the 135th largest in the world as of 2015,[70] stated an intention to relocate R&D operations into the U.K. to take advantage of the patent box.[71] Though promising, it is unclear the extent to which this may be indicative of other companies following suit. Lastly, another potential efficacy metric, arguably in alignment with stated objectives,[72] might be the extent to which patent filings have increased after or in anticipation of the tax regime's implementation.[73] Patent application filings in the U.K. totaled 22,256 in 2011; 23,229 in 2012; 22,936 in 2013; and 23,040 in 2014.[74] Patent publications totaled 10,043 in 2011; 10,653 in 2012; 11,021 in 2013; and 12,227 in 2014.[75] Based on the data thus far, there is no clear indication that the patent box has affected filings. In light of all presented data, further evidence is needed to assess the efficacy of the U.K. patent box.

### 2. Innovation Policy in the US

In contrast to the U.K. patent box, U.S. federal law provides two tax incentives for firm R&D investment, both of which were enacted to overcome market failures.[76] Section 174 of the Internal Revenue Code (IRC) offers an unlimited expensing allowance for qualified research spending, while Section 41 of the IRC offers a non-

---

[70] The World's Biggest Public Companies, FORBES.COM, http://www.forbes.com/global2000/list/3/#tab:overall (last visited May 14, 2016).
[71] Bob Stembridge, Patent Box Tax Incentives Show Positive Signs, THOMPSON REUTERS, http://stateofinnovation.thomsonreuters.com/patent-box-tax-incentives-show-positive-signs (last visited May 14, 2016) ("GlaxoSmithKline is on record as taking advantage of the U.K. Patent Box by relocating some of its R&D operations back to the U.K. from offshore locations. Chief Executive Andrew Witty said recently, 'Since the Patent Box, we've invested in upgrading 15 or 16 of our sites in the UK. It has made Britain the go-to place for our industry.'").
[72] See supra Section II.B.1.
[73] See CAMBRIDGE DESIGN PARTNERSHIP AND MARKS & CLERK, supra note 63, at 3 (comparing patent application numbers between countries that have enacted Patent Box schemes to those that have not).
[74] INTELLECTUAL PROP. OFFICE, Facts and figures: Patent, trade mark, design & hearing administrative data 2013 and 2014 calendar years 5 (June 2015), https://www.gov.uk/government/uploads/system/uploads/attachment_data/file/456097/Facts_and_Figures_2015.pdf.
[75] Id.
[76] See Gary Guenther, Research Tax Credit: Current Law and Policy Issues for the 114th Congress, CONG. RESEARCH SERV. RL31191 at 2 (March 13, 2015), https://www.fas.org/sgp/crs/misc/RL31181.pdf; W. Wesley Hill & J. Sims Rhyne, Opening Pandora's Patent Box: Global Intellectual Property Tax Incentives and Their Implication for the United States, 53 IDEA 371, 377 (2013).

refundable tax credit for qualified research spending above a base amount ("the R&D credit").[77] The former, enacted in 1954,[78] allows a taxpayer "to deduct currently all 'research and experimental expenditures' made in connection with the taxpayer's trade or business or to amortize the expenditures over a period of not less than 60 months."[79] The latter, and the focus of this section, provides an income tax credit for qualified R&D expenditures.[80]

### a.   History of the U.S. R&D Tax Credit

Responding to the decline in research and development expenditures relative to the real gross national product from 1968 to 1979,[81] Congress established a temporary research tax credit in Section 41 of the Economic Recovery Tax Act of 1981 ("ERTA").[82] Section 41 of the ERTA provided a tax credit to firms "equal to 25% of qualified research spending above a base amount, which was equal to average spending on such research in the three previous tax years, or 50% of current-year spending, whichever was greater."[83] Since its inception, the R&D credit has been modified and extended numerous times.[84] In

---

[77] Guenther, *supra* note 76, at 2; *see* 26 U.S.C. § 174 (2012); 26 U.S.C. § 41 (2012).

[78] Guenther, *supra* note 76, at 2.

[79] David L. Cameron, *Research Tax Credit: Statutory Construction, Regulatory Interpretation and Policy Incoherence*, 9 COMP. L. REV. & TECH. J. 63, 72 (2004); Hill & Rhyne, *supra* note 76, at 376.

[80] Graetz & Doud, *supra* note 6, at 353.

[81] Staff of Joint Comm. on Taxation, 97th Cong., *General Explanation of the Economic Recovery Tax Act of 1981*, at 119 (Comm. Print 1981) ("In the case of research and development activities conducted by business, company-financed and Federal expenditures over the 12-year period 1968-1979 remained at a fairly stable level in real terms, fluctuating between $19 and $22.8 billion in constant dollars. Relative to real gross national product, such expenditures for company research declined from 2.01 percent in 1968 to 1.58 percent in 1975, essentially remaining at that level since then.").

[82] *Id.* at 120 ("In order to reverse this decline in research spending by industry, the Congress concluded that a substantial tax credit for incremental research and experimental expenditures was needed to overcome the reluctance of many ongoing companies to bear the significant costs of staffing and supplies, and certain equipment expenses such as computer charges, which must be incurred to initiate or expand research programs in a trade or business."). *See* Hill & Rhyne, *supra* note 76, at 377; Graetz & Doud, *supra* note 6, at 352.

[83] Guenther, *supra* note 76, at 11.

[84] Tyson & Linden, *supra* note 24, at 7 ("Since then [1981], the credit has been restructured several times and renewed 13 times. With a single 12-month exception in 1995–1996 (during which the credit ceased to be in effect), each extension has continued from the previous date of expiration."); Guenther, *supra* note 76, at 11.

the first such alteration, Congress revised the research tax credit in the Tax Reform Act of 1986 and extended the credit until December 31, 1988.[85] Other noteworthy modifications occurred in the Omnibus Budget Reconciliation Act of 1989 and the Energy Policy Act of 2005. The Omnibus Budget Reconciliation Act of 1989 raised the base amount so that it was equal to the greater of 50% of a firm's current-year qualified research expenditures, or the product of the firm's average annual gross receipts in the previous four tax years and a "fixed-base percentage."[86] The Energy Policy Act "added a fourth component to the research tax credit by establishing a credit equal to 20% of payments for energy research performed under contract by qualified research consortia, colleges and universities, federal laboratories, and eligible small firms."[87] Now, with the passage of the Protecting Americans from Tax Hikes Act of 2015, the R&D tax credit been extended indefinitely.[88]

### b.    Design of the U.S. R&D Tax Credit

In an effort spanning decades, the U.S. has developed a quadripartite R&D credit, comprising: (1) a regular research credit, (2) an alternative simplified credit, (3) a basic research credit, and (4) an energy research credit.[89] The regular research credit equals the sum of 20% of a company's qualified research expenditures for the taxable year over the base amount.[90] With the alternative simplified credit, a firm may elect to receive a credit equal to 14% of the qualified research expenses "for the taxable year as exceeds 50 percent of the average qualified research expenses for the 3 taxable years preceding the taxable year for which the credit is being determined."[91] The basic research credit, under IRC Section 41(e), allows companies that partner with non-profit organizations to receive a credit equal to 20% for qualified research above the qualified organizational base period

---

[85] Guenther, *supra* note 76, at 11.

[86] *Id.*

[87] *Id.* at 13.

[88] *See* Kevin Brady, *Section-by-Section Summary of the Proposed "Protecting Americans from Tax Hikes Act of 2015,"* COMMITTEE ON WAYS AND MEANS 3 (2015), http://waysandmeans.house.gov/wp-content/uploads/2015/12/SECTION-BY-SECTION-SUMMARY-OF-THE-PROPOSED-PATH-ACT.pdf.

[89] Guenther, *supra* note 76, at 3.

[90] 26 U.S.C. § 41(a)(1) (2012); Guenther, *supra* note 76, at 13.

[91] 26 U.S.C. § 41(c)(5).

amount.[92] Lastly, the energy research credit provides firms with a tax credit that equals "20 percent of the amounts paid or incurred by the taxpayer in carrying on any trade or business of the taxpayer during the taxable year (including as contributions) to an energy research consortium for energy research."[93]

The regular research credit and the alternative simplified credit rely on calculations using qualified research expenses and a base amount.[94] Qualified research expenses refer to the sum of in-house research expenses or contract research expenses that are paid or incurred by a firm during the taxable year.[95] In-house expenses include wages and supply costs.[96] Contract research expenses refer to 65% of the amount paid to another for qualified research.[97] The base amount is calculated from the product of the fixed-base percentage and the average gross receipts of the taxpayer for the four taxable years prior to the credit year.[98]

### c.   Efficacy of the U.S. R&D Tax Credit

Much like the U.K. patent box,[99] the effectiveness of the U.S. R&D credit remains unclear.[100] "In theory, the credit stimulates increased investment in qualified research by lowering the after-tax cost of undertaking another dollar of research."[101] Economic studies have attempted to measure the efficacy of the R&D tax credit using cost-benefit or R&D price elasticity analyses.[102] This cost-benefit method compares the increase in R&D spending to the loss in tax revenue, while the price elasticity method "measures the percent change in R&D in response to a 1% change in the user cost of R&D."[103] A review of such studies found that there was a "dollar-for-dollar increase in reported R&D spending on the margin" as a result of

---

[92] Guenther, *supra* note 76, at 8.
[93] 26 U.S.C. § 41(a)(3) (2012).
[94] *Id.* at § 41.
[95] *Id.* at § 41(b).
[96] *Id.* at § 41(b)(3).
[97] *Id.*
[98] *Id.* at § 41(c).
[99] *See supra* Part II.B.1.iii.
[100] Graetz & Doud, *supra* note 6, at 355.
[101] Guenther, *supra* note 76, at 8.
[102] Graetz & Doud, *supra* note 6, at 355.
[103] *Id.* at 356.

the R&D tax credit from 1980 to 1991.[104] A study specific to the pharmaceutical industry from 1982 to 1985, however, found the credit to be much less beneficial, calling into question the reliability of such analyses.[105] Even in more recent studies, the efficacy of the R&D tax credit remains debated.[106]

### III.    AN INNOVATION POLICY MIX

Policy makers and scholars increasingly tout the use of a *policy mix* to address the intricacies affecting a nation's ability to stimulate innovation.[107] Although the scope of the term itself is subject to debate,[108] a policy mix[109] can be understood as the combination of and interaction between the domain areas covered, the rationales proposed, the strategic tasks pursued, and the policy instruments deployed to address a country's innovation goals.[110] The policy mix approach accounts for the interdependence of actors, ideas, structures, institutions, and policies that contribute to a nation's innovation performance and provides a tool for assessing the effectiveness of the entirety of a nation's innovation policies and the interactions thereof.[111] "Using the policy mix concept . . . helps draw attention to inconsistencies and redundancies" that may arise from the incremental deployment of policy instruments.[112] If it does not consider the entire

---

[104] *See* BRONWYN H. HALL, EFFECTIVENESS OF RESEARCH AND EXPERIMENTATION TAX CREDITS: CRTITICAL LITERATURE REVIEW AND RESEARCH DESIGN (1995), https://eml.berkeley.edu/~bhhall/papers/BHH95%20OTArtax.pdf.
[105] Graetz & Doud, *supra* note 6, at 356.
[106] *See* Guenther, *supra* note 76, at 8.
[107] Kieron Flanagan, Elvira Uyarra, & Manuel Laranja, *Reconceptualising the 'policy mix' for Innovation,* RESEARCH POLICY, Vol. 40 702–13 (2011); OECD, *OECD Science, Technology and Industry Outlook,* OECD PUBLISHING 254 (2010), http://www.keepeek.com/Digital-Asset-Management/oecd/science-and-technology/oecd-science-technology-and-industry-outlook-2010_sti_outlook-2010-en#page265.
[108] Flanagan, Uyarra, & Laranja, *supra* note 107, at 4–5; OECD, *supra* note 107, at 254.
[109] The policy mix concept originated in the 1960s in the context of monetary and fiscal policy and has since migrated to other policy arenas, including innovation. Flanagan, Uyarra, & Laranja, *supra* note 107, at 3.
[110] OECD, *supra* note 107, at 257. This understanding can be debated; however, in this paper, this use is preferred.
[111] *Id.* at 255–56; *see also Innovation policy mix for business R&D and Innovation,* OECD, http://www.oecd.org/sti/outlook/e-outlook/stipolicyprofiles/competencestoinnovate/innovationpolicymixforbusinessrdandinnovation.htm (last visited May 14, 2016).
[112] *Innovation policy mix for business R&D and Innovation, supra* note 111.

innovation ecology assessed by the policy mix, a nation, though
interested in stimulating domestic innovation, might implement policy
instruments that focus too heavily on too small of an area, minimizing
its potential returns.[113] Developing this framework will inform the
patent box efficacy analysis.

*A.   Domain Areas*

All of innovation policies can be bifurcated into *domain areas*:
framework condition policies and dedicated science, technology, and
innovation policies.[114] The complementary nature, or lack thereof, of
these domain areas may augment or reduce intended policy effects.[115]
Accordingly, a considered approach addressing the interaction of these
policies can "promote positive feedback responses in the tightly-
coupled parts of the economy, or at least . . . mitigate the force of
negative feedbacks that can damp, or effectively counteract, the
intended effects of the policy intervention targets."[116]

Framework condition policies affect the broad economic
factors relating to innovation and may not relate solely to innovation
goals.[117] Exemplary economic factors include, among others,
macroeconomic policy, tax policy, labor market policy, competition
policy, education and training, infrastructure, and intellectual property
rights.[118] Although these policies may not be innovation-specific, they
can be foundational.[119] For example, a strong education system will

---

[113] *See id.*

[114] *See* OECD, *supra* note 107, at, 259.

[115] *See id.* at 260–61.

[116] PHILIPPE AGHION, PAUL A. DAVID & DOMINQUE FORAY, SCIENCE, TECHNOLOGY AND
INNOVATION FOR ECONOMIC GROWTH: TOWARDS LINKING POLICY RESEARCH AND
PRACTICE IN 'STIG SYSTEMS' 22 (Stanford Inst. for Econ. Policy Research Discussion
Paper No. 06-39, Oct. 2008), http://siepr.stanford.edu/sites/default/files/publications/06-
39_0.pdf.

[117] OECD, *supra* note 107, at 260.

[118] OECD, *supra* note 107, at 260–62; OECD, INTELLIGENT DEMAND: POLICY
RATIONALE, DESIGN AND POTENTIAL BENEFITS 54–57 (OECD Sci, Tech and Industry
Policy Papers No. 13, 2014), http://www.oecd-
ilibrary.org/docserver/download/5jz8p4rk3944.pdf?expires=1462395748&id=id&accnam
e=guest&checksum=A0747E344EF9D325F9BD0AF914380578 [hereinafter
INTELLIGENT DEMAND].

[119] *See* OECD, OECD REVIEWS OF INNOVATION POLICY: CHINA 395 (2008),
http://climatesolver.org/sites/default/files/pdf/0809.pdf ("It is widely acknowledged that
innovative capacity is determined not only by a country's research and development
(R&D) system but also by the interplay of factors which enable knowledge to be

provide the highly-skilled workforce necessary to drive innovation.[120] In another example, a stable macroeconomic environment may relieve some of a firm's more immediate concerns and allow it to invest in long-term R&D projects.[121] "There is a strong link between innovation performance and innovation framework conditions."[122] "Supportive framework conditions enable and facilitate innovation throughout the economy" and have recently become more of a focal point for fostering innovation.[123]

Dedicated science, technology, and innovation policies, by contrast, target specific market, system, or even framework condition policy failures relating to innovation.[124] These policies incorporate both supply- and demand-side measures—for example, R&D tax incentives schemes or grants, and procurement policies, respectively—to support direct investment in science, technology, and innovation, to enhance the innovation competencies of firms, or to strengthen linkages within innovation systems.[125] Both the U.K. patent box and U.S. R&D tax credit are examples of dedicated science, technology, and innovation polices, as each focused on correcting specific market failures.[126]

## B.   Rationales

The fundamental rationales justifying policy intervention address market failure, systems failure, or societal missions and challenges.[127]

---

converted into new products, processes and organisational forms which in turn enhance economic development and growth.").
[120] OECD, *supra* note 107, at 261.
[121] *Id.*
[122] INSIDE CONSULTING, BENCHMARKING INNOVATION POLICY AND INNOVATION FRAMEWORK CONDITIONS 2 (Jan. 2004), http://www.oecd.org/site/worldforum/33705586.pdf.
[123] OECD, *supra* note 107, at 260.
[124] *Id.* at 260, 262.
[125] *Id.* at 260, 268.
[126] *See supra* Section II.
[127] JAKOB EDLER, HUGH CAMERON & MOHAMMAD HAJHASHEM, WORLD INTELLECTUAL PROPERTY ORGANIZATION [WIPO], THE INTERSECTION OF INTELLECTUAL PROPERTY RIGHTS AND INNOVATION POLICY MAKING – A LITERATURE REVIEW 7 (Jul. 2015), http://www.wipo.int/edocs/pubdocs/en/wipo_report_ip_inn.pdf.

### 1. Market Failure

Market failure describes both the inability of price-market institutions to facilitate desirable activities or to halt undesirable ones and the inefficient allocation of resources.[128] These failures stem from indivisibilities, uncertainties, and externalities in the market economy.[129] Innovation market failures, in particular, primarily manifest in three ways:

> i) R&D activity often incurs high fixed costs and economies of scale, while learning-by-doing gives rise to dynamic economies of scale; ii) investment in R&D is inherently risky and information asymmetries abound in markets for knowledge and technology, where they exist; and iii) because knowledge has properties of a public good as performers of R&D can only imperfectly appropriate the results of their effort and the use of knowledge does not preclude its simultaneous use by others.[130]

Underinvestment in R&D in the face of market failure has long been the principle reason for policy intervention.[131] These failures, it is argued, prevent investment in innovation at the socially optimal level.[132] The U.K. patent box and U.S. R&D credit were predicated on addressing market failures.[133]

---

[128] Frances M. Bator, *The Anatomy of Market Failure*, 72 Q. J. ECON. 3 (1958), http://opim.wharton.upenn.edu/~sok/papers/b/Bator-market-failure.pdf; CLIFFORD WINSTON, GOVERNMENT FAILURE VERSUS MARKET FAILURE: MICROECONOMICS POLICY RESEARCH AND GOVERNMENT PERFORMANCE 2 (2006), http://www.brookings.edu/~/media/research/files/papers/2006/9/monetarypolicy-winston/20061003.pdf; *see also* ELLEN SEWELL, MARKET FAILURE 26, http://www.ncpublicschools.org/docs/curriculum/socialstudies/rigorous-ap/economics/microeconomics.pdf (Apr. 10, 2016).

[129] Kenneth Arrow, *Economic Welfare and the Allocation of Resources for Invention, in* THE RATE AND DIRECTION OF INVENTIVE ACTIVITY: ECONOMIC AND SOCIAL FACTORS 609, 609 (1962), http://www.nber.org/chapters/c2144.pdf; INTELLIGENT DEMAND, *supra* note 118, at 8.

[130] INTELLIGENT DEMAND, *supra* note 118, at 8 (emphasis in original).

[131] *Id.*; OECD, *supra* note 107, at 262.

[132] INTELLIGENT DEMAND, *supra* note 118, at 8.

[133] *See supra* Section II.

## 2. System Failure

System failures describe the barriers to innovation that arise from inertia in the economy and hinder the production, distribution, and adoption of knowledge.[134] Innovation often requires cooperation or the exchange of ideas to generate knowledge.[135] System failures are framework conditions—such as network effects, slow technological transitions, slow-changing norms and values, and lack of infrastructure[136]—that inhibit these necessary interactions.[137] "System failures block the functioning of the innovation system, hinder the flow of knowledge and technology and, as a result, reduce the overall efficiency of the system-wide R&D and innovation effort."[138] Overcoming these failures, however, necessitates building up capability, intermediation, training, and cooperative programs.[139]

## 3. Societal Missions and Costs

Societal missions and challenges direct the focus of technology development in order to satisfy certain societal needs: "[I]t is a primary duty of politics to provide direction for technological development and innovation in order to satisfy state needs (e.g. defence, security) and citizen needs (health, education)."[140] These measures incentivize actors to invest or pool resources to achieve a predetermined goal.[141]

## C. Strategic Tasks

Strategic tasks are the objectives addressed by policy instruments.[142] Complementary strategic tasks provide an optimal

---

[134] OECD, *supra* note 107, at 263; INTELLIGENT DEMAND, *supra* note 118, at 9.
[135] EDLER, CAMERON & HAJHASHEM, *supra* note 127, at 7.
[136] INTELLIGENT DEMAND, *supra* note 118, at 9–10.
[137] EDLER, CAMERON & HAJHASHEM, *supra* note 127, at 7.
[138] OECD, *supra* note 107, at 263.
[139] EDLER, CAMERON & HAJHASHEM, *supra* note 127, at 7.
[140] *Id.*
[141] *Id.*
[142] OECD, *supra* note 107, at 264–65.

arrangement of policy instruments for supporting innovation.[143] These
objectives include educating a potential workforce, ensuring proper
development and use of knowledge, providing supportive
infrastructures, enhancing public research contributions, and unleashing
the potential of firms.[144] In the case of the U.K. patent box, one
strategic task, among others, was to increase patent related
commercialization.[145] The U.S. R&D tax credit, by contrast, sought to
incentivize firms to invest in R&D.[146]

## D.  Instruments

Policy instruments are the regulatory tools used to achieve
particular strategic tasks and can be divided into five different
binaries.[147]

### 1.  Population vs. Non-Population Specific

This distinction characterizes *who* is the focus of the policy
intervention.[148] Population-targeted instruments focus on the type of
firm or sector to be supported, whereas non-population targeted
instruments will apply broadly.[149] Population-targeted instruments may
be directed toward facilitating innovation in small and medium-sized
enterprises ("SMEs").[150] The U.K., for instance, has implemented
several policy measures focused on SMEs.[151] In non-population-
targeted instruments, policy intervention may affect firms of all types.

---

[143] *See* Zeting Liu, *The Research Tax Credit in the Policy Mix for Innovation: The French
Case*, J. INNOVATION ECON. no. 12, at 199, ¶ 3 (2013), http://www.cairn.info/revue-
journal-of-innovation-economics-2013-2-page-199.htm.

[144] OECD, *supra* note 107, at 265.

[145] *See supra* Section II.B.1.

[146] *See supra* Section II.B.2.

[147] *See* OECD, *supra* note 107, at 267–70; *Innovation policy mix for business R&D and
Innovation, supra* note 111.

[148] *Innovation policy mix for business R&D and Innovation, supra* note 111.

[149] *Id.*

[150] *Id.*

[151] *See* OECD, *OECD Science, Technology and Industry Outlook*, OECD PUBLISHING
441 (2014), http://www.keepeek.com/Digital-Asset-Management/oecd/science-and-
technology/oecd-science-technology-and-industry-outlook-2014_sti_outlook-2014-
en#page1.

Both the U.K. patent box and the U.S. R&D tax credit exemplify non-population-targeted instruments, as each applies broadly.[152]

### 2.   Technology vs. Non-Technology Targeted

Technology-targeted policy instruments focus on developing specific technologies, whereas non-technology-targeted instruments apply broadly.[153] For example, a nation may have an interest in developing its biotechnology sector and intervene accordingly.[154] Policy instruments may instead encourage all technologies. The U.K. patent box and U.S. R&D tax credit typify the latter, as neither focuses on incentivizing one particular technology.[155]

### 3.   Competitive vs. Non-competitive

Competitive policy instruments confer a benefit once certain performance threshold criteria have been met.[156] Non-competitive instruments, on the other hand, apply universally or after a selection process based on eligibility requirements.[157] Recently, countries have moved toward more competitive instruments for public sector research institutions.[158] The U.K. patent box and U.S. R&D tax, however, exemplify non-competitive policy instruments, as applicants can simply elect to apply these measures to eligible income or expenditures.[159]

### 4.   Financial vs. Non-financial

Policy instruments can be financial or non-financial in nature.[160] Financial instruments can be further divided into direct and indirect instruments.[161] Direct financial instruments include loans, grants and innovation vouchers, while tax incentives are an example of

---

[152] See supra Section II.

[153] Innovation policy mix for business R&D and Innovation, supra note 111.

[154] See id.

[155] See supra Section II.

[156] See Innovation policy mix for business R&D and Innovation, supra note 111.

[157] See id.

[158] OECD, supra note 107, at 267.

[159] See supra Section II.B.

[160] OECD, supra note 151, at 153.

[161] Innovation policy mix for business R&D and Innovation, supra note 111.

an indirect financial instrument.[162] Accordingly, the U.K. patent box and the U.S. R&D tax credit are both examples of indirect financial policy instruments.[163] Non-financial instruments include information campaigns or providing services.[164] More often than not, nations deploy financial instruments.[165]

### 5.   Supply-side vs. Demand-side

Lastly, "[p]olicy instruments to accelerate innovation have been described as either technology (supply) push or demand (market) pull."[166] Supply-side instruments foster knowledge production in order to accelerate knowledge spillovers and externalities.[167] Providing tax incentives to encourage R&D spending is one example of a supply-side measure.[168] Both the U.K. patent box and U.S. R&D tax credit exemplify supply-side measures. In contrast, demand-side instruments foster market opportunities for innovation and encourage suppliers to meet consumer innovation needs.[169] Public procurement is one example of demand-side measure.[170] Although innovation policy has traditionally favored supply-side instruments, interest in demand-side instruments has grown in recent years.[171]

### IV.    CONSTRUING THE PATENT BOX IN VIEW OF THE POLICY MIX

A policy prescription based solely on a comparison of pertinent regulatory measures and the effects thereof would necessarily ignore numerous dissimilarities and empirical uncertainties.[172] The U.K., or any country for that matter, has a unique set of actors, ideas, structures, institutions, and policies that shape its innovation performance.[173] No single policy instrument is implemented in a

---

[162] *Id.*

[163] *See supra* Section II.B.

[164] *Innovation policy mix for business R&D and Innovation, supra* note 111.

[165] *Id.*

[166] INTELLIGENT DEMAND, *supra* note 118, at 3.

[167] *Innovation policy mix for business R&D and Innovation, supra* note 111.

[168] *See supra* Section II.B.

[169] *Innovation policy mix for business R&D and Innovation, supra* note 111.

[170] OECD, *supra* note 151, at 187–88.

[171] OECD, *supra* note 107, at 267–68; INTELLIGENT DEMAND, *supra* note 118, at 3; *see also* OECD, *supra* note 151, at 188.

[172] *See supra* Section II.B.

[173] OECD, *supra* note 107, at 254.

vacuum. Proclaiming the efficacy of a patent box based on the number of participating companies or the patents filed in the U.K. alone likely neglects other important factors at play. To the extent this can be overcome, a policy mix approach provides a means for normalization and contextualization in performing such a comparison.[174] In other words, there is something to be gained from comparing the U.K.'s adoption of the patent box in the context of the policy mix and from the policy mix approach *per se*.

## A.    Redundancy

A patent box provides a similar yet less effective incentive scheme compared to the already deployed R&D tax credit. Applying the policy mix reveals that both the patent box and the R&D tax credit are substantially similar policy instruments.[175] Both, as dedicated science, technology, and innovation policies,[176] target specific market failures rather than framework conditions.[177] In particular, the patent box pushes companies to commercialize patent-related products,[178] while the U.S. R&D tax credit incentivizes companies to invest in R&D.[179] In terms of the binaries, each is broadly applicable and without significant thresholds, and thus non-population targeted, non-technology specific, and non-competitive.[180] Each provides firms with a tax credit, characteristic of an indirect financial instrument.[181] Lastly, both measures seek to foster the production of innovation rather than the market demand for it, making them supply-side instruments.[182]

Nevertheless, instruments sharing these attributes do not necessarily share effectiveness. An important distinction can be made regarding where a given policy instrument acts within the innovation development cycle.[183] Here, the R&D tax credit applies when a firm incurs expenses (a front-end incentive),[184] whereas the patent box

---

[174] *See id.*
[175] *See supra* Section III.
[176] *See supra* Section III.A.
[177] *See supra* Section III.A.
[178] *See supra* Section II.B.1.i.; CIRD200110, *supra* note 43.
[179] *See supra* Section II.B.2.
[180] *See supra* Section III.D
[181] *See supra* Section III.D.5.
[182] *Id.*
[183] Graetz & Doud, *supra* note 6, at 363.
[184] Hill & Rhyne, *supra* note 76, at 377.

applies upon earning qualified income (a back end incentive).[185]
Regarding these particular instruments, it is likely more beneficial to
subsidize front-end activity than it is to subsidize back-end activity.[186]
"Rather than incentivizing private investment in technologies that are
under-explored (those with large and hard-to-capture benefits), a patent
box incentivizes firms to invest in new technologies that return the
largest private profits with the fewest externalities."[187] Put differently,
patent boxes may encourage profit at the expense of innovation.
Additional difficulties in defining what income is sufficiently related to
a patent in order to qualify may further tip the scales.[188]

     Patent box proponents argue that the policies in tandem might
provide synergistic returns outweighing the social cost.[189] Based on the
understanding of the UK's innovation landscape provided by the policy
mix, however, nothing suggests that this would be the case.[190] The U.K.
has implemented both policies, and nothing yet suggests such a
benefit.[191] This may be made more compelling by the fact that there is a
commercialization market failure in the U.K. that is not present,
comparatively, in the US.[192] If one was to expect a combined effect
from adding a patent box, it seems like it might occur in the instance
where the patent box, by its nature, addresses the specific market
failure of that country. All told, using these supply-side measures in
conjunction would be granting similar tax breaks to firms without a
clear social benefit in doing so.

---

[185] Graetz & Doud, *supra* note 6, at 363.

[186] GRAVELLE, *supra* note 2 ("Economic theory also suggests that it may be more
desirable to subsidize investment in R&E rather than reduce the tax rates on the returns:
higher tax rates reduce variance (the variation in return that occurs depending on the
success of the research) as well as return and may, in some circumstances, increase risk
taking."); FICHTNER & MICHEL, *supra* note 7, at 3 ("Contrary to sound economic policy,
a patent box explicitly subsidizes corporate profits that are captured by the private
firm.").

[187] FICHTNER & MICHEL, *supra* note 7, at 3

[188] *See id.*

[189] ATKINSON & ANDES, *supra* note 3, at 1.

[190] *See supra* Section II.B.1.iii.

[191] *Id.*

[192] *See supra* Section II.B.

## B. Remedying Market and System Failures

It is also uncertain to what extent the patent box resolves the failures it purportedly addresses.[193] One reason the U.K. implemented the patent box was to provide incentives for companies to retain and commercialize existing patents and to develop new patented products.[194] In this regard, "[t]he data paint[s] a somewhat unclear picture as to whether or not patent boxes are serving their intended purpose to 'attract R&D and increase commercialization of innovation from domestic firms.'"[195] Beyond mere anecdotes,[196] the adoption of the U.K. patent box has done little so far to discharge this uncertainty.[197] For at least this reason, it seems prudent to wait until more data provides clarity on how well it overcomes this market failure and whether it is worth implementation in the U.S.

Another reason proffered for deploying the patent box was to prevent tax base shifting, a system failure, and instead incentivize firms to relocate manufacturing operations to the adopting country.[198] A recent study, however, has confirmed that patent boxes generate "significant effect on patent location without a change in real research activity, aiming only at the tax benefits."[199] In other words, firms are moving holdings to patent box countries while maintaining operations elsewhere. The recent OECD recommendations suggest that this may be the case with the current U.K. patent box.[200] It is possible that these recommendations will resolve certain issues, but only time will tell if these changes will result in the relocation of manufacturing. Again, it

---

[193] *Id.*

[194] *Id.*

[195] ATKINSON & ANDES, *supra* note 3, at 12.; *see supra* Section II.B.

[196] *See supra* Section II.B.

[197] *Id.*

[198] Alexandra Thornton, *Patent Tax Dodge: Why the Patent Box Does Not Answer America's Need for Tax Reform*, CENTER FOR AMERICAN PROGRESS (June 1, 2015), https://www.americanprogress.org/issues/economy/news/2015/06/01/114088/patent-tax-dodge-why-the-patent-box-does-not-answer-americas-need-for-tax-reform/; *see* Knight & Maragani, *supra* note 3, at 41.

[199] Annette Alstadsæter et al., *European Commission, Patent Boxes Design, Patents Location and Local R&D* 25 (Taxation Papers, Working Paper No. 57, June 2015), *available at* http://ec.europa.eu/taxation_customs/resources/documents/taxation/gen_info/economic_analysis/tax_papers/taxation_paper_57.pdf

[200] *See supra* Section II.B.

seems sensible to see how well the UK's new patent box produces the intended results before acting.

## C. Recommendations

Expending political capital to enact a patent box as a cure-all for the U.S.'s innovation and tax woes would likely miss the mark. Instead, the U.S., once a leader in innovation policy,[201] might well benefit from the measured and holistic approach provided by the policy mix model. Rather than simply following suit as other countries enact patent boxes, the U.S. could deploy any number of coherent and synergistic policy instruments to better foster innovation. For example, the U.S. could address certain framework conditions or perhaps target instruments to aid the innovation of SMEs.[202] Looking into demand-side policies may also provide a worthy compliment to the R&D tax credit, as studies have shown a clear interaction between such policies.[203] Technology-targeted policy instruments might also help by providing resources to underfunded technology spaces.[204]

Additionally, an ever-present undercurrent to patent box discussions seems to be corporate tax regulation as a whole.[205] Some even see these proposals as a platform to address corporate tax reform.[206] While tax policy is one of the framework conditions affecting innovation,[207] it may be better to address these issues head on rather than attempting to solve with the patent box. "[P]roviding tax benefits for patent box income, especially if broadly defined, will lose revenues and make lowering overall corporate tax rates more difficult to achieve in a revenue-neutral tax reform."[208]

Lastly, measuring the efficacy of policy instruments can be quite difficult.[209] In engineering control theory, feedback loops are used

---

[201] See ATKINSON & EZELL, *supra* note 11, at 245.

[202] OECD, *supra* note151, at 441–46.

[203] INTELLIGENT DEMAND, *supra* note 118, at 35.

[204] See ATKINSON & EZELL, *supra* note 11, at 254–56.

[205] See *supra* Section II.

[206] Brett Nowak, *U.S. Patent Box: Will It Be a Box of Chocolates or Pandora's Box for Taxpayers?*, A & M TAX ADVISOR WEEKLY (Oct. 6, 2015) ,
http://www.alvarezandmarsal.com/us-patent-box-will-it-be-box-chocolates-or-pandoras-box-taxpayers ("[M]any lawmakers welcome the Boustany-Neal proposal and view it as an initial step towards U.S. tax reform . . . .").

[207] See *supra* Section III.

[208] GRAVELLE, *supra* note 2.

[209] See *supra* Section II.B.

to monitor dynamic systems.[210] These feedback loops provide data for further corrective or adaptive modification.[211] This concept may have value in forming policy instruments. Perhaps part of the policy development process could focus on how an instrument's effectiveness might be evaluated in the future and ways in which pertinent data could be collected. In that way, the true impact could be assessed for more informed policymaking.

## V.    CONCLUSION

Emerging Congressional support for a patent box has afforded an opportunity to assess its potential use as an innovation policy tool.[212] Evaluating the U.K.'s recent adoption of a patent box in light of existing U.S. policy and within a policy mix framework has revealed certain redundancy and efficacy concerns. Innovation in the U.S. might be better served by adopting a policy mix approach, addressing certain framework conditions critical to innovation, and implementing additional policy tools to complement its R&D tax credit. Doing so may ensure continued prosperity in an increasingly competitive and innovation focused global economy.

---

[210] S. Simrock, *Control Theory*, DESY, https://cds.cern.ch/record/1100534/files/p73.pdf (last visited May 14, 2016).
[211] Yuriy Brun et al., *Engineering Self-Adaptive Systems through Feedback Loops, in* SOFTWARE ENGINEERING FOR SELF-ADAPTIVE SYSTEMS (Betty H. Cheng et al. eds. 2009), http://people.cs.umass.edu/~brun/pubs/pubs/Brun09SEfSAS.pdf.
[212] *See supra* Section I.

# WHAT'S IN A NAME, BROTHER—PROFIT OR PUBLICITY: AN ANALYSIS OF TRADEMARKING RING NAMES IN PROFESSIONAL WRESTLING

### ALISSA M. HARRINGTON[1]

---

[1] Alissa M. Harrington is a Juris Doctor Candidate at Mitchell Hamline School of Law, expected to graduate in 2017. She would like to thank her husband, Chris, for his patience, support, and access to and guidance through his voluminous collection of wrestling resources.

I.      INTRODUCTION: ENTER THE WRESTLERS

The bell tolls. The stadium goes dark. Every cell phone camera glows eerily, pointed at the empty space where he is about to appear. He appears in smoke and fire as the infamous first bars of Chopin's funeral march are met with a roaring crowd. Mark William Calaway appears to step into the ring as his wrestling persona—the Undertaker.[2] It is unlikely anyone but the most die-hard professional wrestling fans would care if Mark William Calaway was going to show up at an event. But many a child of the 90s would shiver if the Undertaker were coming to dinner.[3]

Ring names in professional wrestling are the calling cards by which fans and the general public know the athletes who perform in the ring.[4] Children ask for Seth Rollins[5] action figures, Roman Reigns[6] t-

---

[2] *The Undertaker Walks into Hell in a Cell: WrestleMania 28*, WWE.COM,
http://www.wwe.com/videos/playlists/undertakers-eerie-arrivals-at-wrestlemania (last visited May 14, 2016).
[3] *See Mark Calaway Biography*, IMDB.COM,
http://www.imdb.com/name/nm0130587/bio (last visited May 14, 2016).
[4] *See* Richard Moran, *WWE: 20 Worst Wrestling Ring Names Ever*, WHATCULTURE.COM (Feb. 28, 2014) http://whatculture.com/wwe/wwe-20-worst-wrestling-ring-names-ever.php ("You can tell that good old Bill [Shakespeare] was never a wrestling booker though because if he were, he'd know that names are important. Very important indeed."); Aubrey Sitterson, *The 11 best professional wrestling names*, GEEK.COM (Aug. 28, 2015) http://www.geek.com/news/the-11-best-professional-wrestling-names-1632336/ ("In pro wrestling, however, your name is as crucial of a choice as your ring gear, finisher, entrance music or catchphrase, and as such, phenomenal wrestler names are as abundant as the kickpads."); *see also* Titan Sports, Inc. v. Hellwig, No. 3:98-CV-467(EBB), 1999 U.S. Dist. LEXIS 10523 at 5–6 (D. Conn. Apr. 22, 1999) (citation omitted) ("3.2 If WRESTLER does not own, possess or use service marks, trademarks or distinctive and identifying indicia and PROMOTER develops such service marks, trademarks, and distinctive and identifying indicia for WRESTLER, they shall belong to PROMOTER and PROMOTER shall have the exclusive license and right in perpetuity,

shirts, and Luke Harper[7] standees. They would not know what to do with Colby Lopez[8], Leati "Joe" Anoa'i[9], and Jon Huber[10] merchandise. But do these ring names rise to the level of personal names for purposes of barring trademark registration without permission from the individual? Or are the ring names representing fictitious characters that are portrayed by wrestlers? The United States Patent and Trademark Office ("USPTO") seems to be unclear: trademark requests from World Wrestling Entertainment ("WWE") for marks relating to the names of wrestlers have received inconsistent treatment—some require the signatures of the real person whose ring name is at issue, while others pass by without comment.

This article sets out to answer the question—how should the USPTO and courts treat the ring names of wrestlers? Specifically, this article looks at several examples showcasing the variety of situations that can arise with wrestling names—names created by the company, names based on or identical to the real name of the wrestler, names used by more than one person as the same character, and names used prior to the individual's association with the company—then explores the competing interests of the company and the individual in name-based trademark law, and concludes with suggestions on how each situation should be treated moving forward.

---

to use, and to authorize others to use, WRESTLER's ring name, likeness, voice, signatures, costumes, props, gimmicks, routines, themes, personality, character and caricatures as used by or associated with WRESTLER's performance as a professional wrestler (collectively 'Name and Likeness').").

[5] *Seth Rollins*, WWE.COM, http://www.wwe.com/superstars/seth-rollins (last visited May 14, 2016).

[6] *Roman Reigns*, WWE.COM, http://www.wwe.com/superstars/roman-reigns (last visited May 14, 2016).

[7] *Luke Harper*, WWE.COM, http://www.wwe.com/superstars/lukeharper (last visited May 14, 2016).

[8] *Colby Lopez*, IMDB.COM, http://www.imdb.com/name/nm2497048/?ref_=fn_al_nm_1 (last visited May 14, 2016).

[9] *Joe Anoa'i Biography*, IMDB.COM, http://www.imdb.com/name/nm5195221/bio?ref_=nm_ov_bth_nm (last visited May 14, 2016).

[10] *Jon Huber*, IMDB.COM, http://www.imdb.com/name/nm3829606/ (last visited May 14, 2016).

II.     LAYING DOWN THE LAW: TRADEMARKS AND NAMES

A.   *Lanham Act and Names*

     The Lanham Act prohibits the use of a name "identifying a
particular living individual except by his written consent."[11] Case law
has clarified that the name must also "identify and distinguish the
[product] and not merely the individual or group."[12] The same is true of
character names—the name must service to identify the source, not just
the character.[13] In other words, character names and other names are
descriptive marks that will only become registrable if the mark gains
secondary meaning. Secondary meaning, in this sense, would be the use
of the name in a way that leads to the public associating the name with
a particular product or service.[14] Separately, the Lanham Act bars
registration of marks that are "merely a surname."[15]

     Of course, the more interesting question becomes—what is a
name that identifies a particular living individual, and when does it
serve to identify the source of the product and not just the individual or
character? Where is the line between the use of a name merely to
identify an individual who is found in an entertainment setting and the
use of a name as an identifier of the service of entertainment or the
source of a product of the company? The courts and the USPTO have
approached those questions differently. Performers have sometimes
been granted the ability to trademark their own names[16] while at other
times, performers have been unable to use their names as trademarks.[17]

B.   *TMEP—Trademark Manual of Examining Procedure on Names*

     The Trademark Manual of Examining Procedure (TMEP)
controls how the examiners of the USPTO proceed in the registration of
trademarks.[18] Trademarks arising from names are subject to a variety of

---

[11] 15 U.S.C. § 1052(c) (2012).
[12] TMEP § 1301.02(b) (Oct. 2015).
[13] *Id.*
[14] Yvette Joy Liebesman, *When Selling Your Personal Name Mark Extends To Selling Your Soul*, 83 TEMP. L. REV. 1, 47 n.17 (2010).
[15] 15 U.S.C § 1052(e)(4).
[16] *See In re* Carson, 197 U.S.P.Q. 554 (T.T.A.B. 1977).
[17] *In re* Lee Trevino Enters., Inc., 182 U.S.P.Q. 253 (T.T.A.B. 1974).
[18] TMEP Introduction (Oct. 2015).

different inquiries according to the TMEP.[19] Examiners are asked to determine if the name is barred as "merely a surname,"[20] if the name has obtained secondary meaning,[21] and if the name is a name that identifies a person or a fictitious character to determine if consent would be required for registration.[22] Names identifying living persons require the consent of the person, while names of fictitious characters do not.[23]

If a name is that of a person, which includes not just a legal name, the following is provided as guidance:

> *First Name, Pseudonym, Stage Name, Surname, Nickname, or Title.* If the mark comprises a first name, pseudonym, stage name, nickname, surname, or title (e.g., 'Mrs. Johnson' or 'Aunt Sally'), the examining attorney must determine whether there is evidence that the name identifies an individual who is generally known or is publicly connected with the business in which the mark is used and, as a result, the relevant public would perceive the name as identifying a particular living individual.[24]

In contrast, fictitious character names do not require the consent of any individual:

> *Fictitious Character.* The examining attorney should not make an inquiry if it is clear from the record, or from the examining attorney's research, that the matter identifies a fictitious character. For example, no inquiry is necessary as to whether 'Alfred E. Neuman,' 'Betty Crocker,' or 'Aunt Jemima' is the name of a particular living individual because they are names of well-known fictitious characters. Likewise, no inquiry is necessary as to a design that is obviously that of a cartoon character.[25]

---

[19] TMEP §1301; TMEP § 1206.
[20] TMEP § 1301.
[21] *Id.*
[22] TMEP § 1206.
[23] *Id.*
[24] TMEP § 1206.03 (Oct. 2015)
[25] *Id.*

Comparing the two standards, it is clear that the requirements for registration depend heavily on whether or not the examiner considers a wrestler's ring name to be that of an identifiable person or a fictitious character. Mainly at issue here is whether or not the consent of the individual must be given before registration is granted by the USPTO.

Regardless of whether the ring name is determined to be an identifier of a living person or a fictitious character, the examiner must also determine if the name has obtained secondary meaning as an indicator of the source of the product.[26] "The name of a character or person *is* registrable as a service mark if the record shows that it is used in a manner that would be perceived by purchasers as identifying the services in addition to the character or person."[27]

## C.   TMEP—Authorities for Names as Trademarks

The TMEP lists a number of cases as precedent in deciding how to address the issue of names as trademarks,[28] and may be used to help the examiners decide whether to issue a trademark registration.[29] The cases provide a framework that is helpful to understand why the USPTO's decisions have varied on what type of rights are available and if permission is required to register wrestler's ring names.

### 1.   In re Lee Trevino[30]

Lee Trevino, famed PGA golfer[31] perhaps better known in some circles for his cameo in the Adam Sandler film *Happy Gilmore*,[32] attempted to register his name as a service mark of Lee Trevino Enterprises, Inc. for promoting goods and services.[33] The registration was refused by the examiner because the specimens filed showed "LEE TREVINO" being used to identify Lee Trevino as an individual

---

[26] TMEP § 1301; *see also* TMEP § 1212.
[27] TMEP § 1301.02(b).
[28] TMEP § 1206; TMEP § 1301.
[29] 4 ANNE GILSON LALONDE, GILSON ON TRADEMARKS § 15.11 (2015).
[30] *In re* Lee Trevino Enters., 182 U.S.P.Q. 253 (T.T.A.B. 1974).
[31] *Lee Trevino Biography*, BIO.COM, http://www.biography.com/people/lee-trevino-9510248 (last visited May 14, 2016).
[32] *Lee Trevino Biography*, IMDB.COM,
http://www.imdb.com/name/nm0005504/?ref_=ttfc_fc_cl_t11 (last visited May 14, 2016).
[33] *In re* Lee Trevino Enters., 182 U.S.P.Q. at 253.

performing services, instead of the source of the services as Lee Trevino Enterprises, Inc.[34]

The applicant appealed citing nineteen instances where a service mark registration was granted for a mark containing or wholly comprised of the name of a famous individual.[35] The board pointed out the difference between the nineteen instances cited by the applicant and the "LEE TREVINO" mark, mainly that the specimens filed with the applicant must "demonstrate use of the name in question to identify goods sold or transported in commerce or services rendered by the applicant corporation as distinguished from use merely to identify the particular individual who endorses the goods or performs the services set forth in the application."[36] The specimens in the application were posters and other materials listing Lee Trevino's accomplishments, the "availability of Lee Trevino, the individual, for endorsements, advertisements, exhibitions of golf, and sales meetings," endorsements by Lee Trevino, and, subsequent to the initial application, documents showing Lee Trevino as a consultant.[37]

The specimens, according to the board, represented examples of Lee Trevino as a person who endorsed products, rather than as an indicator of the Lee Trevino Enterprises, Inc. brand.[38] The board affirmed the registration refusal.[39]

### 2.   In re Burger King Corp.[40]—BURGER KING

Burger King Corp. applied to register the "fanciful figure" of a king as a service mark for restaurant and carry-out food services.[41] At issue was whether or not the depicted king was a service mark or

---

[34] Id.

[35] Id. ("including 'ARTHUR MURRAY' for instruction in dancing, 'BILLY GRAHAM' for religious educational services, 'EVELYN WOOD' for conducting courses of instruction in rapid and perceptive reading techniques, 'DOROTHY CARNEGIE' for educational services, 'AL HIRT'S' for restaurant services, 'MICKEY MANTLE'S' for restaurant services, 'EDDY ARNOLD'S' for restaurant services, 'ROY ROGERS' for restaurant services, and 'COLONEL SANDERS INN' for hotel and motel services.").

[36] Id. (quoting In re Generation Gap Prods., 170 U.S.P.Q. 423 (T.T.A.B. 1971)).

[37] Id. at 254.

[38] Id.

[39] Id.

[40] In re Burger King Corp., 183 U.S.P.Q. 698 (T.T.A.B. 1974).

[41] Id.

merely a character in advertising the products.[42] The registration application was refused, and the applicant appealed.[43]

The applicant argued for a "liberal view" of the registration statute, which would allow the design of the burger king to be used as a service mark in addition to the name "BURGER KING."[44] In response, the board upheld the refusal and ruled that the fanciful design of the king did not rise to the level of identifying the brand, but rather only identified an advertising character.[45]

### 3.   In re Steak & Ale Restaurants[46]—PRINCE CHARLES

This textbook classic involves the American steakhouse— Steak & Ale Restaurants—attempt to register "PRINCE CHARLES" as a trademark for fresh and cooked meat.[47] The examiner refused the registration under 2(c) of the Lanham Act because "PRINCE CHARLES" consists of or compromises a particular living individual.[48] Namely, Charles Philip Arthur George, the Prince of Wales.[49] Prince Charles, as he is most often known, is a member of the English royal family.[50] The examiner based the registration refusal on the belief that "PRINCE CHARLES" is the name of this British Prince Charles.[51]

The applicant appealed to the Trademark Trial and Appeal Board (T.T.A.B.) arguing that the name represented multiple individuals, including another member of the English royal family and a member of the Swedish royalty.[52] Alternatively, the applicant argued that "PRINCE CHARLES" is a historical title used to identify multiple

---

[42] Id.
[43] Id.
[44] Id. at 700.
[45] Id.
[46] In re Steak & Ale Rests., Inc., 185 U.S.P.Q. 447, 448 (T.T.A.B. 1975).
[47] Id. at 447.
[48] Id.
[49] The Prince of Wales Biography, The Prince of Wales and Duchess of Cornwall, http://www.princeofwales.gov.uk/the-prince-of-wales/biography (last visited May 14, 2016). He is also known by a number of other titles, including the Duke of Cornwall, Duke of Rothesay, Earl of Carrick, Baron Renfrew, Lord of the Isles, and Prince and Great Steward of Scotland. Id.
[50] Id.
[51] In re Steak & Ale Rests., Inc., 185 U.S.P.Q. at 447.
[52] Id.

members of various royal families.[53] Finally, the applicant argued it is a royal title and not a name.[54]

The T.T.A.B. did not agree with any of the applicant's arguments.[55] The board responded to the three arguments in order. First, even if more than one person has a name, it "does not make any one of them any less of a particular living individual."[56] Second, the board used similar logic to address the argument that the existence of historical figures lacked probative value.[57] "Thus, the existence in the past of one or more individuals with a name or a combination of a title and a name such as that herein involved cannot negate the proposition that a contemporary with the same or a similar name or title is a particular living individual."[58] Finally, the board addressed the title argument by clarifying that given names are not the only names barred under 2(c).[59] A title or combination of title and name could be used as a nickname, and thus, would be barred.[60]

> [T]he statute uses the words 'a name' and not the words 'the name.' Hence 'name' in section 2(c) is not restricted to the full name of an individual but refers to any name regardless of whether it is a full name or a surname or given name, or even a nickname, which identifies a particular living individual.[61]

On these bases, the board upheld the registration refusal.[62]

### 4.   In re Carson[63]—JOHNNY CARSON

John W. Carson took the stage as the host of *The Tonight Show* in 1962, beginning a thirty-year career as the King of Late Night

---

[53] *Id.*
[54] *Id.*
[55] *Id.* at 447–48.
[56] *Id.* at 447.
[57] *Id.* at 448.
[58] *Id.*
[59] *Id.*
[60] *Id.*
[61] *Id.* (quoting Reed v. Bakers Eng'g & Equip. Co., 100 U.S.P.Q. 196 (PTO 1954)).
[62] *Id.*
[63] *In re* Carson, 197 U.S.P.Q. 554 (T.T.A.B. 1977).

TV.[64] Johnny Carson applied to trademark "JOHNNY CARSON" for
entertainment services, including "monologues, comedy routines and
the hosting of guest appearances of others."[65] The examiner refused the
registration based on the ground that "JOHNNY CARSON" identified
the individual John W. Carson, rather than as a mark to identify
services rendered by the applicant.[66] The examiner suggested "THE
JOHNNY CARSON SHOW" as an alternative mark, but Carson
refused and appealed the registration refusal to the T.T.A.B.[67]

Carson argued "JOHNNY CARSON" acted both as an
identifier of an individual and as the identifier of the source of services
performed by the same individual.[68] Additionally, the applicant argued
the word "show" acted as a generic description of the services rendered
by the individual, and no additional distinctiveness would be added to
the mark by adding the word to the mark "JOHNNY CARSON."[69]

The specimens submitted with the appeal and the original
application included numerous posters, newspaper copy, and other
advertisements.[70] One specimen was a newspaper page showing a
picture of Carson with the words: "JOHNNY CARSON is in the Congo
Room at Del Webb's hotel Sahara with Bette Midler."[71] The board
found that this specimen used the mark simply as an identifier of the
individual, not as a source identifier.[72] In contrast, the board found that
many of the other specimens showed the use of the mark as an indicator
of source of entertainment services.[73] Specifically, the board calls out
the advertisements using the mark in conjunction with the words "IN
CONCERT" or "3 BIG PERFORMANCES AT THE MUSIC HALL!"
and information on how to obtain tickets to the advertised
performances, as examples of how the mark is used as an indicator of
source.[74] The board additionally recognizes the specimens containing

---

[64] *Johnny Carson Biography*, IMDB.COM,
http://www.imdb.com/name/nm0001992/bio?ref_=nm_ov_bth_nm (last visited May 14,
2016); *Johnny Carson Biography*, BIO.COM, http://www.biography.com/people/johnny-
carson-9239714 (last visited May 14, 2016).
[65] *In re* Carson, 197 U.S.P.Q. at 554.
[66] *Id.*
[67] *Id.*
[68] *Id.* at 555.
[69] *Id.* at 554.
[70] *Id.* at 555.
[71] *Id.*
[72] *Id.*
[73] *Id.*
[74] *Id.* at 555–56.

ticket information and "THE JOHNNY CARSON SHOW" as illustrative of how the mark alone serves as an indicator of services, without the need for the additional words describing the service ("the show").[75]

The T.T.A.B. took the time to distinguish the "JOHNNY CARSON" mark from the refused mark "LEE TREVINO" by noting that "LEE TREVINO" was never used in the specimens provided as a service mark.[76] Instead, the specimens showed three uses: the mark used as a "textual reference to Lee Trevino as an individual" in combination with the identification of services; the mark used with "services not listed in the identification of goods set forth in the application;" and the mark not used in a service mark manner with no reference to services.[77] The board held that applications should be determined based on the specimens in the record.[78] The record for Carson supported the registration of the mark, and the board reversed the examiner's registration refusal.[79]

### 5. In re Whataburger[80]—WHAT-APOTAMUS

Whataburger attempted to register the image of a hippopotamus with the name "WHAT-APOTAMUS" directly below the image on an iron-on patch as a service mark for restaurant services.[81] The applicant also filed a poster displayed at the cashier counter depicting a group of different animals about to consume food and drink with the words "Your Whatapatch Zoo is here for you" as a specimen.[82] Patches were distributed without charge to customers with children as the main recipients.[83] The application was refused because the mark did not identify the restaurant services of the applicant.[84]

On appeal, the T.T.A.B. upheld the refusal based on the finding that the characters were part of a collect-them-all advertising

---

[75] Id.
[76] Id. at 556.
[77] Id.
[78] Id.
[79] Id.
[80] In re Whataburger Sys., Inc., 209 U.S.P.Q. 429 (T.T.A.B. 1980).
[81] Id. at 429–30.
[82] Id.
[83] Id.
[84] Id. at 429.

character gallery rather than an indicator of source.[85] The board found
that the animals were a "promotional gambit" more in line with giving
away toy balloons emblazoned with familiar nursey rhyme characters
than with something the purchasers would use to indicate the source of
hamburgers.[86] In refusing the registration, the board held "[n]ot only
must the matter presented for registration be intended primarily to
indicate origin, but as previously indicated, it must also be of such a
nature that purchasers would be likely to consider that it indicated such
origin."[87]

6.   *In Re Fla. Cypress Gardens Inc.*[88] —*CORKY THE CLOWN*

Everybody loves (or hates) a clown.[89] The T.T.A.B. is no
exception. Cypress Gardens Inc. applied for a service mark in
"CORKY THE CLOWN" for entertainment services, including live
performances by a clown.[90] The examiner refused the registration on
two grounds: (1) the mark identifies a character rather than a service
and (2) the mark is used "inconspicuously as part of informational
textual material" rather than as a service mark.[91] The applicant
appealed, and the T.T.A.B. reversed the registration refusal in favor of
Cypress Gardens.[92]

"CORKY THE CLOWN" appeared on handbills alongside
other acts advertising the attractions at Cypress Gardens in the
specimens for the application.[93] The T.T.A.B. found that "CORKY
THE CLOWN" is the name of a character played by one or more
people rather than any type of name for a living individual.[94] As such,
the board looked to the previous case of *In re Folk* and "THE
LOLLIPOP PRINCESS" for guidance.[95] Lin Folk sought to trademark
the name of the character she portrayed when she told children's stories

---

[85] *Id.* at 430–31.
[86] *Id.* at 431.
[87] *Id.*
[88] *In re* Fla. Cypress Gardens Inc., 208 U.S.P.Q. 288 (T.T.A.B. 1980).
[89] GARY LEWIS & THE PLAYBOYS, EVERYBODY LOVES A CLOWN (Liberty Records
1965).
[90] *In re* Fla. Cypress Gardens Inc., 208 U.S.P.Q. at 288.
[91] *Id.*
[92] *Id.*
[93] *Id.*
[94] *Id.* at 290.
[95] 160 U.S.P.Q. 213 (T.T.A.B. 1968).

on the radio and in-person.[96] The T.T.A.B. also overturned the registration refusal of the examiner in *Folk*, holding, "There can be no question on the record herein but that 'THE LOLLIPOP PRINCESS' identifies and distinguishes the services performed by applicant."[97]

In *Cypress Gardens*, the board cited the holding in *Folk* to support its decision to allow the registration of "CORKY THE CLOWN" by arguing that the difference in medium—radio vs. only in-person performances—is not sufficient to break down the analogy.[98] In both cases, the service mark identified the character as well as the act.[99] The board continued to say that they find no reason why the name of the act would not be as registerable as the name of Cypress Gardens.[100] "In fact, this situation is somewhat anal[o]gous to the registration of marks which identify a particular feature, such as an ingredient, a finish, etc., of goods."[101]

Addressing the examiner's second reason for refusal, the board shortly stated that there is no requirement that a mark be conspicuous "[s]o long as it is used in such a manner as to be readily recognizable as a trademark."[102] Since neither of the examiner's reasons for registration refusal were upheld, the board overruled the examiner and allowed registration of the mark.[103]

### 7. *In re Mancino*[104]—*BOOM BOOM*

Raymond M. "Boom Boom Mancini" Mancino applied to register the service mark "BOOM BOOM" for "entertainment services, namely, conducting boxing exhibitions and matches."[105] The applicant submitted specimens of the cover of boxing match programs, leaflets, and newspaper articles.[106] Specimens showed the applicant's ring record, nickname, and participation in boxing matches.[107] The examiner

---

[96] *Id.* at 214.
[97] *Id.*
[98] *In re* Fla. Cypress Gardens Inc., 208 U.S.P.Q. 288, 291–92 (T.T.A.B. 1980).
[99] *Id.* at 292.
[100] *Id.*
[101] *Id.*
[102] *Id.*
[103] *Id.*
[104] *In re* Mancino, 219 U.S.P.Q. 1047 (T.T.A.B. 1983).
[105] *Id.* (citing U.S. Trademark Application Serial No. 327,710 (filed Sept. 14, 1981)).
[106] *Id.* at 1047–48.
[107] *Id.*

found the specimens showed the mark was used only to identify the applicant as a participant rather than as an identifier of the source of boxing services.[108] The T.T.A.B. agreed and upheld the refusal of registration, holding that people would see the words "BOOM BOOM" in connection with the applicant merely as his boxing nickname and not as the identifier of any source of services.[109]

  8.   *In re Sauer*[110]—*BO BALL*

   In 1989, Debbie Sauer applied for a mark of "BO BALL" on "an oblong shaped ball made of white leather with red stitching at the seams."[111] The mark appears to be a hybrid of a football and a baseball.[112] The registration was refused based on a violation of 2(a) and 2(c) because the allusion to football and baseball with the name "Bo" suggested a false connection with Bo Jackson, and the mark is the use of Jackson's name without his consent.[113] Bo Jackson, as the examining attorney showed, "is a famous athlete who has played both professional football and baseball."[114] The applicant appealed, arguing that other celebrities have the first name "Bo," therefore there would not be an automatic connection to Bo Jackson.[115]
   The board confirmed the examiner's use of a four-part test to determine if a mark falsely suggests a connection with an individual in violation of 2(a).[116] First, the "mark must be shown to be the same or a close approximation of the person's previously used name or identity."[117] Second, "[i]t must be established that the mark (or part of it) would be recognized as such."[118] Third, it must be established that "the person in question is not connected with the goods or services."[119] And, finally, "the person's name or identity must be of sufficient fame that when it is used as part or all of the mark on applicant's goods, a

---

[108] *Id.*
[109] *Id.*
[110] *In re* Sauer, 27 U.S.P.Q.2d 1073 (T.T.A.B. 1993).
[111] *Id.*
[112] U.S. Trademark Application Serial No. 73,822,435 (filed Aug. 30, 1989).
[113] *In re* Sauer, 27 U.S.P.Q.2d 1073 (T.T.A.B. 1993).
[114] *Id.* at 1074.
[115] *Id.*
[116] *Id.* at 1073.
[117] *Id.*
[118] *Id.*
[119] *Id.*

connection with that person is likely to be made by someone considering purchasing the goods."[120]

All four parts of the test were met, according to the board.[121] Bo Jackson is widely known as "Bo" and has been known as such since childhood.[122] As a professional athlete who excels at both football and baseball, the connection of "Bo" with the word "ball" on a football-baseball hybrid would be recognized as identifying Jackson.[123] There is no established connection between the applicant and Jackson.[124] Finally, specimens including Cheerios boxes, magazines, figurines, trading cards, and other materials establish that Bo Jackson "has achieved great fame and notoriety, so that when his nickname is used . . . purchasers will likely make a connection between him and the applicant's products."[125] The board upheld the refusal based on 2(a) as well as on the basis of 2(c).[126]

The board also laid out the test for a refusal under 2(c).[127] Mainly, that without the consent of an individual, a name that identifies a living individual may not be registered as a mark.[128]

> A name is deemed to 'identify' a particular living individual, for purposes of Section 2(c), only if the 'individual bearing the name in question will be associated with the mark as used on the goods, either because that person is so well known that the public would reasonably assume the connection, or because the individual is publicly connected with the business in which the mark is used.'[129]

---

[120] *Id.*
[121] *Id.*
[122] *Id.*
[123] *Id.*
[124] *Id.*
[125] *Id.*
[126] *Id.*
[127] *Id.*
[128] *Id.*
[129] *Id.* (quoting Martin v. Carter Hawley Hale Stores, Inc., 206 U.S.P.Q. 931 (T.T.A.B. 1979)).

Again, the board found that the "BO BALL" mark satisfies the test and also confirms the refusal of the registration under 2(c).[130]

9.  *In re Hoefflin*[131] —*OBAMA PAJAMA, OBAMA BAHAMA PAJAMAS, BARACK'S JOCKS DRESS TO THE LEFT*

The applicant applied for three separate marks for pajamas and undergarments, all of which were denied registration based on 2(c) and the connection of the marks to President Barack Obama.[132] All three cases were appealed by the applicant, and given the similarities between the cases, the T.T.A.B. combined them into a single decision.[133]

The applicant argued the refusals under 2(c) were inappropriate because the mark is used for a product (pajamas) not connected to Barack Obama, the mark did not use the entire name of Barack Obama, and the mark only coincidentally refers to the forty-fourth president.[134] In upholding the registration refusals, the board refined some of its earlier holdings.

First, the board clarified that an individual could be identified by a mark either because the person is connected to the product or because the individual is famous enough that a connection would be made absent a connection between the person and the product.[135] The board also presented a connection between the bar in 2(c) and the right to publicity.[136] "This provision is intended to protect the intellectual

---

[130] *Id.*

[131] *In re* Hoefflin, 97 U.S.P.Q.2d 1174 (T.T.A.B. 2010).

[132] *Id.*

[133] *Id.* at 1175 ("Inasmuch as all three of these appeals involve common questions of law and fact, and each has been treated in substantially the same manner by the applicant and by the Trademark Examining Attorney, we have consolidated these three separate appeals and are issuing a single decision herein.").

[134] *Id.* at 1175–76.

[135] *Id.* at 1175–76 (citation omitted) ("In determining whether a particular living person bearing the 'name' would be associated with the mark as being used on the goods, we must consider (1) if the person is so well known that the public would reasonably assume the connection, or (2) if the individual is publicly connected with the business in which the mark is being used.").

[136] *Id.* at 1176.

property right of privacy and publicity that a living person has in his/her identity."[137]

    In the case at hand, the examining attorney presented a wide range of sources indicating the fame of Barack Obama, including an article about "Obamafication," the practice of using Obama's name as part of made up words either for political or merchandising goals.[138] The board found the evidence presented "the obvious" to support a finding that Barack Obama is famous enough that he need not be connected to the pajama industry for any of the marks to be identified with him.[139]

    Second, the board addressed the issue of coincidence in using the name Obama. While 2(c) does not protect an individual who coincidentally shares a name with an applied-for mark, the board found that the evidence showed the purchasing public would make such an association.[140] Furthermore, the board pointed out that while other presidential names such as "Bill," "George," "Ronald," and "Jimmy" had been successfully used in registered marks, the names were also "consistently among the most popular male names in the country."[141] Given the unusual nature of "Barack," said the board, it is distinguishable from the highly common names of other former presidents.[142]

    Third, the board quickly clarified that full, given names were not the only names offered protection under 2(c). "Rather, this statutory sub-section operates to bar the registration of marks containing not only full names, but also surnames, shortened names, nicknames, etc., so long as the name in question does, in fact, 'identify' a particular living individual."[143] And for all of the reasons discussed, the board upheld

---

[137] *Id.* (citing 2 J. MCCARTHY, MCCARTHY ON TRADEMARKS AND UNFAIR COMPETITION, §§ 10.07, 28.1 and 28.46 (4th ed. 2010)).

[138] *In re* Hoefflin, 97 U.S.P.Q.2d 1174, 1176 (T.T.A.B. 2010). The examining attorney also presented evidence from the online Urban Dictionary entry for "Obamapajamas" and noting the inherent rhyming scheme to Obama Pajama. *See id.*

[139] *Id.* at 1177.

[140] *Id.* at 1176 ("Of course, the fact that applicant filed these three particular applications together just weeks before President Obama's historical swearing-in would seem to belie this representation.").

[141] *Id.*

[142] *Id.* at 1177–78.

[143] *Id.* at 1177 (citing *In re* Sauer, 27 U.S.P.Q.2d 1073, 1074 (T.T.A.B. 1993)).

the refusal of registration for all three marks, absent the consent of the
Forty-Fourth President, Barack Obama.[144]

    *10.  In re Morrison & Foerster LLP[145]—FRANKNDODD*

       Former Congressman Barney Frank and Former Senator Chris
Dodd are the namesakes and "co-architects" of the Dodd-Frank Wall
Street Reform and Consumer Protection Act.[146] The applicant wished
to register "FRANKNDODD" as a service mark for legal and
legislative update services.[147] Based on the association with the former
Congressman and former Senator, the examining attorney refused the
registration under 2(c).[148]

       The board overturned the refusal on the grounds that the name
"Dodd-Frank" is publicly connected with the legislation, not the
individuals.[149] "FRANKNDODD" is a reversal of the name order from
the legislation in order to create an allusion to Mary Shelley's
*Frankenstein*, since the bill was pieced together from fifteen separate
laws and the allusion had already been made by the media.[150] The
board also distinguishes the case at hand from *In re Hoefflin* by
pointing out that, unlike Obama in "OBAMAPAJAMA,"
"FRANKNDODD" is the name of a statute and also a commentary on
said legislation rather than just the names of individuals.[151] In
overturning the registration refusal, the board found that the mark
"would be understood by the relevant consuming public as referencing

---

[144] *In re* Hoefflin, 97 U.S.P.Q.2d 1174, 1176 (T.T.A.B. 2010).
[145] *In re* Morrison & Foerster LLP, 110 U.S.P.Q.2d 1423 (T.T.A.B. 2014).
[146] *Id.* at 1424; *Dodd-Frank Wall Street Reform and Consumer Protection Act*, U.S.
COMMODITY FUTURES TRADING COMMISSION (Jan. 5 2010),
http://www.cftc.gov/idc/groups/public/@swaps/documents/file/hr4173_enrolledbill.pdf.
[147] *In re* Morrison & Foerster LLP, 110 U.S.P.Q.2d 1423, 1423 (T.T.A.B. 2014).
[148] *Id.* at 1423–24.
[149] *Id.* at 1427–28.
[150] *Id.* The author would note that the T.T.A.B. misidentifies the character "Frankenstein"
as the monster who is put together with the parts of numerous people in *Frankenstein*
rather than the name of the doctor. Of course, as has been pointed out by numerous online
sources, "Knowledge is knowing Frankenstein isn't the monster; wisdom is knowing
Frankenstein is the monster." Brian McGackin, *Culling the Classics: Frankenstein*, LIT
REACTOR (Oct. 31, 2014) https://litreactor.com/columns/culling-the-classics-
frankenstein.
[151] *In re* Morrison & Foerster LLP, 110 U.S.P.Q.2d 1423, 1428 (T.T.A.B. 2014).

and commenting on the Dodd-Frank Act rather than as specifically identifying Congressman Barney Frank and Senator Chris Dodd."[152]

III.     DIVIDING UP THE ROSTER: CATEGORIES OF NAMES AND EXAMPLES OF WRESTLER TRADEMARK PROCEEDINGS

All of the cases cited in the TMEP leave wrestler names—arguably nicknames, stage names, character names, given names, or names identifying individuals—up for interpretation, depending on what category an examiner chooses to use in classifying the mark. Further complicating the analysis, it is not always clear if the name of a wrestler is a given name or a name previously used before joining the entity seeking to register the trademark. Since there is scant case law on the subject of wrestlers' names,[153] it is up to balancing competing analogies to figure out what should apply. The various decisions by the USPTO show that there is not a universally accepted criteria to determine if wrestlers' names (whether they are based on real names or not) should require the consent of the wrestler or if the wrestling promoter registering the wrestler's name as a mark is distinguishable as the source of the product or service.[154]

---

[152] *Id.*

[153] The Ultimate Warrior cases: Warrior v. Titan Sports, Inc., No: CV96-15377 (Ariz. Sup. Ct. 1997) (trademark case); Titan Sports, Inc. v. Hellwig, 1999 U.S. Dist. LEXIS 10523 (D. Conn. Apr. 26, 1999) (subsequent character copyright case mentioning details of earlier trademark case not found in the record otherwise) provides an example of how a state court ruled on a very specific issue—the ownership of a trademark of the name "Warrior." In that case, Mr. Hellwig entered the WWF (now WWE) with his given name—James Brian Hellwig. Warrior v. Titan Sports, Inc., No: CV96-15377 (Ariz. Sup. Ct. 1997). He had already worked as the Dingo Warrior for a year in another wrestling federation—World Class Championship Wrestling—before joining the WWF performing under the name "Dingo Warrior." *Id.* His contract, as stated in the lawsuit, specifically addressed the issue of intellectual property in the character name. *Id.* However, Hellwig claimed that he was the one who made the change to the Ultimate Warrior name that would eventually make him a household name. *Id.* In 1993, he legally changed his name to the one-word Warrior (and his children's surnames to Warrior). *Id.* While an interesting case, it is difficult to gather much precedent from the case. Not only were the lawsuits decided in state court, but the combination of the timing of the legal name change, the character's creation, and the contract terms make the case only good for general principles, which will be discussed later on.

[154] The most common source of the product or service is usually the WWE. "The WWE has dominated its market and has established its brand in the minds of the American public." Sungick Min et. al., *An Empirical Analysis of the Effectiveness of World Wrestling Entertainment Marketing Strategies*, SPORT J. (Feb. 6, 2014),

The purpose of professional wrestling, particularly the WWE, is to sell entertainment.[155] The entertainment provided by the world-class athletes employed by WWE is based on the storylines and characters.[156] One perspective says the wrestlers become "akin to literary characters or characters in a play individually spinning their author's character conception."[157] The company follows this perspective, saying "[o]ur creative team develops compelling and complex characters and weaves them into dynamic storylines that combine physical and emotional elements."[158] In order to draw a profit from these characters and stories, WWE not only provides live events, televised events, consumer products, and productions, but also licenses the rights to "substantially all of the [their] characters."[159]

Wrestling ring names are more than names, they represent identities. Ring names convey an alter ego for the athlete, an identity that extends beyond the ring and into the real world. The line between the characters gets blurred even further when the wrestlers are often asked to adhere to a code of conduct that suggests the reality of the show into real life.[160] Conversely, the private lives of wrestlers can also enter the ring.[161] Romantic entanglements behind the scenes show up

---

http://thesportjournal.org/article/an-empirical-analysis-of-the-effectiveness-of-world-wrestling-entertainment-marketing-strategies/.

[155] Daniel Bilsky, *From Parts Unknown: WWE v. Jim Hellwig in the Ultimate Battle for Character Copyright*, 19 MARQ. SPORTS L. REV. 419, 421 (2009).

[156] *Id.* at 422.

[157] *Id.* at 419.

[158] *Company Overview*, WWE.COM, http://corporate.wwe.com/company/overview (last visited May 14, 2016).

[159] *Id.*

[160] *See* Philip Frazer, *Top 15 Times Wrestling Got Real*, SPORTSTER (Dec. 12, 2014), http://www.thesportster.com/wrestling/top-15-times-wrestling-got-real/?view=all ("Once upon a time kayfabe—the act of portraying staged events as real—was an unbreakable tangent, used to try and get the audience as invested as possible in the clashes of heroes and villains."); *see also* David Shoemaker, *Grantland Dictionary: Pro Wrestling Edition*, GRANTLAND.COM (Aug. 13, 2014), http://grantland.com/features/grantland-dictionary-pro-wrestling-edition/ ("kayfabe (n.; adj.) — The code of secrecy that undergirds the pro wrestling industry by which the secret of its unreality is protected. Keeping kayfabe is the act of staying in character before, during, and after shows so as to maintain the illusion. As an adjective, it separates real from fake, as in, "He's not my real brother, he's just my kayfabe brother." The term comes from carnie slang (possibly a variation on Pig Latin) for "be fake" or "keep secret.").

[161] Dave Meltzer, WRESTLING OBSERVER NEWSL. (April 18, 2011) (article on file with author) ("The Edge/Lita/Matt Hardy angle started out as legit, and after an incident in real life where Edge's car was defaced (not an angle) while on the road in the Carolinas,

on TV.[162] Drug and alcohol problems in real life turn into redemption stories.[163] Deaths of loved ones become reasons to hire people.[164] Pets and tragedies are dragged into the ring.[165] Even lawsuits and government investigations have been dramatized into scripted angles.[166] With the close connections between real life and what happens for entertainment, a wrestler's name is possibly not just a character.

    The names of professional wrestlers come from a variety of sources—some use their real names or a variation on their real name,[167]

---

the company either believed Hardy did it, or in some form was responsible for it, as Hardy was fired.").

[162] Bryan Alvarez, FIGURE FOUR WKLY. NEWSL. (July 2, 2007) (article on file with author) ("Nancy Benoit, formerly Nancy Sullivan and Nancy Daus, performed under the stage name Woman for years. In a very famous story, her husband and WCW booker at the time Kevin Sullivan put Benoit and Nancy together in storyline. In order to convince people that the two were really a couple, he booked them together on the road and in hotel rooms. As is often the case in this business, storyline became reality, and Nancy separated from Sullivan and married Benoit in 2000 after living together for three years.").

[163] Dave Meltzer, WRESTLING OBSERVER NEWSL. (September 13, 2010) (article on fle with author) ("With all the people who went through rehab, the WWE's two most notable success stories they used to brag about years ago were William Regal and Eddy Guerrero.").

[164] Dave Meltzer, WRESTLING OBSERVER NEWSL. (Jun. 30, 2014) (article on file with author) ("Vickie returned in 2006, after Eddy's death, first as the widow of the beloved Eddie, but then making her own name as a heel.").

[165] Kevin Eck, *Q&A with Jeff Hardy*, BALT. SUN RING POSTS (October 3, 2008), http://weblogs.baltimoresun.com/sports/wrestling/blog/2008/10/qa_with_jeff_hardy.html ("[T]hat Friday night I lost everything, and the saddest thing is I lost my dog Jack. You hear about fires all the time, but then you experience it, man, it's just like, 'Wow, this really happens to people.' It's a night I'll never forget, naturally. A week or so later I found Jack's body in the ruins. I got a little closure to that and cried a lot, was sad a lot and had bad dreams. When I came back we actually made that somewhat of a story line[.]"); Dave Meltzer, WRESTLING OBSERVER NEWSL. (April 13, 2009) (article on file with author) ("They pushed that Matt was the one who set fire to Jeff's trailer and killed his dog in both the video package, and it was talked about in the commentary for the match.").

[166] Dave Meltzer, WRESTLING OBSERVER NEWSL. (May 25, 2010) (article on file with author) ("The 11/2 Raw, on election eve, will be from Bridgeport, CT. The WWE has never been the master of subtlety when it comes to attempting to sway last minute close elections and the next few weeks of television and releases should be at least interesting. This past week, the company has started a "Stand up for WWE" campaign, which they encourage fans to voice their support claiming the company has come under unfair and biased attacks from politicians and media outlets.").

[167] John Cena, Randy Orton, Bryan Daniel (Bryan Danielson) to name a few. *See infra* Part III A.

some use a name from previous wrestling experience,[168] some use a name portrayed by more than one person,[169] or, most commonly in the modern era, the company creates the characters.[170] Each source creates specific challenges when trying to identify who should own trademark rights, if any are available, to the name.

The next section of this article looks at examples of each of four origins for wrestling names that WWE has trademarked in the past fifteen years: real names, names from previous wrestling experience, names represented by more than one person, and names solely created by the company. At least one example of a trademark application and the correspondence between WWE and the USPTO is discussed, as well as a short analysis of the laws mentioned by both sides in their correspondence.

## A.   Real Names Are Easy: John Cena

John Cena was born John Felix Anthony Cena.[171] He started his televised WWE career on June 27, 2002 on WWE Smackdown.[172] On October 28, 2003, WWE filed an application to register "JOHN CENA" as a service mark for entertainment wrestling performances and wrestling news.[173] On April 28, 2014, the USPTO replied noting that "JOHN CENA" was a name identifying an individual and therefore barred from registration without the consent of the individual.[174] WWE replied on October 19, 2004, with the signed consent of John Cena,

---

[168] Rey Mysterio, Chris Jericho, Hulk Hogan, Sting, Lance Storm, Ultimo Dragon, Ricky Steamboat, Ric Flair, etc. are all examples. *See infra* Part III A.

[169] *See e.g.*, *Doink the Clown*, WIKIPEDIA, https://en.wikipedia.org/wiki/Doink_the_Clown (last visited May 14, 2016) (Doink the Clown); *Sin Cara*, WIKIPEDIA, https://en.wikipedia.org/wiki/Sin_Cara (last visited May 14, 2016) (Sin Cara); *Dr. X*, WIKIPEDIA, https://en.wikipedia.org/wiki/Doctor_X_(wrestler) (last visited May 14, 2016) (Dr. X).

[170] The "bookers" would traditionally be the ones who would create the characters. Bookers are the people who would book the talent and decide who would win and lose the matches. *supra* note 160.

[171] *John Cena Biography*, IMDB.COM, http://www.imdb.com/name/nm1078479/bio (last visited May 14, 2016).

[172] *WWE Smackdown*, (Titan Entertainment broadcast June 27, 2002).

[173] JOHN CENA, U.S. Registration No. 2957043 (Application).

[174] *Id.* (Priority Action).

dated May 10, 2004.[175] On May 31, 2005, the registration was granted for "JOHN CENA."[176]

　　While WWE did not include John Cena's consent in the original application, the company submitted it without further comment on the record. Given the trademark sought is the first name and surname of John Cena, the case law seems to present an easy solution—get the consent of the individual and get the mark registered. [177]

## B.　Previous Wrestling: Rey Mysterio[178]

　　The 27-year-old Óscar Gutiérrez had already been flying from the turnbuckles for over a decade in Mexico[179] by the time he literally exploded onto the scene accompanied by fireworks to debut on WWE Smackdown on July 25, 2002.[180] Óscar is the nephew of Miguel Ángel López Díaz, more widely known as the luchador and trainer Rey Misterio Sr.[181] Diaz premiered in 1976 as Rey Misterio (King Mystery) and went on to train other wrestlers, including his nephew Óscar.[182]

---

[175] *Id.* (Response to Office Action).

[176] *Id.* (Registration).

[177] *See* 15 U.S.C. §§ 1051, 1052(c) (2012); *In re* Sauer, 27 U.S.P.Q.2d 1073, 1075 (T.T.A.B. 1993).

[178] This article does not talk about the end of Rey Mysterio's career with the WWE and the possible international trademark issues. Rumors flew about possible contract issues between Rey Mysterio and WWE over the use of the name, since it was used with only a slightly altered spelling of the addition of "Jr." for many years prior to his time in the WWE when wrestling in Mexico and Japan. David Meltzer, WRESTLER OBSERVER NEWSL. (Mar. 9, 2015) (article on file with author) ("Over the past year there were a number of issues back-and-forth which neither side went public with, due to wanting a quiet resolution that would allow Mysterio to do what he wanted. There were threats about usage of the Rey Mysterio name, although he'd have almost surely won that in court because he had started using the name Rey Misterio Jr., in AAA back in 1992 and used it on major shows including PPV in the U.S. as well as in Japan before coming to ECW and WCW (the intellectual property of both that WWE currently owns). But such a legal fight could be long and costly. There were also issues both sides could have used, regarding drug testing failures by Mysterio and alleged racial remarks within the WWE that had been talked about that were one of the reasons of the quick resolution and dropping of the non-compete in the Jose Alberto Rodriguez (Del Rio) case.").

[179] John M. Milner, *Rey Mysterio Jr. Bio*, CANOE – SLAM! SPORTS WRESTLING, http://slam.canoe.com/Slam/Wrestling/Bios/mysterio.html (last visited May 14, 2016).

[180] *WWE SMACKDOWN* (Titan Entertainment broadcast July 25, 2002)

[181] *Rey Mysterio (Mystery King) Profile*, LUCHAWIKI, http://www.luchawiki.org/index.php?title=Rey_Misterio (last visited May 14, 2016).

[182] *Id.*

Óscar made his professional debut at age fourteen in 1989 as Colibri
(Hummingbird).[183] Two years later in 1991, his uncle ceremoniously
gave Oscar a luchador mask and the name Rey Misterio, Jr.[184] The
sixteen-year-old continued to wrestle in Mexico, Japan, and eventually
made the jump to World Championship Wrestling (WCW) in the
United States.[185] By the time Rey Mysterio climbed in the ring for
WWE, fans were already holding up "Rey Mysterio, Jr." signs as the
announcer Michael Cole hailed him as "the most celebrated luchador to
invade the U.S. since Mil Mascaras."[186]

On December 2, 2002, the WWE filed an intent to use
application for the mark REY MYSTERIO in connection with
entertainment services, mainly wrestling exhibitions.[187] As expected,
on July 16, 2003, the USPTO file shows a notice of publication stating,
"The mark of the application appears to be entitled to registration."[188]
On August 5, 2003, the mark was published in the Official Gazette.[189]
The mark continued to follow the normal course of registration when
the WWE amended the application to show use on April 27, 2004.[190]
The amendment alleges the mark's use in commerce beginning on July
25, 2002,[191] the day Rey Mysterio premiered on Smackdown.[192]

Nearly two years later, on March 12, 2004, the WWE applied
for an intent to use registration for REY MYSTERIO on action figures
and other toys.[193] A few months later, on July 19, 2004, the trademark
examiner sent a notice to WWE in regards to the entertainment service
mark saying "Does Not Function as Service Mark—Personal Name."[194]
The action claimed that the "Rey Mysterio is clearly the name of the

---

[183] *Rey Mysterio Jr. Profile*, LUCHAWIKI, http://www.luchawiki.org/index.php?title=
Rey_Misterio_Jr. (last visited May 14, 2016).
[184] *Id.*
[185] *Id.*
[186] *WWE SMACKDOWN* (Titan Entertainment broadcast July 25, 2002). Mil Mascaras
(Spanish for 1,000 masks) is considered to be one of the most internationally successful
luchadores with a career spanning back to the mid-1960s. *See Mil Máscaras Bio*,
WWE.COM, www.wwe.com/superstars/mil-mascaras (last visited May 14, 2016).
Entertainingly, he is the uncle of current WWE wrestler Alberto Del Rio. *Id.*
[187] REY MYSTERIO, Registration No. 2972939 (Application).
[188] *Id.* (Notice of Publication).
[189] *Id.*
[190] *Id.* (Amendment to Allege Use).
[191] *Id.*
[192] Milner, *supra* note 179.
[193] REY MYSTERIO, Registration No. 3124385 (Application).
[194] REY MYSTERIO, Registration No. 2972939 (Office Action Outgoing).

wrestler in [the specimen]" and will be refused registration unless there is a showing of secondary meaning.[195] A month later, the USPTO also sent a correspondence on the toy mark application noting that Rey Mysterio was the name of an individual and written consent was required to use the name.[196]

In January of 2005, WWE responded to the entertainment mark action with a response arguing that Rey Mysterio was the name of a character, akin to "PETER PAN, Registration No. 1,831,779, SUPERMAN, Registration No. 1,181,536, BATMAN, Registration No. 1,652,640, BARNEY, Registration No. 1,860,039, TWEETY, Registration No. 1,869,692."[197] The response also notes that a number of WWE wrestlers' names had already been granted registration, such as THE ROCK, THE UNDERTAKER, EDGE, and LITA.[198] Several months later, WWE responded to the toy trademark on March 25, 2005, with the written consent of Óscar Gutierrez to the registration of REY MYSTERIO by the WWE.[199] By doing so, the WWE provided written consent for both trademark applications, and both were granted in short order.[200]

The case of Rey shows one of the points of tension within the law: should the USPTO require the consent of a performer who plays a character whose name predates the performer's contract with the trademark applicant and is widely associated with the individual? Or should the USPTO leave well enough alone and allow the WWE to register the trademark of any character on its roster, given the close association between the characters and the company? The attorney for WWE points to a variety of character trademarks in her response, suggesting that we should use the analogy of characters in works of literature, television, or film to make the decision about how to treat the marks that are previously associated with a performer.[201] Certainly, there are similarities between a character like Barney and wrestlers. Both appear in taped television performances portraying characters in storylines written by other people. Both are providing an entertainment

---

[195] *Id.*
[196] REY MYSTERIO, Registration No. 3124385. (Office Action Outgoing).
[197] REY MYSTERIO, Registration No. 78198695. (Response to Office Action).
[198] *Id.*
[199] REY MYSTERIO, Registration No. 3124385. (Response to Office Action).
[200] REY MYSTERIO, Registration No. 3124385; REY MYSTERIO, Registration No. 2972939.
[201] REY MYSTERIO, Registration No. 78198695. (Response to Office Action).

service. But there are also differences. For one thing, Barney was created by Lyons Partnership.[202] Although WWE claims in its response "the mark is a fictitious character name, created by Applicant,"[203] it is questionable whether or not the small changes in the name (the removal of "Jr." and the changing of the spelling, though not the sound, from Misterio to Mysterio) would stand up to much scrutiny.[204] Of course, since both Rey Misterio and Rey Misterio Jr. had operated primarily in Mexico[205], there was not a prior trademark registration for either name. It would still be uncertain how the USPTO would rule in a case where the previously used name was used in the United States without registration. Perhaps, more importantly, this should serve as a warning to professional wrestlers to register their names as service marks and trademarks in the United States before entering into a contract with the WWE if the wrestlers want to ensure their consent is necessary for WWE to transfer the mark.

C.  *More Than One Person Under a Mask: the Sin Caras*[206]

    In 2011, the WWE applied to register the mark "SIN CARA" in four categories: wrestling entertainment,[207] clothing,[208] toys,[209] and

---

[202] BARNEY, Registration No. 1860039.

[203] REY MYSTERIO, Registration No. 2972939.

[204] LALONDE, *supra* note 29, at §1.3 ("The applicant may be able to argue that the trademarks are dissimilar in sound, appearance and meaning . . . .").

[205] *See Rey Mysterio Jr. Profile, supra* note 183.

[206] This article will not address the more interesting international issue with the Sin Cara trademark. WWE did not register the trademark in the United States or in Mexico in time to block the registration of the name mark and the design of the mask in Mexico. David Meltzer, WRESTLING OBSERVER NEWSL., Jun. 6, 2011, at 6 (article on file with author) ("WWE forgot to trademark the name Sin Cara, so when CMLL found this out, as a nuisance, they trademarked the name Sin Cara for use in Mexico."). Another theory is that CMLL was attempting to block the first man behind the Sin Cara mask from using the name Sin Cara or his signature mask if he were to return to Mexico after leaving the WWE. David Bixenspan, *CMLL trademarks Sin Cara name/mask in Mexico to block a post-WWE run*, CAGESIDESEATS.COM (Jun. 15, 2011, 7:42 PM), http://www.cagesideseats.com/2011/6/15/2226054/cmll-trademarks-sin-cara-name-mask-in-mexico-to-block-a-post-wwe-run ("The idea is that if he eventually leaves WWE and comes back to work full time in Mexico, not only could he not be Mistico in other companies like AAA, but he couldn't be Sin Cara, either.").

[207] SIN CARA, Registration No. 4440573.

[208] SIN CARA, Registration No. 85353048.

[209] SIN CARA, Registration No. 85353056.

paper products.[210] Sin Cara debuted on television as a masked luchador on April 4, 2011.[211] Under the mask that night was Luis Ignascio Urive Alvirde.[212] Alvirde already had a career as a luchador in Mexico under the name Mistico but took over the Sin Cara name when he moved to the WWE.[213] Quickly, though, Jorge Arias also started to wrestle as Sin Cara when Alvirde was suspended for violating the WWE wellness policy.[214] Both men wrestled as Sin Cara, eventually with two different colored masks, and even competed against each other over the name with Alvirde winning the right to compete under the name.[215] After several rocky years though, Alvirde left the company and Arias ended up as Sin Cara in the WWE by 2014.[216] Sin Cara is still listed on the WWE website with the accomplishments of both Alvirde and Arias listed in the Sin Cara Bio.[217]

At the same time that the two men portrayed the character, the four trademark intent to use applications moved through the USPTO.[218] All four applications received the same concern from the examining attorney: that "SIN CARA" was a stage name for Luis Ignascio Urive Alvirde.[219] The responses from WWE varied slightly: most just denied that it was a stage name identifying an individual, while the response in

---

[210] SIN CARA, Registration No. 85353064.

[211] *WWE RAW* (Titan Entertainment broadcast Apr. 4, 2011), *available at* http://www.wwe.com/shows/raw/2011-04-04.

[212] *See* Ryan Dilbert, *Comparing Hunico and the Original Sin Cara's Ring Work*, BLEACHER REP. (Dec. 11, 2013), http://bleacherreport.com/articles/1884807-comparing-hunico-and-the-original-sin-caras-ring-work (naming Alvirde as the original Sin Cara).

[213] *Id.*

[214] *WWE News: Smackdown news & notes - IC Title change, "Sin Cara" returns, Beth & Natalya get a team name*, PRO WRESTLING TORCH (Aug. 12, 2011 9:39:07 PM), http://pwtorch.com/artman2/publish/WWE_News_3/article_52014.shtml#.Vq6eBSorKhd

[215] Joey Styles, *Who deserves to be called Sin Cara?*, WWE.COM (Oct. 4, 2011), http://www.wwe.com/shows/smackdown/2011-09-30/both-sin-caras-talk-to-wwe.com.

[216] *Sin Cara*, WWE.COM, http://www.wwe.com/superstars/sin-cara (last visited May 14, 2016); Nick Pagliano, *Breaking: Original Sin Cara Confirms His Release from WWE, Claims He Owns the Gimmick Rights, Is the Character Done in WWE?*, WRESTLEZONE (Jan. 24, 2014) http://www.wrestlezone.com/news/447345-sin-cara-confirms-his-wwe-release.

[217] *Sin Cara, supra* note 216.

[218] SIN CARA, Registration No. 4440573; SIN CARA, Registration No. 85353048; SIN CARA, Registration No. 85353056; SIN CARA, Registration No. 85353064.

[219] SIN CARA, Registration No. 4440573 (Offc Action Outgoing); SIN CARA, Registration No. 85353048 (Offc Action Outgoing); SIN CARA, Registration No. 85353056 (Offc Action Outgoing); SIN CARA, Registration No. 85353064 (Offc Action Outgoing).

the entertainment services mark file included the addition, "The mark represents a stage name that is owned by Applicant."[220] The examining attorney did not initially accept the response but did eventually move the application forward without the need for anyone's written consent.[221]

The record does not provide a great deal of insight into the thinking of either the examining attorney or the WWE attorney in this case. It appears the examining attorney believed the mark to be a stage name; WWE said no; the examining attorney disagreed; and then, somehow, the two came to an understanding.[222] The scant information makes it hard to determine what law either is depending on, other than the standard recitations to 2(c) of the Lanham Act and the TMEP 1206 and 1301.[223] More importantly, it can be inferred from the initial issue presented and eventual registration of the mark that the examiner was convinced that SIN CARA did not identify an individual as a stage name.[224] Without more in the record, it is nearly impossible to figure out which facts in the case changed the examiner's mind. Was it the entrance of Arias under the mask of Sin Cara on television during the time the application was pending? Was it the recognition of Sin Cara as a character rather than a stage name? Or was it something else entirely?

Working from analogy, it seems the most logical comparison to the earlier case law would be to *In re Florida Cypress Gardens.*[225] The character of Corky the Clown, at issue in *Cypress Gardens*, was a character who was portrayed by one or multiple people, in live entertainment, and acted as an identifier of entertainment services for Cypress Gardens.[226] Sin Cara, it seems from the record, is also a character portrayed by multiple people, in live entertainment, and acting as an identifier of wrestling entertainment services for WWE.[227] Given the similarities, it would seem that the type of precedent set by *Cypress Gardens* should lead to a similar outcome under the current law of registration without consent for future characters portrayed by more than one individual.

---

[220] SIN CARA, Registration No. 4440573 (Response to Office Action).
[221] SIN CARA, Registration No. 4440573.
[222] *See id.*
[223] *Id.* (Outgoing Office Action).
[224] *See id.*
[225] *In re* Fla. Cypress Gardens Inc., 208 U.S.P.Q. 288 (T.T.A.B. 1980).
[226] *Id.* at *5.
[227] SIN CARA, Registration No. 4440573.

### D. Company Men

#### 1. Man? Men? Lunatic Fringe aka Dean Ambrose aka Jonathan Good

On June 18, 2013, WWE filed an application to register the trademark DEAN AMBROSE in entertainment services.[228] The application came approximately seven months after the November 18, 2012, debut of Dean Ambrose at the pay-per-view Survivor Series.[229] Jonathan "Jon" Good had been wrestling under the name Dean Ambrose since he started in the WWE developmental league in 2011.[230] On September 18, 2013, the examiner noted a phone conversation with the applicant's attorney and made the note "The name DEAN AMBROSE is a fictitious ring name owned solely by the applicant to refer to a particular character in the WWE storylines. The name does not refer to a living individual."[231] The examiner then amended the record to note "[t]he name DEAN AMBROSE does not identify a living individual."[232] Without any more issues or drama, the registration was granted on January 21, 2014.[233]

The drama returned, however, when on August 19, 2014, WWE filed an intent to use application for the mark LUNATIC FRINGE.[234] The application proceeded normally with the specimen for use offered on September 10, 2015.[235] The specimen shows a still from a video with three men and a referee in the middle of a wrestling ring with the headline "Dean Ambrose v. Sheamus & Kane—2-on-1 Handicap Match: Smackdown, June 18, 2015 (2:24)" and the caption "The Lunatic Fringe battles the Corporate Demon & The Celtic Warrior."[236] On September 19, 2015, the examiner sent an Office Action saying LUNATIC FRINGE was the name of a living individual,

---

[228] DEAN AMBROSE, Registration No. 4470627.
[229] See WWE Survivor Series (Titan Entertainment broadcast Nov. 18, 2012), available at https://www.youtube.com/watch?v=AuDUiOh_mr8.
[230] Dean Ambrose, WIKIPEDIA, https://en.wikipedia.org/wiki/Dean_Ambrose#WWE (last visited May 14, 2016).
[231] DEAN AMBROSE, Registration No. 4470627 (Notation to the file).
[232] Id. (Examiners Amendment).
[233] Id. (Registration Certificate).
[234] LUNATIC FRINGE, Serial No. 86,370,179 (Application).
[235] Id. (Specimen).
[236] Id.

namely Dean Ambrose.[237] The examiner goes on to quote the two-part test found in a number of cases, including the previously discussed *In re Hoefflin*.[238] The examiner continues by saying that since LUNATIC FRINGE is obviously the nickname or stage name of a wrestler and the industry the service mark is to be used for is wrestling, there is sufficient connection between the individual and the industry to require the consent of the individual pictured in the specimen.[239] To date, the WWE has not offered a response.[240]

The facts here seem somewhat straightforward. The WWE has already registered DEAN AMBROSE and is now registering a secondary nickname for the wrestling persona, LUNATIC FRINGE. It is unclear if the change in perspective from the registration of DEAN AMBROSE to the LUNATIC FRINGE specimen has to do with a sudden realization on the part of the examiner that wrestlers are people or a change in policy. If the policy did change between the 2014 registration of DEAN AMBROSE and the 2015 examination of the specimen of use for LUNATIC FRINGE, it was outside of the updates to the TMEP in April 2014 and July 2015.[241] The only updates to the relevant sections—1206 and 1301—were stylistic updates and a single update to the case citations.[242]

Perhaps the difference has more to do with the previously mentioned questions on how to handle a wrestler's name. It is clear from the correspondence with the USTPO on the DEAN AMBROSE and LUNATIC FRINGE marks that some examiners are more easily swayed that a wrestler's ring name is a character name of the WWE, while others insist it is the stage name of a wrestler, requiring the signature of the wrestler before it can be registered.[243]

---

[237] *Id.* (Office Action Outgoing).
[238] *In re* Hoefflin, 97 U.S.P.Q.2d 1174, 1175-76 (T.T.A.B. 2010).
[239] LUNATIC FRINGE, Serial No. 86,370,179 (Office Action Outgoing).
[240] *See id.*
[241] *See* TMEP at Change Summary.
[242] *Id.*
[243] LUNATIC FRINGE, Serial No. 86,370,179; DEAN AMBROSE, Registration No. 4470627.

## 2. *Gone and Abandoned: Val Venis*

Sean Allen Morley has a long and storied wrestling career, spanning multiple decades, federations, and ring names.[244] After returning to the ring name of Val Venis in 2003,[245] he was released from his WWE contract.[246] In his waning years, the WWE sought to register VAL VENIS as a mark for wrestling entertainment services.[247] On June 11, 2007, the USPTO sent an outgoing office action stating that the mark is a name that identifies a particular individual.[248] The response from WWE was the same as has been seen in other cases, the simple statement that the mark does not identify a particular living individual.[249] On January 14, 2008, the USPTO issued a final office action containing pointed language about the applicant's denial that the mark VAL VENIS simply does not identify a particular living individual.[250]

> The examining attorney is at a loss to understand how the applicant can aver, through a signed verification, that the name in the trademark does NOT identify a particular living individual when said individual is a professional wrest[l]er, who has wrestled for the applicant. The trademark examining attorney refers to the excerpted materials from the Google® search engine in which "VAL VENIS" appeared in reference to "WRESTLING" in approximately 137,000 stories.[251]

The examiner presented a distinctly different perspective on the question of whether ring names are characters or are nicknames or stage names of living individuals.

---

[244] *Val Venis*, WIKIPEDIA, https://en.wikipedia.org/wiki/Val_Venis (last visited May 14, 2016).
[245] *Id.* Val Venis originally debuted on WWE television on May 18, 1998. *Id.*
[246] *D-Lo Brown, Bam Neely, Val Venis released*, WWE.COM (Jan. 9, 2009) http://www.wwe.com/inside/news/dloreleased.
[247] U.S. Trademark Application Serial No. 77,142,336 (filed Mar. 28, 2007).
[248] *Id.*
[249] *Id.*
[250] *Id.*
[251] *Id.*

The WWE did send in a request for reconsideration.[252] In return, the examiner sent back a denial of the reconsideration along with an additional fifty-nine attachments showing various references to the real names of wrestlers and the use of ring names along to identify wrestlers.[253] Again, this examiner showed a particular flare in his response to the WWE denying the reconsideration and affirming the original final action.

> Although the applicant avers that the mark is a character name that can be used by more than one actor, at the applicant's choosing, there is no evidence that any wrestler's stage name is passed along to a successor. In fact, while a plethora of websites exist about professional wrestlers, and their stage names, the trademark examining attorney was unable to discover any evidence that it is the practice of professional wrestlers to take over the stage name of another. See attached evidence from Google® and Ask Jeeves®. Accordingly, while the applicant's argument is rejected as it is unsupported by any evidence and appears to be contrary to manner in which stage names are used by professional wrestlers.[254]

The WWE did not appeal the finding or respond to the USPTO on this matter. Instead, the USPTO sent the notice of abandonment to the applicant on December 16, 2008.[255] It could be inferred from the timing of the abandonment that WWE might have chosen to pursue and fight the findings of the examiner, had Val Venis not been close to the end of his career at WWE.

Even if WWE did not respond to the examining attorney, we can still glean some information from the attorney's writing. The response of the examiner represents a departure from the other cases in that it shows the examiner clearly stating that the ring name of a wrestler should be considered as a stage name, rather than as a character name.[256] The examiner points out that he or she is "at a loss"

---

[252] Id.
[253] Id.
[254] Id.
[255] Id.
[256] Id.

to understand how someone who has wrestled under a name for over a decade could deny that the ring name of the wrestler identifies the living person of the wrestler.[257] In contrast to the other applications discussed, where the examiner takes the simple rejection that the mark identifies a living individual or allows for the argument that a ring name is more akin to a character name, this examiner does not buy it.

Underneath the argument of the examiner is also a number of unspoken assumptions. First, the examiner assumes that the ring name or stage name of the wrestler must be used by the public to identify the person who is employed by WWE as the wrestler because a name is generally only used by one wrestler. The assumption is not without support or merit. In the second correspondence, the examining attorney did provide comprehensive lists of individuals who only use one wrestling name.[258] Given the list the examiner provides, it would be easy to assume a one-to-one identification of wrestlers to their names.

Second, the examining attorney consistently uses the word "stage name" when referring to the character or ring name of the wrestler.[259] When this one-to-one association exists, stage names may be a good analogy for ring names in some cases.[260] Like the stage name LOLLIPOP PRINCESS in *In re Folk*,[261] wrestler ring names are generally used consistently by one person to identify themselves to an audience. Stage names are put in the category of "first names, surnames, shortened names, pseudonyms, stage names, titles, or nicknames" in TMEP 1206.[262] Individuals who use stage names are entitled to protection from unwanted registration of the stage name under 15 U.S.C. § 1052(c).[263]

As the examples discussed in this article show, however, it is not a hard and fast rule that only one person plays a character.[264] On this point, the examiner is clearly missing some of the facts. Given the type of research the examiner provides in his attachments, it does not

---

[257] *Id.*

[258] *Id.* (Attachments to Reconsideration Letter).

[259] *Id.*

[260] Stage name is defined as "the name, different from his or her real name, that an actor or performer is publicly known by." *Stage Name*, CAMBRDIGEDICTIONARIESONLINE, http://dictionary.cambridge.org/us/dictionary/english/stage-name (last visited May 14, 2016).

[261] 160 U.S.P.Q. 213 (T.T.A.B. 1968).

[262] TMEP 1206.01 (Oct. 2015).

[263] TMEP 1206.

[264] *See e.g., In re* Fla. Cypress Gardens Inc., 208 U.S.P.Q. 288 (T.T.A.B. 1980).

appear that the examiner knew how to search for exceptions.[265] The examiner searches for "'wrestler's successor' + 'ring name'" and comes up with no results.[266] It seems the examiner might be able to take a lesson away from this—sometimes people in the industry are able to find information more readily than a trademark examiner.

The lesson for WWE and the general public attempting to register a ring name as a service mark is that the examiners at the USPTO do not appear to be in agreement on how to treat the requests. With various outcomes for ring names that seem to defy easy categorization, the USPTO should push toward consistency in a few areas where consistency does not currently exist—whether to treat ring names not based on the given name of the wrestler as personal names identifying individuals or to treat them as character names. In the next section, I offer a model that would provide consistency and serve the needs of both the company and the individual wrestlers.

IV.     THE AUTHORITY VS. THE WRESTLERS—COMPETING
INTERESTS IN TRADEMARK PROTECTION AND A POSSIBLE MODEL TO
MOVE FORWARD

A.   The Company Line: Economic Incentives to Continue to Create

Wrestlers in the WWE are employed as independent contractors by WWE.[267] The company must invest in order to develop the storylines and promotions.[268] The company provides writers, infrastructure, venues, and overhead necessary to create live wrestling events.[269] As such, the company has an economic interest in the intellectual property of its card of wrestlers.[270] To provide an arena—both literally and figuratively—for the wrestlers to practice their craft,

---

[265] U.S. Trademark Application Serial No. 77,142,336 (filed Mar. 28, 2007) (Attachments to Reconsideration Letter).

[266] *Id.*

[267] David Cowley, *Employees vs. Independent Contractors and Professional Wrestling*, 53 U. LOUISVILLE L. REV. 143, 148 (2014) ("Yet the WWE circumvents providing almost all benefits by ingeniously classifying their wrestlers as independent contractors rather than employees, despite the resemblance to a classic employer-employee arrangement.").

[268] Daniel Bilsky, *From Parts Unknown: WWE v. Jim Hellwig in the Ultimate Battle for Character Copyright*, 19 MARQ. SPORTS L. REV. 419, 436 (2009).

[269] *Id.* at 435.

[270] *Id.* at 436.

the company should be able to register the trademarks for which they helped to create.

The case of CORKY THE CLOWN most resembles these situations.[271] As such, when the company creates the ring name of the wrestlers, the company should be able to register the ring name as a trademark or service mark without the consent of the individual who portrays the character in the ring. Like the names of the individual performances and performers in *Cypress Gardens*, the ring names of the wrestlers act as "registration of marks which identify a particular feature" from the larger entertainment company.[272]

### B.    *Everybody Roots for the Face: Independent Contractors and Right to Publicity*[273]

Wrestlers who work for WWE are treated by the company as independent contractors.[274] The wrestlers lack many of the protections of the classic employer-employee relationship.[275] "[T]he wrestlers are unable to bargain collectively through a union, and the company is absolved from providing health insurance, Social Security and Medicare contributions, and unemployment insurance."[276] It should be noted that "[i]n many respects, the WWE takes good, if not exceptional, care of its talent."[277] Still, most of the 140–150 wrestlers on the roster are not necessarily in a place to bargain.[278] The contracts are generally standard contracts and contain a provision assigning the rights of the name and likeness of the wrestler to the company.[279] The contractors, therefore, do not leave much room for the protection of the wrestler as a celebrity after leaving the employment of the company.

---

[271] *In re* Fla. Cypress Gardens Inc., 208 U.S.P.Q. 288 (T.T.A.B. 1980).

[272] *Id.*

[273] For a more complete look at the issues of misclassification in the wrestling industry, particularly WWE, see David Cowley, *Employees vs. Independent Contractors and Professional Wrestling*, 53 U. LOUISVILLE L. REV. 143 (2014) and Stephen S. Zashin, *Bodyslam from the Top Rope*, 12 U. MIAMI ENT. & SPORTS L. REV. 1 (1995).

[274] David Cowley, *Employees vs. Independent Contractors and Professional Wrestling*, 53 U. LOUISVILLE L. REV. 143, 148 (2014).

[275] *Id.*

[276] *Id.*

[277] *Id.* at 150.

[278] *Id.* at 149.

[279] *See* Titan Sports, Inc. v. Hellwig, 1999 U.S. Dist. LEXIS 10523, at 3–6 (D. Conn. Apr. 26, 1999) (Example of standard contract language for talent).

The wrestlers may also have some additional protections at the state level through the right of publicity. The right of publicity is the right of individuals to protect "any symbol that the public associates primarily with the plaintiff, including names and nicknames, visual images, vocal likeness and other 'signature' symbols."[280] The right protects the "commercial exploitation" of people's identities through state-level actions either in statute or at least at common law.[281] Notably, celebrities from Muhammad Ali[282] to Johnny Carson[283] have been able to stop others from not only using their given names but also from using their nicknames and stage names.[284] An actor can even become so inextricably linked with their character that the character may be indistinguishable by the public from the actor.[285]

The Supreme Court in *Zacchini v. Scripps-Howard Broadcasting Co.* argued the purpose of the right is to both prevent unjust enrichment and to provide an economic incentive (protection) for performances.[286] Importantly, the right to publicity is usually treated as a form of property in that it can be assigned or contracted to another.[287] Given the contracts of the WWE, the wrestler is likely contracting the rights of publicity to the company as well. If the wrestlers are not careful, they may be signing away more than they know.

## C. You Get What You Brought In: A Model Based on Prior Identification

Based on the case law, analysis of some example cases, and needs of both parties, the USPTO should create a standard for the registration of wrestling ring names as marks that both provides some

---

[280] LALONDE, *supra* note 29, at § 2B.02.
[281] 4-57 INTELLECTUAL PROPERTY COUNSELING & LITIGATION § 57.07 (2015).
[282] Ali v. Playgirl, Inc., 447 F. Supp. 723, 726–27 (S.D.N.Y. 1978) (prohibiting use of "the Greatest" in association with a portrait drawing of a black man in a boxing ring).
[283] Carson v. Here's Johnny Portable Toilets, Inc., 698 F.2d 831 (6th Cir. 1983) (prohibiting the portable toilet company from using "Here's Johnny").
[284] LALONDE, *supra* note 29, at § 2B.02.
[285] McFarland v. Miller, 14 F.3d at 912 (3d Cir, 1994) ("We also hold that there is evidence on this record which shows that the name Spanky McFarland has become so identified with McFarland that it could be considered his own name or the name of a character so associated with him as to be indistinguishable from him in public perception.").
[286] Zacchini v. Scripps-Howard Broad. Co., 433 U.S. 562 (U.S. 1977).
[287] LALONDE, *supra* note 29, at § 2B.05.

consistency and balances the needs of the company with those of the wrestlers. In order to provide consistency, the USPTO should treat the wrestling ring name marks in two categories: (1) names directly related or identical to the real world name of the wrestler or the name commonly used by the wrestler before contracting with the trademark applicant; and (2) names created by the company.

For the first category, the USPTO should treat the names as "identifying a particular living individual."[288] Names you bring in should be treated as names—both your own and ones used before as stage names in a professional capacity. Not only would this allow the wrestlers a choice in bargaining, albeit a fairly weak one, it would still allow names brought to the company to be treated as assets in a contract negotiation. The USPTO should use the same principles expressed in the cases involving non-character names to determine how far to extend the protection.

For the second category, the USPTO should treat created characters names as just that—names of characters. As such, the USPTO should not require the consent of the wrestler known by the company-created name to register the name as a mark. As mentioned above, the USPTO should turn to *In re Cypress Gardens*[289] for guidance in these cases, as well as *In re Folk*.[290]

By applying the two different categories to all wrestling ring name related trademarks, the USPTO would provide consistency and balance to a currently inconsistent area of practice. The examiners and attorneys could get in the ring, run the ropes, take some bumps,[291] and know exactly what the outcome would be every time. Just like the pros.

---

[288] 15 U.S.C. § 1052(c) (2012).

[289] *In re* Fla. Cypress Gardens Inc., 208 U.S.P.Q. 288 (T.T.A.B. 1980).

[290] *In re* Folk, 160 U.S.P.Q. 213 (T.T.A.B., 1968).

[291] Shoemaker, *supra* note 160 ("[B]ump (n.) — A move taken in the ring resulting in a hard fall or landing, or (as a verb) to take such a move. It can also refer to the act of selling.").

VIDEO GAMES AND INTELLECTUAL PROPERTY:
SIMILARITIES, DIFFERENCES, AND A NEW APPROACH TO
PROTECTION
JOHN KUEHL[1]

This article will explore how the video game industry has integrated itself into the framework of copyright law.[2] This article will discuss how digital piracy and weak copyright laws abroad have shifted traditional video game pricing models to a free-to-play model, and how the mobile industry's sudden growth and embrace of the free-to-play model has altered the video game landscape.[3]

While the free-to-play model has become profitable and successful at curbing piracy, its sudden success has given rise to an

---

[1] J.D. Candidate 2017, Mitchell Hamline School of Law. The author would like to thank the Staff and Board of *Cybaris*® for their edits and invaluable feedback; specifically, Bryan Jarvis and Caitlin Kowalke. Many thanks to Valerie Hathaway-Kuehl, Professor Kenneth Port, Chad Pawlenty, John Pawlenty, and many other family and friends for their support.
[2] *Infra* Parts II & III.
[3] *Infra* Part II.B.4.

increase in copyright infringement suits. While creative fields have always borrowed from and built upon existing works, whether or not a game has been outright copied has not always been easy to determine. To date, courts have been hesitant to draw a bright-line rule. More recently, it is clear that courts are trying to strike a balance between preventing theft of ideas without limiting creativity. This, however, remains challenging, and the market should be allowed to find the equilibrium it had before the explosion of free-to-play games.

## I.          INTRODUCTION

On October 27, 2015, *Halo 5: Guardians* was released on Microsoft's video game console, the Xbox One. As a first-person shooter game, *Halo 5: Guardians* is the tenth game released in the best selling *Halo* video game series, which has sold over sixty-five million titles in the fourteen-year history of the series.[4] In the first twenty-four hours, the release of *Halo 5: Guardians* generated the most revenue in franchise history, with over $400 million in worldwide sales.[5] In terms of revenue generated, each release in the *Halo* series is the equivalent of a blockbuster film. The series has a deep fan base, with consumers spending $4.6 billion on *Halo* products over the last fourteen years.[6]

The *Halo* series, however, is an aberration of current video game industry trends. Mobile gaming appears to be unstoppable: in 2015, 85% of all mobile app revenue was generated by video games.[7] Video game console sales of both PlayStation 4 and Xbox One are lagging behind the previous generation.[8] While console sales have slowed, there has been a rapid rise in popularity of the mobile video game market over the past decade, which is expected to grow 51% year

---

[4] Eddie Makuch, *Halo Series Reaches 65 Million Units Sold*, GAMESPOT (July 13, 2015), http://www.gamespot.com/articles/halo-series-reaches-65-million-units-sold/1100-6428844.

[5] Erik Kain, *'Halo 5' Was the Biggest Launch in 'Halo' History*, FORBES (Nov. 4, 2015), http://www.forbes.com/sites/erikkain/2015/11/04/halo-5-was-the-biggest-launch-in-halo-history/#16c38e2052e5.

[6] Joshua Brustein, *Can the Woman Behind Halo 5 Save the Xbox?*, BLOOMBERG BUS. (Oct. 22, 2015), http://www.bloomberg.com/features/2015-halo-5-bonnie-ross/.

[7] Dean Takahashi, *Mobile games hit $34.8B in 2015, taking 85% of all app revenues*, VENTUREBEAT (Feb. 10, 2016), http://venturebeat.com/2016/02/10/mobile-games-hit-34-8b-in-2015-taking-85-of-all-app-revenues/.

[8] ZhugeEX, *Console Market Growth: Gen 7 Vs Gen 8 (USA)*, ZHUGEEX BLOG (Oct. 19, 2015), https://zhugeex.com/2015/10/console-market-growth-gen-7-vs-gen-8-usa/.

over year in North America alone.[9] Recently released mobile games
have Super Bowl ads starring supermodels and famous actors.[10] They
are free to play and can be played any time from a mobile phone or
through social networking sites like Facebook.

The number of people who play free-to-play games is
staggering. King Digital Entertainment, creator of the popular mobile
game *Candy Crush Saga*, reported that 408 million people play *Candy
Crush* every month,[11] and these numbers are only likely to rise. Mobile
gaming is predicted to control 42% of the gaming market by 2020.[12]

In November 2015, King Digital was purchased by video
publisher Activision Blizzard for $5.9 billion.[13] The acquisition was
viewed by many as a way for Activision to make a move into the
booming mobile video game market.[14] More than 150 million
Americans play video games.[15] With an average age of thirty-five, 42%
of video gamers play for at least three hours a week.[16] In 2015, the
global video game industry was projected to have revenue over $91
billion.[17] Of those total sales, China and the United States were

---

[9] John Gaudiosi, *Mobile Game Revenues Set to Overtake Console Revenues in 2015*,
FORTUNE (Jan. 15, 2015, 10:56 AM), http://fortune.com/2015/01/15/mobile-console-
game-revenues-2015/.
[10] *See* Jeff Grubb, *Watch Swimsuit Model Kate Upton's Game of War Super Bowl Ad
Right Here*, VENTUREBEAT (Feb. 1, 2015, 4:05 PM),
http://venturebeat.com/2015/02/01/watch-swimsuit-model-kate-uptons-game-of-war-
super-bowl-ad-right-here/; Jeff Grubb, *Liam Neeson Stars in $9M Clash of Clans Super
Bowl Commercial*, VENTUREBEAT (Feb. 1, 2015, 5:50 PM),
http://venturebeat.com/2015/02/01/liam-neeson-stars-in-9m-clash-of-clans-super-bowl-
commercial/.
[11] Matt Krantz, *Candy Crush King IPO: $22.50, Trades Wednesday*, USA TODAY (March
25, 2014, 8:19 PM), http://www.usatoday.com/story/money/markets/2014/03/25/candy-
crush-king-ipo-price/6879681/.
[12] Dean Takahashi, *Game-software Revenues to Grow from $90B to $115B by 2020*,
VENTUREBEAT (Jan. 25, 2016, 4:00 AM), http://venturebeat.com/2016/01/25/game-
software-revenues-expected-to-grow-from-90b-in-2016-to-115b-by-2020/.
[13] Michael J. de la Merced & Nick Wingfield, *Bobby Kotick's Activision Blizzard to Buy
King Digital, Maker of Candy Crush*, N.Y. TIMES (Nov. 2, 2015),
http://www.nytimes.com/2015/11/03/business/dealbook/activision-blizzardto-buy-king-
digital-maker-of-candy-crush.html?_r=0.
[14] Chris Morris, *Why Activision Spent $5.9 Billion on Candy Crush Creator King Digital*,
FORTUNE (Nov. 3, 2015, 6:30 AM), http://fortune.com/2015/11/03/activision-blizzard-
king-digital/.
[15] *More than 150 Million Americans Play Video Games*, ENT. SOFTWARE ASS'N. (Apr.
14, 2015), http://www.theesa.com/article/150-million-americans-play-video-games/.
[16] *Id.*
[17] Brendan Sinclair, *Gaming will hit $91.5 billion this year - Newzoo*,
GAMESINDUSTRY.BIZ (Apr. 22, 2015, 2:46 PM),

expected to spend a combined \$44 billion on video games in 2015.[18] While there are still triple-A console releases like *Halo* and *Call of Duty*, the mobile video game industry is thriving, as 19% of all video game software sales were attributed to mobile games.[19]

With this massive amount of global revenue, it is surprising to see that China, the largest purchaser of video games, also has one of the highest rates of piracy in the world.[20] It should not be surprising to see that "[a]s games have become more and more complicated, so have the intellectual property ('IP') related issues."[21] While video games are a new and exciting frontier for the law, courts have often relied upon the black-letter law for determining legal outcomes.

II.     THE TROUBLE DEFINING VIDEO GAMES IN COPYRIGHT LAW

Copyright law is grounded in the Constitution, providing authors and inventors with the "exclusive Right to their respective Writings and Discoveries."[22] Despite video games existing before 1976, there is no mention of them in the Copyright Act of 1976.[23] This is not to say that the Act was unprepared; 17 U.S.C. § 102 of the original 1976 Act established that intangible works could come under copyright protection.[24] A 1980 amendment to the Copyright Act established that computer programs fell under the scope of the Copyright Act, defining a computer program as "a set of statements or instructions to be used directly or indirectly in a computer to bring

---

http://www.gamesindustry.biz/articles/2015-04-22-gaming-will-hit-usd91-5-billion-this-year-newzoo.

[18] Jeff Grubb, *Here Are the Countries that Make up Most of the \$91.5B Global Gaming Business (Spoiler: China Rules)*, VENTUREBEAT, (Oct. 15, 2015, 11:30 AM), http://venturebeat.com/2015/10/15/here-are-the-countries-that-make-up-most-of-the-91-5b-global-gaming-business-spoiler-china-rules/.

[19] Morris, *supra* note 14.

[20] Jiarui Liu, *Copyright for Blockheads: An Empirical Study of Market Incentive and Intrinsic Motivation*, 38 COLUM. J.L. & ARTS 467 (2015).

[21] Kyle Gross, *Game On: The Rising Prevalence of Patent-Related Issues in the Video Game Industry*, 12 SMU SCI. & TECH. L. REV. 243 (2009).

[22] U.S. CONST. art. 1, § 8, cl. 8.

[23] Joshua I. Miller, *Unknown Futures and the Known Past: What Can Patent Learn from Copyright in the New Technological Age?*, 21 ALB. L.J. SCI. & TECH. 1, 32–33 (2011).

[24] 17 U.S.C. § 102(a) (2012).

about a certain result."[25] However, establishing whether or not a video game is copyrightable is no simple task.[26]

Recognition of video games as copyrightable has been in place since the 1980s. In *Midway Manufacturing Co. v. Artic International, Inc.*, the court directly addressed the dilemma of trying to figure out where exactly video games fit within the copyright spectrum.[27] The problem, at least in the court's view, was determining "whether the creative effort in playing a video game is enough like writing or painting to make each performance of a video game the work of the player and not the game's inventor."[28] The court found that the creator of the game was entitled to copyright protection for what happened within their creation.[29] At the same time, the court also concluded that, "the video game does not fit with complete ease the definition of derivative work."[30]

Because of the incompatibility of video games in the realm of copyright, even with the 1980 amendment, determining the boundaries of where video games fit within the Copyright Act illustrates what distinguishes intellectual property from real property.[31] Video games are protected as intellectual property, rather than real property, because they contain both literal and non-literal elements.[32] However, differentiating between those elements can be tricky because, as Thomas Hemnes once wrote, "[V]ideo games themselves are in many ways perversely unsuited to traditional forms of legal protection, particularly protection against copyright infringement."[33] And while video games do fall within the "audiovisual works" definition of the Copyright Act, this classification is somewhat of a difficult fit. [34]

---

[25] Deborah F. Buckman, Annotation, *Intellectual Property Rights in Video, Electronic, and Computer Games*, 7 A.L.R. Fed. 2d 269 (2005).

[26] *See* 17 U.S.C. § 101 (2012).

[27] 704 F.2d 1009, 1012 (7th Cir. 1983).

[28] *Id.* at 1011.

[29] *Id.*

[30] *Id.* at 1014.

[31] Nichols v. Universal Pictures Corp., 45 F.2d 119, 121 (2d Cir. 1930) ("Nobody has ever been able to fix that boundary, and nobody ever can.").

[32] Lilith Games (Shanghai) Co. Ltd. v. UCool, Inc., 2015 WL 5591612, at *5 (N.D. Cal. Sept. 23, 2015) (citing Miller v. Facebook, Inc., 2010 WL 2198204, at *4 (N.D. Cal. May 28, 2010)).

[33] Thomas M. S. Hemnes, *The Adaptation of Copyright Laws to Video Games*, 131 U. PA. L. REV. 171 (1982).

[34] 17 U.S.C. § 101 (2012) ("'Audiovisual' works are works that consist of a series of related images which are intrinsically intended to be shown by the use of machines, or

A modern video game series such as *Call of Duty* parallels the film industry with its realistic graphics, high production costs and values, and results (along with sales figures). Yet, while these games may look and sound like movies, the experience of a video game is quite different from watching a film.[35] Mass entertainment like books, films, television, or music are separate and often individualized experiences. While it is possible for a person to become immersed in the world created on the page or screen, a video game is different.[36] Unlike in a film, the progression of a video game is guided by the player.[37] While each game has a pre-set and linear story, the choices of the player have a significant impact on the duration of that story, as well as how it ends.

Further complicating matters is a decades long debate concerning whether video games or computer software should even be copyrightable.[38] These complications often make it easier for video games to be compared to movies. For obvious reasons this comparison does not always work. As one court has stated:

> [T]o assume that computer programs are just one more new means of expression, like a filmed play, may be quite wrong. The "form"—the written source code or the menu structure depicted on the screen—look hauntingly like the familiar stuff of copyright; but the "substance" probably has more to do with

---

devices such as projectors, viewers, or electronic equipment, together with accompanying sounds, if any, regardless of the nature of the material objects, such as films or tapes, in which the works are embodied.").

[35] *See generally*, Irini A. Stamatoudi, *Are Sophisticated Multimedia Works Comparable to Video Games?*, 48 J. COPYRIGHT SOC'Y U.S.A. 467 (2001). Here, Stamatoudi looked to define a 'multimedia work,' which was a hybrid of an audiovisual work: "The mere inclusion of different kinds of expressions does not allow a work to qualify as a multimedia work. On top of that, these expressions have to be integrated. They have to be combined with each other to such an extent that any distinction or any attempt at distinguishing between the various expressions and elements initially included in the work is either impossible or makes no sense." *Id.* at 469.

[36] *See* Michael A. Gunn, *Silicon Knights v. Epic Games: When Intellectual Property Is Regrettable*, 12 J. INTERNET L. 9, 9 (2015).

[37] *Id.*

[38] *See generally*, Stephen Breyer, *The Uneasy Case for Copyright: A Study of Copyright in Books, Photocopies, and Computer Programs*, 84 HARV. L. REV. 281, 347 (1970) ("In the face of this uncertain need it would seem unwise to extend copyright protection to virtually all computer programs . . . for such an extension may cause considerable harm."); *see also* Stamatoudi, *supra* note 35, at 472 ("Video games were initially denied copyright protection altogether.").

problems presented in patent law or, as already noted,
in those rare cases where copyright law has
confronted industrially useful expressions.[39]

Even though some difficulty remains in determining where
video games fall within the greater copyright ecosystem, there is some
clarity. The producer of a video game has the exclusive right to sell and
distribute his or her creation, like all copyright owners.[40] If one
infringes this exclusive right, the determination of infringement is
guided by the same requirements for establishing copyright
infringement as are used for all other types of works, which are best
stated by the Court in *Feist Publication, Inc. v. Rural Telephone
Service Co.*: "To establish infringement, two elements must be proven:
(1) ownership of a valid copyright, and (2) copying of constituent
elements of the work that are original."[41] Yet, a violation of rights is
not easy to determine because of the infancy of the video game
industry, the philosophical implications of gaming, and the unclear
limits on copyright protection.

Typically, there are three individual elements of a video game
that can be copyrighted: the look and feel, the mechanics, and the art.[42]
These elements have different tests to determine whether there has been
a copyright violation. Unsurprisingly, there has been difficulty in
adapting the law to new technology where there has been substantial
innovative progress or a cultural shift. This, along with other flaws in
the copyright system, has had a dramatic impact on the video game
industry.

A.  *Flaws in the Copyright System*

The Internet has broken down international borders causing
some unique legal problems. "Because the Internet makes it extremely
easy to engage in cross-border activities, it enables all Internet actors to
engage in such activities, and even actors who are not versed in the

---

[39] Lotus Dev. Corp. v. Borland Int'l, Inc., 49 F.3d 807, 820 (1st Cir. 1995).
[40] 17 U.S.C. § 106 (2012).
[41] Feist Publ'n, Inc. v. Rural Tel. Serv. Co., 499 U.S. 340, 361 (1991).
[42] Christopher Lunsford, *Drawing a Line Between Idea and Expression in Videogame
Copyright: The Evolution of Substantial Similarity for Videogame Clones*, 18 INTELL.
PROP. L. BULL. 87, 96–99 (2013).

intricacies of international copyright are exposed to cross-border dealings involving copyright issues."[43]

> Digital technology empowers average consumers to make near-perfect copies of information products and distribute such copies globally with just a few clicks on their keyboards. Despite the potential for numerous non-infringing uses, many digital platforms such as peer-to-peer (P2P) networks have become a breeding ground for the infringing practice commonly called "file sharing," for most users are primarily interested in exchanging copyrighted music and video files without due authorization.[44]

The courts have been helpful in defining the law, but there has not been substantial progress made towards enforcing the law. While the famous *Napster*[45] and *Grokster*[46] anti-piracy cases received a great deal of media attention, they had little effect in stopping piracy. Now, video games are just as vulnerable to file-sharing theft as other media was at the time of *Napster* and *Grokster*.

China, a major player in the video game industry, has the distinction of being both rampant with piracy and having the highest rate of copyright enforcement in the world.[47] Four out of every five copyrighted works in the Chinese marketplace are potentially pirated. Due to the proportionally low rate of enforcement relative to the occurrences of piracy, the copyright system in China has been referred to as "copyright anarchy."[48] There are a few reasons for this. First,

---

[43] Marketa Trimble, *The Multiplicity of Copyright Laws on the Internet*, 25 FORDHAM INTELL. PROP. MEDIA & ENT. L.J. 339, 344 (discussing issues in great detail such as the organization, creation, and difficulties of creating an international copyright scheme).

[44] Jiarui Liu, *Copyright Complements and Piracy-Induced Deadweight Loss*, 90 IND. L.J. 1011, 1020 (2015) (comparing video game consoles to a razor blade system, in that gaming consoles that play only a specific set of titles are similar to that of a razor only using a specific blade, and suggesting that this razor blade ecosystem creates profitability by keeping consumers within one specific ecosystem).

[45] *See* A&M Records, Inc. v. Napster, Inc., 284 F.3d 1091 (9th Cir. 2002).

[46] *See* Metro-Goldwyn-Mayer Studios Inc. v. Grokster, Ltd., 545 U.S. 913 (2005).

[47] Eric Priest, *Copyright Extremophiles: Do Creative Industries Thrive or Just Survive in China's High-Piracy Environment?*, 27 HARV. J.L. & TECH. 467, 474 (2014).

[48] Jiarui Liu, *The Tough Reality of Copyright Piracy: A Case Study of the Music Industry in China*, 27 CARDOZO ARTS & ENT. L.J. 621, 626 (2010).

China operates under a civil law system.[49] Because there are no codified laws for copyright infringement in China, there has been a lack of uniform decisions.[50] Second, China is a communist nation, and individual protections run contrary to collectivist ideals.[51] This further complicates China's piracy problem.

It is important to note that problems facing copyright do not begin and end with China. China is often spotlighted because, as one of the largest economies in the world outside of the United States, it is viewed as a technological rival.[52] In Russia, online piracy and copyright infringement are also rampant.[53] Because of the lack of proper cross-border intellectual property protections, the market needs to adapt to find solutions to copyright infringement.

## B.   Solutions to Copyright Infringement

If an individual procures a copy of a video game through a channel not authorized by the exclusive copyright holder, that individual is committing copyright infringement.[54] While a great deal of piracy-based copyright infringement claims and media attention focus on the music and film industries, the piracy rate for video games is also quite high.[55] All that is required to illegally download a film, television show, or the latest pop album is an Internet connection and a computer. A video game can just as easily be illegally downloaded in this same manner. Because of this, "[v]ideo game piracy arguably

---

[49] Guangliang Zhang, *Rules for Denying Copyright Permanent Injunctions in China: Fog Needs to be Cleared*, 62 J. COPYRIGHT SOC'Y 341, 359 (2015).

[50] *Id.*

[51] Vincent Brodbeck, *Using the Carrot, Not the Stick: Streaming Media and Curbing Digital Piracy in China*, 19 B.U.J. SCI. & TECH. L. 127, 138 (2013).

[52] *See* Joseph E. Stiglitz, *The Chinese Century*, VANITY FAIR (Jan. 2015), http://www.vanityfair.com/news/2015/01/china-worlds-largest-economy ("Now China is the world's No. 1 economic power. . . . The world economy is not a zero-sum game, where China's growth must necessarily come at the expense of ours. In fact, its growth is complementary to ours.").

[53] Robert O. Lindefjeld, *It's Time for the Internet to Start Acting Like an Adult*, 6 NO. 5 LANDSLIDE 1, 7 (2014).

[54] *See* 17 U.S.C. § 506(a)(1)(C) (2012).

[55] Don Reisinger, *Study: $42 Billion Worth of PSP, DS Games Pirated*, CNET (June 7, 2010, 1:38 PM), http://www.cnet.com/news/study-42-billion-worth-of-psp-ds-games-pirated/.

represents a more damaging form of copyright infringement than piracy in the wider entertainment industry."[56]

While some video games require high end computers to function at a playable level, peer-to-peer ("P2P") file sharing networks have made it possible to illegally download almost every classic video game and play them with emulation software.[57] Because of these challenges, the video gaming industry has taken a few proactive approaches to combat piracy.

### 1. Digital Rights Management

The video game industry has tried many different ways to protect itself. "[The video gaming industry] has pursued the traditional enforcement routes that other industries have used to combat piracy, with the same middling results."[58] One of these "traditional" routes is digital rights management ("DRM").[59] "[These] mechanisms . . . allow only certain types of access to, or uses of, the underlying copyrighted work and forbid all others."[60] The purpose of DRM in a pirated copy of a video game is to prevent it from working by alerting the copyright owner of an unauthenticated copy.[61] Some would argue DRM has not slowed the rate of piracy and has proven, for the most part, to be unpopular within the video gaming community.[62] However, the video game community has been more receptive to "Endogenous DRM," a form of DRM that causes the game to be unplayable, often with humorous results.[63]

---

[56] See Andrew V. Moshirnia, *Giant Pink Scorpions: Fighting Piracy with Novel Digital Rights Management Technology*, 23 DEPAUL J. ART, TECH. & INTELL. PROP. L. 1, 3–4 (2012).

[57] See Jeffrey S. Libby, *The Best Games in Life are Free?: Videogame Emulation in a Copyrighted World*, 36 SUFFOLK U.L. REV. 843, 844–45 (2003).

[58] Moshirnia, *supra* note 56, at 2.

[59] *Id.*

[60] Timothy K. Armstrong, *Digital Rights Management and the Process of Fair Use*, 20 HARV. J.L. & TECH. 49, 50 (2006).

[61] Moshirnia, *supra* note 56, at 33.

[62] Moshirnia, *supra* note 56, at 35 (providing an outstanding discussion on the history of DRM and how DRM in video games continues to evolve).

[63] *Id.* ("Croteam, developer of the Serious Sam first person shooter ("FPS") franchise, inserted [DRM] into its game *Serious Sam 3: Before First Encounter*. . . . If the game detects an unlicensed copy, it triggers a giant, invincible, pink scorpion armed with two shotguns that relentlessly hunts the player. This enemy appears after the player secures the weakest gun in the game. . . . The DRM scheme imparts powerlessness on the player, who inevitably fails to survive.")

While extreme versions of DRM are divisive within the gaming community, there is evidence that DRM may be becoming too sophisticated for modern pirates. A prominent hacker was recently quoted as saying, "I still believe that this game can be compromised. But according to current trends in the development of encryption technology, in two years time I'm afraid there will be no free games to play in the world."[64] Even though the gaming industry has recently had success in reducing the piracy of video games, it continues to develop other ways to curb piracy.

   2.  *Controlled Ecosystems*

The most popular extension of DRM is a controlled ecosystem, like a video game console. While video games themselves have DRM, closing the ecosystem is another layer of the same idea. The Nintendo Entertainment System featured a cartridge-based system, which was known to be more difficult to copy than a floppy disk.[65] A more recent example is the Microsoft's Xbox. The original Xbox console was released in 2001.[66] "Microsoft hoped that it could recoup the costs of its investment through the sale of games, accessories, and other services. This proved to be a fairly risky strategy as the company is reported to have lost up to $150 on each Xbox."[67] Microsoft included DRM controls to prevent piracy.[68] But just as early computer hackers circumvented DRM for PC titles, they worked around the DRM of the Xbox, and piracy continued.[69] Still, this did not stop Microsoft from attempting to alter the traditional delivery method with their most recent gaming console, the Xbox One.

When the Xbox One was announced at the Electronic Entertainment Expo in 2013, Microsoft sought to do away with

---

[64] Angus Morrison, *Could Piracy be Scuppered in Two Years?*, PC GAMER (Jan. 8, 2016), http://www.pcgamer.com/could-piracy-be-thwarted-within-two-years/.
[65] Stephen McIntyre, *Game over for First Sale*, 29 BERKELEY TECH. L.J. 1, 13 (2014) (citing DAVID SHEFF, GAME OVER: HOW NINTENDO ZAPPED AN AMERICAN INDUSTRY, CAPTURED YOUR DOLLARS, AND ENSLAVED YOUR CHILDREN 33 (1993)) ("The system would play games on cartridges, not disks. Floppy disks were threatening to computerphobes and, more important, they were copiable.").
[66] Christopher Soghoian, *Caveat Venditor: Technologically Protected Subsidized Goods and the Customers Who Hack Them*, 6 NW. J. TECH. & INTELL. PROP. 46, 48 (2007).
[67] *Id.*
[68] *Id.* This method of subsidization is known as the razor blade model. *See* Liu, *supra* note 44 at 1020.
[69] *Id.* at 51.

traditional used-game sales.[70] Developers loved the idea; consumers were skeptical.[71] The idea was simple: a disk in a brick and mortar store would carry the license to the game, could be used one by a primary user, and shared to specified individuals.[72] The roll out of the new delivery method did not go over well. "The way Microsoft rolled out its vision of the brave new digital-focused future was full of concrete negatives and only fuzzy, imagined positives."[73] Due to the highly negative reaction from consumers, Microsoft changed directions and stuck to traditional game sales.[74]

Another version of the controlled ecosystem is the smartphone. Owners of Android, Windows, and Apple users are able to purchase and download games from markets specifically designed for the operating systems of the phones. Use of this controlled ecosystem is on the rise. "Mobile devices now outsell personal computers by double and in 2016, mobile devices in use worldwide will exceed the number of people on the planet, with each person owning approximately 1.4 devices."[75] On Apple's App store, video games account for 20% of all applications available for download.[76]

### 3. Video Game Pricing Models

The further advancement of technology and the adaptation of the industry has led to video games being offered through many different ways: a flat-fee model, a subscription-based model, an open-pricing model, and a free-to-play model.[77] Games sold at a flat fee are

---

[70] Kyle Orland, *Xbox One, Discs, and Downloads: Better than Feared, Worse than Hoped*, ARSTECHNICA (June 7, 2013, 10:40 AM),
http://arstechnica.com/gaming/2013/06/xbox-one-discs-and-downloads-better-than-feared-worse-than-hoped/.
[71] *Id.*
[72] *Id.*
[73] Kyle Orland, *Xbox One Eighty: Microsoft Fails to Sell the Future, Retreats to the Past*, ARSTECHNICA (June 19, 2013, 6:40 PM), http://arstechnica.com/gaming/2013/06/xbox-one-eighty-microsoft-fails-to-sell-the-future-retreats-to-the-past/.
[74] *Id.*
[75] Alexandra McDonald, Jason McDonell & Caroline Mitchell, *Mobile Apps: Redefining the Virtual California Economy and the Laws that Govern It*, 24 Competition: J. ANTI. & UNFAIR COMP. L. SEC. ST. B. CAL. 86 (2015) (citing *The Future of Mobile Application Development*, ENTREPENEUR.COM, http://assets.entrepreneur.com/article/1409068924-by-2017-app-market-will-be-77-billion-dollar-industry-infographic.jpg (last visited May 14, 2016)).
[76] *Id.*
[77] *Id.*

traditionally offered digitally and at brick-and-mortar stores. Subscription-based models were made popular by massive multiplayer online games such as World of Warcraft.

The open-pricing model of anti-piracy protection works under market principles. The idea behind open pricing is consumers pay what they want to pay for the use of copyrighted material.[78] There are various open-pricing models that the video gaming industry has adopted from the music and film industries.[79] One of the more popular open-pricing models is the Humble Bundle.[80] The Humble Bundle allows consumers to pay what they want for a selection of games, and a portion of the proceeds goes to charity.[81] While some analysts have seen this method as a success, open pricing models continue to have issues with piracy. It appears that no matter what something costs, some people are always going to pirate.[82]

No matter which way a person chooses to purchase a video game, the way the purchase is made is dramatically changing. Over the last five years, there has been a 23% increase in the digital sale of video games.[83] This increase in sales has been linked to an increase in mobile device sales.[84] Of these mobile game sales, Apple earned nearly half of the mobile game market revenue.[85] Of these sales, free-to-play games generated the most revenue.

### 4. Free-to-play Video Games as a Middle Ground to Piracy

Producing a video game is an effort on par with releasing a motion picture[86] but is perhaps considerably riskier. "The process of video game development, while exciting and worthwhile, can be a torturous expedition[.] . . . Most modern console video games take from

---

[78] Moshirnia, *supra* note 56, at 40.

[79] *Id.*

[80] *Id.* at 41.

[81] *Id.*

[82] *Id.* at 42.

[83] *2015 Sales, Demographic and Usage Data: Essential Facts About the Computer and Video Game Industry*, ENT. SOFTWARE ASS'N, 8 (2015) http://www.theesa.com/wp-content/uploads/2015/04/ESA-Essential-Facts-2015.pdf.

[84] Gaudiosi, *supra* note 9.

[85] *Id.*

[86] *See* Luke Villapaz, *'GTA 5' Costs $265 Million To Develop And Market, Making It The Most Expensive Video Game Ever Produced: Report*, INTERNATIONAL BUSINESS TIMES (Sept. 8, 2013, 3:36 PM), http://www.ibtimes.com/gta-5-costs-265-million-develop-market-making-it-most-expensive-video-game-ever-produced-report.

one to three years and over ten million dollars to fully develop . . . [and o]nce completed, only four percent of all games are profitable."[87]

In the real world, the consumer is offered the opportunity to download a game digitally, within an open or closed ecosystem.[88] Xbox, iPhone, and Facebook are examples of closed ecosystems while the PC is considered an open ecosystem.[89] According to Yves Guillermot, the CEO of video game publisher and developer Ubisoft, around 95% of PC video games played are pirated.[90] One cause of the high rate of international piracy is that the gaming industry started to produce games that are free to play.[91] "The free-to-play business model for video games first originated in the early 2000s in South Korea. The approach, embodied by games such as Nexon's MapleStory, allowed frustrated developers to evade rampant piracy and lower the bar for casual gamers to join massive multiplayer online games."[92]

Free-to-play computer games are produced by using already produced assets and typically have older, more dated graphics to lower the cost of production.[93] The free-to-play games that were once popular only in China have become increasingly popular in the United States, and it is now a $30 billion dollar industry.[94] What began as a few companies embracing the concept has mushroomed into something much larger and more lucrative. Microsoft has gotten on board the free-to-play bandwagon with *Halo Online*.[95] The title, which is currently in a testing phase, is seen as a way to spread brand awareness and to combat rampant Russian piracy.[96] Like Ubisoft's free-to-play titles,

---

[87] Suzanne Jackiw, Article, *Title Defense: Creating Consistency in Video Game Title Trademark Law*, 96 J. PAT. & TRADEMARK OFF. SOC'Y 1, 3 (2014).
[88] Symposium, *Paying and Playing*, 15 SMU SCI. & TECH. L. REV. 179, 180 (2012).
[89] *Id.*
[90] Dan Pearson, *Guillemot: As Many PC Players Pay for F2P as Boxed Product*, GAMEINDUSTRY.BIZ (Aug. 22, 2012, 3:00 AM), http://www.gamesindustry.biz/articles/2012-08-22-guillemot-as-many-pc-players-pay-for-f2p-as-boxed-product.
[91] *Id.*
[92] John Gaudiosi, *The Wave of Free-to-play Games is Surging and Sony's Along for the Ride*, FORTUNE (Jan. 15, 2015, 1:00 PM), http://fortune.com/2015/01/13/sony-free-play-video-games/.
[93] Pearson, *supra* note 90.
[94] Dean Takashi, *Arnold Schwarzenegger Stars in Machine Zone's New Mobile Strike Ad*, VENTUREBEAT (Nov. 21, 2015, 1:47 PM), http://venturebeat.com/2015/11/21/machine-zone-starts-advertising-mobile-stirke-game-with-arnold-schwarzenegger/.
[95] Emanuel Maiberg, *In Russia, Halo Is Free*, MOTHERBOARD (Mar. 27, 2015, 9:32 AM), http://motherboard.vice.com/read/in-russia-halo-is-free.
[96] *Id.*

*Halo Online* uses modified game assets to keep costs of development low.[97] There is even a free-to-play version of *Call of Duty* that is exclusive to China.[98] While PC games have embraced the idea of free-to-play games, what really launched the concept of free-to-play into the mainstream was the smartphone.

Smartphones have put games, like the aforementioned *Candy Crush Saga*, into users' pockets. An entire industry has spawned from mobile phone games. Free-to-play games generate revenue not from initial sales but through in-app purchases as well as customer metadata.[99]

What makes in-app purchases interesting is that many consumers believe the game costs less than in normal circumstances even though it is actually more expensive.[100] In-app purchases "generated ten times more revenue than advertising for games and substantially more [revenue] than pre-paid games."[101] Sixty percent of free-to-play gaming revenue comes from in-app purchases.[102] Additionally, depending on the medium, users of free-to-play games will trade their personal information for the right to access free content.[103] Mobile gaming companies then sell the metadata.[104] This metadata was estimated to have generated $5.5 billion in revenue in 2013.[105]

While the games themselves are based on skill, players choose to increase the speed of gameplay by spending real-world money.[106] This reinforces the idea that with stagnant intellectual property laws, the market has adapted on its own.[107] This is not uncharacteristic of the

---

[97] *Id.*

[98] Chris Plante, *Watch a Trailer for Call of Duty Online, Because You May Never Get to Play It*, THE VERGE (Jan. 19, 2015, 10:58 AM), http://www.theverge.com/2015/1/19/7852719/call-of-duty-online-trailer-china.

[99] Alexandra McDonald, Jason McDonell & Caroline Mitchell, *Mobile Apps: Redefining the Virtual California Economy and the Laws That Govern It*, 24 Competition: J. Anti. & Unfair Comp. L. Sec. St. B. Cal. 86, 87 (2015).

[100] *Id.*

[101] *Id.* at 88.

[102] Chris Jay Hoofnagle & Jan Whittington, *Free: Accounting for the Costs of the Internet's Most Popular Price*, 61 UCLA L. REV. 606, 613 (2014).

[103] *Id.* at 613.

[104] *Id.*

[105] *See* McDonald, McDonell & Mitchell, *supra* note 99, at 88.

[106] Mason v. Mach. Zone, Inc., 2015 U.S. Dist. LEXIS 142790, *2 (D. Md. Oct. 20, 2015) (defining free-to-play games within games as part of an overall skill based game).

[107] Kevin Newman, *Don't Copy That Floppy: The IP Enforcement Dilemma in the United States*, 40 NEW ENG. J. ON CRIM. & CIV. CONFINEMENT 191, 192 (2014).

video game industry. The video gaming industry was one of the first industries to adapt to the rapid technological advancements of the last 15 years.[108]

With increased availability there is a very real possibility that free-to-play video game revenues could one day overtake traditional video game revenues. This becomes a legal issue when free-to-play games begin to copy their pay-to-play counterparts.

The market conditions are not the only factor that makes the law in this area challenging. The court reasoned in *Lotus v. Borland International* that "[a]pplying copyright law to computer programs is like assembling a jigsaw puzzle whose pieces do not quite fit."[109] No matter the market conditions, these pieces are often strange and obtuse. But the ever changing pieces show how the gaming industry has grown from table-top *Pac-Man* to a massive entertainment industry where video games such as *Call of Duty* face legal action for depictions of historical figures.[110] While the copyright laws governing video games can be confusing at times, in the free-to-play gaming market, the pieces are beginning to take shape. A great example of where the pieces happened to fit is *Tetris Holding, LLC v. Xio Interactive, Inc.*[111]

III.     TETRIS HOLDING V. XIO INTERACTIVE, A NEW LOOK AT FEIST

In *Tetris Holding v. Xio Interactive*, the defendant, Xio, created a game for the iPhone called *Mino*.[112] The game's appearance was nearly identical to *Tetris*.[113] Tetris Holding argued that there were 14 copyrighted elements in *Mino*.[114] In the suit, Xio admitted to downloading *Tetris* and conducting extensive research to determine which parts of the game could be legally copied.[115] In the suit, Xio argued that what they copied were the rules of the game, which they

---

[108] Christian Genetski & Christian Troncoso, *Copyright Industry Perspectives: The Pivotal Role of TPMS in the Evolution of the Video Game Industry*, 38 COLUM. J.L. & ARTS 359, 361 (2015).

[109] 49 F.3d 807, 820 (1st Cir. 1995).

[110] *See*, Joshua Sinclair, *Noriega v. Activision/Blizzard: The First Amendment Right to Use a Historical Figure's Likeness in Video Games*, 14 DUKE L. & TECH. REV. 69, 70 (2015).

[111] 863 F. Supp. 2d 394 (D.N.J. 2012).

[112] *Id.* at 398.

[113] *Id.*

[114] *Id.* at 397.

[115] *Id.* at 399.

argued were not an "original expression" and, thus, not subject to copyright infringement claims.[116] The court examined each of Xio's defenses, rejected the defenses, and granted Tetris Holding's motion for summary judgment.[117]

In making its ruling, the court used a combination of in-game screen shots, admissions from Xio, and other video game based patents.[118] The court used established tests to determine if there was infringement.[119] What makes the ruling of *Tetris Holding* distinct is the application of copyright doctrine to video games.

*Tetris Holding* began with the traditional two-step copyright infringement analysis applied in *Feist Publications, Inc. v. Rural Telephone Service Co., Inc.*[120] As in *Feist*, the determination is not as straightforward as it sounds, and because of the complexity of applying copyright law to video games, the court took a different approach.

Because video games are an amalgamation of many different copyrighted elements, the court needed to determine which elements were subject to copyright law.[121] To make this determination, the court looked to what is known as the "idea-expression dichotomy."[122] The "idea-expression dichotomy" combines 17 U.S.C. §102(a)[123] and §102(b).[124] The concept appears to be rather simple: copyright will not

---

[116] *Id.*

[117] Tetris Holding v. Xio Interactive, 863 F. Supp. 2d 394, 416 (D.N.J. 2012). For a detailed of analysis of each of Xio's defenses, see Brian Casillas, *Attack of the Clones: Copyright Protection for Video Game Developers*, 33 LOY. L.A. ENT. L. REV. 137, 152 (2013).

[118] *Tetris Holding*, 863 F. Supp. 2d at 410.

[119] *See generally* Casillas, *supra* note 117, at 152.

[120] *Tetris Holding*, 863 F. Supp. 2d at 399 ("To establish a claim of copyright infringement, a plaintiff must establish: (1) ownership of a valid copyright; and (2) unauthorized copying of original elements of the plaintiff's work." Dun & Bradstreet Software Services, Inc. v. Grace Consulting, 307 F.3d 197, 206 (3d Cir. 2002)); *see also* Feist Publ'ns, Inc. v. Rural Tel. Serv. Co., 499 U.S. 340, 361 (1991).

[121] *Tetris Holding*, 863 F. Supp. 2d at 400.

[122] *Id.* at 400.

[123] "Copyright protection subsists, in accordance with this title, in original works of authorship fixed in any tangible medium of expression, now known or later developed, from which they can be perceived, reproduced, or otherwise communicated, either directly or with the aid of a machine or device." 17 U.S.C. §102(a) (2012).

[124] "In no case does copyright protection for an original work of authorship extend to any idea, procedure, process, system, method of operation, concept, principle, or discovery, regardless of the form in which it is described, explained, illustrated, or embodied in such work." *Id.* at § 102(b).

protect an idea, only its expression.[125] As in *Feist*, the determination is not that simple.

The copyright statute requires that works be original to be eligible for copyright protection.

> Originality does not signify novelty; a work may be original even though it closely resembles other works so long as the similarity is fortuitous, not the result of copying. To illustrate, assume that two poets, each ignorant of the other, compose identical poems. Neither work is novel, yet both are original and, hence, copyrightable.[126]

Courts have had trouble applying the doctrine to computer programs.[127] The biggest issue appears to be in determining the difference between the rules of the game and the idea of the game.[128] This is because rules are not copyrightable.[129] To determine what was copyrightable, the *Tetris Holding* court used two additional doctrines, merger and scènes à faire.[130] Merger occurs when an idea and an expression become inseparable.[131] Because this would create a "monopoly" on ideas, merger is not protected by copyright law.[132] Scènes à faire "originated in stock characters and features of dramatic works" and also falls under a similar un-copyrightable umbrella.[133] "Because it is virtually impossible to write about a particular historical

---

[125] *Tetris Holding*, 863 F. Supp. at 400.

[126] Feist Publ'ns, Inc. v. Rural Tel. Serv. Co., 499 U.S. 340, 345–46 (1991).

[127] *Tetris Holding*, 863 F. Supp. at 400 ("As Judge Stahl of the First Circuit aptly wrote: 'Applying copyright law to computer programs is like assembling a jigsaw puzzle whose pieces do not quite fit.'" (quoting Lotus Dev. Corp. v. Borland Int'l, 49 F.3d 807, 820 (1st Cir.1995))).

[128] Sonali D. Maitra, *It's How You Play the Game Why Videogame Rules Are Not Expression Protected by Copyright Law*, LANDSLIDE 34, 35 (2015) ("Most—if not all—courts apply the following test in determining whether a video game infringes another's copyright: whether two games have the same 'idea' only (which means no infringement) or something more in common," (possible infringement)).

[129] *Id.* at 36.

[130] *Tetris Holding*, 863 F. Supp. at 403.

[131] *Id.* (quoting Kay Berry, Inc. v. Taylor Gifts, Inc., 421 F.3d 199, 209 (3d Cir. 2005) ("In some instances, there may come a point when an author's expression becomes indistinguishable from the idea he seeks to convey, such that the two merge.")).

[132] *Id.*

[133] Apple Computer, Inc. v. Microsoft Corp., 799 F. Supp. 1006, 1021 (N.D. Cal. 1992).

era or fictional theme without employing certain 'stock' or standard literary devices, . . . scenes a faire are not copyrightable."[134]

Of Xio's defenses, the weakest was that the two games were not substantially similar.[135] In determining substantial similarity, the court relied upon "case law and common sense" to understand *Tetris* at an abstract level and the game's concepts.[136] The court wrote: "There is such similarity between the visual expression of *Tetris* and *Mino* that it is akin to literal copying."[137] This copying was so clear that both the merger and scènes à faire defenses were quickly dismantled.[138] Another argument that the defendants made was that the way *Tetris* was played was more in the line with a patent and thus not copyrightable.[139] Yet, the court ruled that the idea and rules of *Tetris* were expressed in such a way that it was clear *Mino* copied them too closely to constitute original expression.[140] The court even went so far as to point out how another video game, *Dr. Mario*, had taken the rules of *Tetris* and made a unique expression from them.[141] Because of the substantial similarities between the two titles, the plaintiff's motion for summary judgment was granted.[142]

The *Tetris Holding* ruling was viewed as a victory for the video game industry, giving the industry "a new weapon to prevent the cloning of their work."[143] It was also viewed as a win for creativity.[144] At the same time, there was worry about frivolous lawsuits by copyright owners wanting to protect their interests.[145]

---

[134] Hoehling v. Universal City Studios, Inc., 618 F.2d 972, 979 (2d Cir. 1980).

[135] *Tetris Holding*, 863 F. Supp. 2d at 410–11.

[136] *Id.* at 401–02 (citing Atari, Inc. v. N. Am. Phillips Consumer Elec. Corp., 672 F.2d 607, 617 (7th Cir. 1982) (applying the abstractions test to analyze a video game)).

[137] *Id.* at 410. The court included screenshots from both games in the decision. *Id.*

[138] *Id.* at 412 ("I am not convinced that either the doctrine of merger or scènes à faire applies here. The latter, as discussed earlier, is inapposite because *Tetris* is a wholly fanciful presentation; it is a unique puzzle game and does not have stock or common imagery that must be included. Nor does merger apply because there are many novel ways Xio could have chosen to express the rules of *Tetris*. Xio's own expert admitted there are 'almost unlimited number' of ways to design the pieces and the board and the game would still 'function perfectly well.'").

[139] *Id.* at 404.

[140] *Id.* at 412.

[141] *Id.* at 412 (citing U.S. Patent No. 5,265,888 (filed Feb. 19, 1993)).

[142] *Id.* at 415.

[143] Brian Casillas, *supra* note 117, at 139.

[144] *Id.* at 170.

[145] *Id.* at 169.

The court found it was clear that Xio Interactive had copied Tetris.[146] This does not necessarily mean that creativity is going to be narrowed. The result of *Tetris Holding* does not seem to have created a boom of video game copyright trolls. It is true that there has been an increase in copyright claims since the Xio decision, but the courts have been careful in applying the law in an extreme fashion.

What the *Tetris Holding* ruling has done is reinforce the idea of the importance of placing an original spin on unoriginal concepts. By making a game available for free to anyone who owned an iPhone (and likely profiting from the ad revenue), Xio Interactive was not doing anything wrong. But because Xio Interactive took the concepts of *Tetris* and engaged in wholesale copying of them in production of *Mino*, the court drew a line.[147]

In *Tetris Holding*, the court compared side-by-side screenshots of *Tetris* and *Mino* to come to the conclusion that *Mino* infringed *Tetris*'s copyright.[148] Comparing side-by-side representations in a copyright claim is nothing new, and it was easy for the court to make a substantial similarity determination when comparing the two titles.[149] But what has changed is the technology and the ability of the court to compare in infringement allegations. The ruling was seen as the court adopting a "high level of understanding" of video game mechanics for the first time.[150] It was also viewed as a possible killing blow to "knock-off" games: "improvements in technology significantly expand the creative limits of game developers, developers of [cloned video games] may have diminishing success in arguing that their wholesale copying is permissible because expression has merged with idea."[151]

---

[146] *Id.*

[147] *Tetris Holding*, 863 F. Supp. 2d at 410.

[148] *Id.* at 410–11.

[149] *Id.* at 409 ("Xio has provided the court with links to uploaded videos at www.youtube.com showing the game play of both *Tetris* and *Mino*; Tetris Holding has provided similar video evidence. The Court has reviewed these videos as well as screen shots of the individual game screens, the declarations and attached exhibits, and the parties' respective statements of fact.").

[150] Casillas *supra* note 117, at 168 ("Tetris Holding's victory in the case was only guaranteed once it convinced the court to identify the underlying game rules and game play at a 'high level.'") (quoting Jack Schecter, *Grand Theft Video: Judge Gives Gamemakers Hope for Combating Clones*, SUNSTEIN KANN MURPHY & TIMBERS LLP (June 2012), http:// sunsteinlaw.com/grand-theft-video-judge-gives-gamemakers-hope-for-combating-clones/).

[151] *Id.*

This high level understanding was quickly applied in *Spry Fox LLC v. LOLApps, Inc.*[152]

A.   *Triple Town and Yeti Town: Knock-offs Beware*

      In *Spry Fox LLC v. LOLApps Inc.*, Spry Fox approached LOLApps to develop an iOS game of its popular Amazon Kindle game, *Triple Town*.[153] Five months after development began, LOLApps ended development and announced it was releasing its own game, *Yeti Town*.[154] Spry Fox alleged that *Triple Town* and *Yeti Town* were very, very similar to each other.[155] While there were aesthetic differences between *Triple Town* and *Yeti Town*, the core game concepts were nearly identical:[156]

> In Triple Town, the object at the bottom of the hierarchy is a patch of grass. . . . In Yeti Town, the object at the bottom of the hierarchy is a sapling. . . . In Triple Town, the antagonist is a bear. In Yeti Town, the antagonist is a yeti. . . . In both games, the placement and hierarchical transformation of objects progressively builds the game grid and earns points for the player.[157]

      Both games allowed for in-game purchases.[158] Both games had identical prices and conversion rates in their respective in-game stores.[159] Even early game dialogue box tutorials were similar.[160] The court noted the similarities[161] and looked to determine the differences in the games' ideas and expressions.[162]

---

[152] 2012 WL 5290158, at *1 (W.D. Wash. Sept. 18, 2012).
[153] *Id.*
[154] *Id.*
[155] *Id.*
[156] *Id.* ("The action in both games takes place on a six-by-six grid. Each game provides a player a series of objects to place in the squares of the grid. When a player places an object such that three identical objects connect, those matching objects disappear, replaced by an object that is one step up in the game's hierarchy.").
[157] *Id.* at *1–2.
[158] *Id.* at *2.
[159] *Id.*
[160] *Id.*
[161] *Id.* at *2.
[162] *Id.* at *4.

The court found that certain elements of *Triple Town*, such as the use of points and an in-game market were common in many games and not copyrightable.[163] The court also found the core mechanics of *Triple Town*, like the six-by-six grid the game was played on, not copyrightable.[164] The court refused to dismiss the plaintiff's allegations, finding that "Spry Fox has plausibly alleged substantial similarity between Triple Town and Yeti Town."[165] The court admitted that it did not take as much of a "nuanced" approach as did the court in *Tetris Holding*, but in denying the motion to dismiss, the court noted that its decision was based strongly upon "the application of uncontroversial copyright principles to the ever-evolving field of video games."[166]

B.   *Everyone is Copying Everyone: Blizzard Entertainment v. Lilith Games & Lilith Games v. uCool*

In *Blizzard Entertainment, Inc. v. Lilith Games Co.* (Lilith), Blizzard brought an action for copyright infringement against Lilith for allegedly copying the likenesses and actions of characters from Blizzard's popular game World of Warcraft, and Valve Entertainment's popular game *Defense of the Ancients* (DotA).[167] The suit alleged that characters, settings, terrain, and assets were copied and used in two games, *DotA Legends* and *Heroes Charge*.[168] Just like *Mino* and *Triple Town*, *Heroes Charge* and *DotA Legends* are free-to-play games, and both offer "in app purchases."[169] *Heroes Charge* proved to be so popular that uCool paid $2.25 million to advertise it during Super Bowl XLIX.[170]

It is important to note, however, that Lilith Games is not the creator of *Heroes Charge*. In fact, Lilith Games created another game

---

[163] *Id.* at *5.

[164] *Id.* at *6.

[165] *Id.* at *8.

[166] *Id.*

[167] Blizzard Entm't, Inc. v. Lilith Games (Shanghai) Co. Ltd., 2015 WL 8178826, at *1 (N.D.Cal. Dec. 8, 2015).

[168] *Id.*

[169] uCool, *Heroes Charge*, ITUNES PREVIEW, https://itunes.apple.com/us/app/heroes-charge/id900313219?mt=8 (last updated Mar. 3, 2016).

[170] Dean Takashi, *Ucool Spent $2.25M on the Worst-rated Super Bowl Commercial*, (Feb. 2, 2015, 6:45 PM), http://venturebeat.com/2015/02/02/ucool-spent-2-25m-on-the-worst-rated-super-bowl-commercial/ (last visited May 14, 2016).

called *Sword and Tower*.[171] *Sword and Tower* is also known as *DotA Legends*.[172] It just so happens that *DotA Legends* and *Heroes Charge* look strikingly similar. So similar in fact, that Lilith Games actually brought suit against uCool, the creators of *Heroes Charge*, for copyright infringement.[173] The image below shows the similarities between titles. The top screenshot is from *DotA Legends*, and the bottom screenshot is from *Heroes Charge*.[174]

---

[171] Compl. par. 7, Blizzard Entm't, Inc. v Lilith Games (Shanghai) Co. Ltd., 2015 WL 5244670 (N.D. Cal. Sep. 8, 2015).

[172] Lilith Games (Shanghai) Co. Ltd. v. uCool, Inc., 2015 WL 4128484, slip. op. at *1 (N.D. Cal. Jul. 8, 2015).

[173] Lilith Games (Shanghai) Co. Ltd. v. uCool, Inc., 2015 WL 3523405, at *1 (N.D. Cal. Jun. 4, 2015).

[174] Christian Nutt, *Blizzard Sues a Studio That's Suing a Studio*, http://www.gamasutra.com/ view/news/239626/Blizzard_sues_Soul_Clash_dev_just_as_it_sues_the_Heroes_Charge_ dev.php, (last updated Mar. 24, 2015).

175

The suit brought forward by Lilith alleged that uCool stole and copied the code from their game.[176] The court noted the near identical expressions of both games, as well as the fact that "Heroes Charge includes a portion of Lilith's code that triggers Lilith's copyright notice at a certain point while playing Heroes Charge."[177] Judge Conti did not dismiss Lilith's claims of copyright infringement and the litigation is ongoing.[178] Judge Conti recently denied Lilith's request for a

---

[175] *Id.*
[176] *Lilith Games*, 2015 WL 4128484, at *1.
[177] *Id.*
[178] *Id.*

preliminary injunction.[179]   While these motions and injunction proceedings were being denied, Blizzard was in the process of suing for copyright infringement for character likeness.[180]

When the court approached the *Blizzard* suit to determine if there was infringement of Blizzard's video game characters, they looked at the three-pronged *Towle* test to determine whether or not Blizzard's characters were afforded copyright protection.[181] The *Towle* test was developed in *DC Comics v. Towle* to determine whether the Batmobile was copyrightable.[182] The *Towle* test has three requirements: (1) specific physical qualities, (2) consistency, and (3) distinctiveness.[183] Regarding this test, the court reasoned:

> [A]lthough Plaintiffs allege that 'dozens of characters from 'Heroes Charge' are derived from and substantially similar to Blizzard and Valve's characters,' they plead no facts demonstrating that any one of the dozens of characters are plausibly copyrightable . . . Instead, Plaintiffs make conclusory statements that their characters are 'distinctive . . . with names, distinctive physical appearances, clothing, weapons, traits, abilities, and ongoing stories.'[184]

Because Blizzard made only general allegations of infringement, the court could not find that there was infringement. Unlike *Tetris Holding*, the infringement argument was found to be ineligible for copyright protection under scènes à faire doctrine. Here, the court relied in part on a different video game case, *Capcom v. Data East* to make their scènes à faire determination.[185] The court looked at the differences between generic fighting characters in making their

---

[179] Lilith Games (Shanghai) Co. Ltd. v. UCool, Inc., 2015 WL 5591612, slip. op. at *8 (N.D. Cal. Sep. 23, 2015).

[180] Blizzard Entm't, Inc. v. Lilith Games (Shanghai) Co. Ltd., 2015 WL 8178826, at *2 (N.D. Cal. Dec. 8, 2015).

[181] *Id.* at *4.

[182] DC Comics v. Towle, 802 F. 3d 1012, 1015 (9th Cir. 2015).

[183] *Id.* at 1021. "We read these precedents as establishing a three-part test for determining whether a character in a comic book, television program, or motion picture is entitled to copyright protection."

[184] Blizzard Entm't, Inc. v. Lilith Games (Shanghai) Co. Ltd., 2015 WL 8178826, at *5 (N.D. Cal. Dec. 8, 2015).

[185] Capcom U.S.A., Inc. v. Data E. Corp., 1994 WL 1751482, at *15 (N.D. Cal. Mar. 16, 1994).

ruling: "Street Fighter II and Fighter's History bear more similarities . . . because they contain a greater percentage of reality based moves that are faithful to one or more of the martial arts disciplines and characters drawn largely from a pool of stereotyped human fighters. As a result . . . many of its elements are not protectable."[186]

The *Blizzard* ruling may serve as a limiter to copyright claims for those who feared that *Tetris Holding* could lead to frivolous suits. At the very least, the *Blizzard* ruling establishes the importance of a minimal pleading standard for video game copyright infringement accusations. "If, as Plaintiffs contend, dozens of characters are at issue . . . a plausible claim would require that Plaintiffs submit a representative sampling of infringed content . . . establishing that the content and characters at issue are copyrightable.[187] This makes the pending litigation between Lilith and uCool all the more intriguing.

If Lilith and uCool have not infringed upon the copyright of Blizzard Entertainment's generalized fantasy characters, it may be difficult for a court to find uCool infringed upon the copyright of Lilith. The court, however, could follow the analysis in *Spry Fox* to determine how closely related the two games are by comparing side-by-side screenshots, as included above.[188] From the screenshots above, the two games appear very similar.

There is a great deal of irony in Blizzard bringing suit for copyright infringement, and it shines light on to an important element of success of the video game industry as a whole. *Warcraft*, the real time strategy (RTS) game that served as the inspiration for *World of Warcraft*, was in many ways a copy of another RTS, *Dune II: Building of a Dynasty*.[189] Maybe this was acceptable because this kind of copying has been deemed acceptable by the industry.[190] "Imitation of other manufacturers' games is standard in the industry, and every major industry player does it frequently."[191] So long as the copying is not

---

[186] *Id.* (appendix).

[187] Blizzard Entm't, Inc. v. Lilith Games (Shanghai) Co. Ltd., 2015 WL 8178826 at *6 (N.D. Cal. Dec. 8, 2015).

[188] Spry Fox LLC v. LOLApps Inc., 2012 WL 5290158 (W.D. Wash. Sep. 18, 2012).

[189] Lunsford, *supra* note 42.

[190] *Id.*

[191] Eric Goldman, *EA's Copyright Infringement Lawsuit Against Zynga Is Dangerous-- For EA,* (Aug. 6, 2012), http://www.forbes.com/sites/ericgoldman/2012/08/06/eas-copyright-infringement-lawsuit-against-zynga-is-dangerous-for-ea/ (last visited May 14, 2016).

excessive, it is viewed as an acceptable practice.[192] "Game designs are often based on, and evolve from, other games. Asteroids followed after and improved on Space War, Galaga improved on Space Invaders, Mortal Kombat improved on Street Fighter, etc."[193] "Successful games are made by borrowing ideas."[194]

The copying of ideas did not end with the *Tetris Holding* ruling.[195] Recently, video game development studio Epic War released a new mobile game named *Mobile Strike*.[196] Two things about game were certain: Arnold Schwarzenegger served as spokesman for the game, and *Mobile Strike* bore a striking resemblance to another mobile title, *Game of War: Fire Age*.[197] It was later learned that Machine Zone, the creator of *Game of War: Fire Age* had started another studio to develop *Mobile Strike*.[198] It appears that the only real difference between the two games is the setting.[199] *Game of War: Fire Age* takes place in a fantasy, whereas *Mobile Strike* is a modern military real time strategy game.

The allure of high profits drives the practice of copying.[200] One company with a reputation for such practices, Zynga, faced three

---

[192] Lunsford, *supra* note 42, at 88.

[193] Joe Linhoff, *Video Games and Reverse Engineering: Before and After the Digital Millennium Copyright Act*, 3 J. TELECOMM. & HIGH TECH. 209, 220 (2004).

[194] *Id.*

[195] It appears that some companies even thrive off of copying. "[T]he proliferation of clones has appeared mostly on mobile gaming platforms, such as the iPhone, Android devices, and tablets, as well as arcade titles—smaller games released on Xbox Live and PlayStation Network—as opposed to games released on the three major consoles . . . [c]loning on online marketplaces, such as Apple's 'App Store,' was most evident after the release of the highly successful app, Angry Birds. Reaching over 100 million downloads, Angry Birds quickly sparked clones in Apple's App Store, with titles such as Angry Rhino: RAMPAGE!, Angry Alien, and Angry Pig. While the majority of the Angry Bird clones are accessible for free, some cloned games have the ability to generate an abundance of revenue." Casillas, *supra* note 117, at 143.

[196] Dean Takahashi, *Arnold Schwarzenegger Stars in Machine Zone's Modern Warfare Game Mobile Strike*, VENTUREBEAT (Nov. 11, 2015, 6:02 PM), http://venturebeat.com/2015/11/11/arnold-schwarzenegger-is-the-star-of-machine-zones-new-mobile-strike-modern-warfare-game/.

[197] *Id.*

[198] *Id.*

[199] *Id.*

[200] *See generally*, Goes Int'l, AB v. Dodur Ltd., 2015 WL 5043296, at *1 (N.D. Cal. Aug. 26, 2015). (Goes International ("Goes"), maker of the game "Bubble Bust", brought a copyright infringement suit against Dodur Ltd. ("Dodur"), maker of the games "Puzzle Bubble Free!" and "Puzzle Bubble Sea." Goes alleged Dodur copied their game almost entirely, including level updates. Goes further alleged that Dodur made $27,000 in

separate infringement and breach of contract suits in 2011.[201] Each of the suits was dismissed, and a year later, Zynga was sued again by Electronic Arts for copyright infringement.[202] The suit was settled out of court, but Zynga is consistently in the news for alleged infringement.[203]

In a way, this makes video games very similar to the phonebook at issue in *Feist*. It reinforces the idea that a certain level of copying or imitation has always been acceptable in our culture.[204]

### C.  Keeping Up With the Kardashians: Where Free-to-Play Goes From Here

With games like *Mobile Strike* and the continued dominance of free-to-play apps on Apple's App Store and the Google Play marketplace, it is clear that free-to-play is not going anywhere.[205] While there is no doubt that the knock-offs will continue, that is not necessarily a bad thing. At issue is insuring that the amount of coping does not cross the line the court seems to be drawing. Regarding the *Triple Town* case, Maryland law professor James Grimmelmann wrote:

> On the one hand, it's well established that literal copying of a game's program is copyright

---

advertising revenue, and $8,000 through in-game purchases. While the court never made a decision as to whether or not Dodur infringed upon Goes copyright, this case illustrates just how lucrative free-to-play games can be, and the power of temptation to copy the work of others.)

[201] Kent Jordan & Robert Wilkinson, *A Review of 2011 Video-Game Litigation and Selected Cases*, 15 SMU SCI. & TECH. L. REV. 271, 281 (2012).

[202] Tanner Robinson & Max Metzler, *2012 Video Game Industry Litigation Review*, 16 SMU SCI. & TECH. L. REV. 1, 9–10 (2013).

[203] *See* Lunsford, *supra* note 42, at 115. ("The EA complaint referred to other litigation in which Zynga was involved, trying to suggest a pattern of producing copyright infringing clones. Ultimately, the parties settled for an undisclosed amount of money. Both videogames at issue lost their popularity with users shortly after their launch, and EA has since stopped offering The Sims Social. It is possible that the futility continued litigation over a game with a short life cycle prompted the settlement, as it would be wasteful for both companies.")

[204] *See* Spry Fox LLC v. LOLApps Inc., 2012 WL 5290158, at *7 (W.D. Wash. Sep. 18, 2012).

[205] *See iOS Top App Charts*, APPANNIE.COM (Jan. 31, 2016), https://www.appannie.com/apps/ios/top/united-states/?device=iphone; *Google Play Top App Charts*, APPANNIE.COM (Jan. 31, 2016), https://www.appannie.com/apps/google-play/top/united-states. Of the top ten grossing apps for both Apple and Google, seventeen of them are free-to-play titles. *Id.*

> infringement. This protects the market for making
> and selling games against blatant piracy. . . . On the
> other hand, the weak or nonexistent protection for
> gameplay mechanics means that innovations in
> gameplay filter through the industry remarkably
> quickly.[206]

In the end, it appears there is a catch-22 between copyright
infringement and being left behind in the industry.[207]

The rulings in *Tetris Holding*, *Spry Fox*, and *Blizzard* show
that courts are really only willing to find infringement when it is
terribly egregious. While some did believe that *Tetris Holding* drew a
line regarding visual distinction, the visual differences between *Triple
Town* and *Yeti Town* in *Spry Fox* illustrate that a game does not need to
be completely identical for the court to find infringement.[208]
"Unfortunately, the majority of clones are visually distinct enough that
an observer can tell they are not the same game when placed next to
whichever game they are allegedly copying, making it harder to prove
infringement and more difficult for a future court to reach the same
ruling."[209] In each case where the court found infringement, discovery
revealed just how far the defendants went in copying their creations. In
*Tetris Holding* , it was the significant research prior to development.[210]
In *Spry Fox*, there was termination of a nondisclosure agreement.[211]

It is also true that for the most part, more recent incidents of
this kind of infringement have occurred on mobile gaming platforms, as
opposed to games released on the three major gaming consoles.[212] The

---

[206] James Grimmelmann, *Copyright and the Romantic Video Game Designer*,
PRAWFSBLAWG (Feb. 2, 2012),
http://prawfsblawg.blogs.com/prawfsblawg/2012/02/copyright-and-the-romantic-video-
game-designer.html. Here, the notion of outright copying being established as unlawful
was defined in *Williams Electronics, Inc. v. Artic Int'l., Inc.*, 685 F.2d 870 (3d Cir. 1982).
[207] *See* Grimmelmann, *supra* note 206.
[208] *See* Spry Fox LLC v. LOLApps Inc., 2012 WL 5290158, at *8 (W.D. Wash. Sep. 18,
2012).
[206] Casillas, *supra* note 117, at 169. "This case also establishes that the most important
fight with clones will be 'over the appropriate level of abstraction of the game mechanics
and gameplay.'"
[209] *Id.* at 168.
[210] *Id.* at 154.
[211] *See Spry Fox*, 2012 WL 5290158, at *1.
[212] *See* Casillas, *supra* note 117, at 143. "[V]ideo games developed for the PlayStation
3—a console developed by Sony—are created on Blu-ray discs. The format of these discs

last major console video game copyright infringement ruling was *Capcom v. Data East* in 1994.[213] Gaming consoles as well as the PC gaming market are more established markets with their own restrictions on who can submit content. The mobile gaming market is new and very lucrative. This was made clear in facts noted in *Tetris Holding*, including: a primary motivation of Xio Interactive was money, "some iPhone games . . . 'have made 250K each in 2 months!'"[214]

A real test of the scope of the *Tetris Holding* decision could come soon. In *Just Games Interactive Entertainment v. Glu Mobile*, Just Games Interactive brought suit against Glu Mobile as well as the popular reality television family the Kardashians.[215] In their copyright infringement complaint, Just Games alleges that Glu Mobile and the Kardashian family took ideas and work from a video game proposal made by Kung Fu Games and later produced their own title—*Kim Kardashian: Hollywood*.[216]

On the surface, it seems that this could be similar to what happened with *Triple Town* and *Yeti Town*; yet, there are a few distinct differences. One major difference between the current litigation and the *Spry Fox* decision appears to be that nothing was produced other than a presentation for what the game could be.

> The work Kung Fu Factory did involved, among other things: (1) conceiving in detail how such a game might work, who the characters would be and what they would do, what the gameplay might be like, including how it could be integrated into social media such as Twitter and Facebook on put on platforms such as Android and iOS devices; (2) designing and authoring an original, overall look and feel for the game's graphical user interface; (3) mocking up a particular creative take on a character customization tool; and (4) drawing and authoring various two-dimensional artwork assets for use in the game, such as artistic depictions of locations where

incorporates what is known as ROM-Mark, a serialization technology that acts as a safety guard against piracy, i.e., mass duplication and sale of unauthorized copies of the discs." *Id.*
[213] Capcom U.S.A., Inc. v. Data East Corp., 1994 WL 1751482, at *1 (N.D. Cal. 1994).
[214] 863 F. Supp. 2d 397 (2012).
[215] Just Games Interactive Ent'mt LLC v. Glu Mobile Inc., 2015 WL 6746480, at ¶ 1 (C.D. Cal. 2015).
[216] *Id.*

gameplay would occur, and an artistic vision for how
Kim, Khloe and Kourtney Kardashian would be
depicted as characters.[217]

While this does appear to be similar to the considerable
amount of work in *Spry Fox*, in *Spry Fox*, there had been five months
of development before LOLApps Inc. ceased production of *Triple
Town* and later released a substantially similar *Yeti Town*.[218] Yet, at the
same time, if the court were ever to compare the presentation from Just
Games with the finished Glu Mobile product, maybe the court could
find for Just Games.

The application of the *Blizzard Interactive* decision adds an
interesting wrinkle to the possible outcome. Maybe because the space
the Kardashian family currently occupies in popular culture, their
identifying characteristics could fit within the scope of the three-part
*Towle* test. There could be a legitimate infringement claim if the
characters in the finished product are both nearly identical to Just
Games concepts and are easily identifiable as Kardashian family
members.

If the Kardashians and Glu Mobile were to be found guilty of
infringement, it would be a greater expansion of copyright protection
than *Tetris Holding*. The reason being this is that there were two
finished working products that could be compared side-by-side in
*Tetris Holding*. Expanding copyright protection to unfinished concepts
could have great impact in a wide variety of creative fields and could
do a lot more to inhibit the creative process than litigating against
knock-offs.

## IV.    CHALLENGES TO CHANGE

The mobile video game market is new and growing each day,
largely in part due to the rise of free-to-play games. The rapid rate at
which it is growing can often mean that the law struggles to adapt to
deal with new technologies or that the legal process is overwhelmed by

---

[217] *Id.* at ¶ 14.
[218] Spry Fox LLC v. LOLApps Inc., 2012 WL 5290158, at *1 (W.D. Wash. Sep. 18,
2012) ("In July 2011, 6Waves and Spry Fox entered into a nondisclosure agreement
granting 6Waves privileged access to Triple Town. In December 2011, 6Waves delivered
Spry Fox two pieces of bad news: it would no longer develop an iOS version of Triple
Town.").

the enormous market which has been created. For instance, finding a blanket solution to infringement is quite difficult. One suggestion is to create a certification process that would ensure copyright is not being violated before a game hits the market.[219] This suggestion would gather various online markets and publishers and ask them to come up with a certification process on their own.[220] On its face, this seems to make a great deal of sense. At the same time, there are a few problems with this concept. While the cost of developing and releasing a game may be expensive, game creation is an inherently creative process, and creating codified certification rules could constrict the creative process.[221]

Creating a standard also seems to be somewhat duplicative. The doctrines of merger and scènes à faire exist to ensure creative freedom. "If the law were to protect expression in such instances, then the copyright holder would have an unacceptable monopoly over that idea."[222] A certification requirement would create rules that stifle creativity through a layer of certification bureaucracy, and could possibly make uncopyrightable elements quasi-copyrightable. A certification process makes even less sense when consideration is given to the fact that copyrights are already registerable.[223] It is true registration does not guarantee protection,[224] but it does give rise to the

---

[219] See Casillas *supra* note 117, at 170 ("To further ensure that copyright infringement is no longer a point at issue, online marketplaces, stores, and publishers, should come together to develop a committee that awards copyright certification to a title before it is released for public consumption.").

[220] *Id.*

[221] See generally, David A. Simon, *Culture, Creativity, & Copyright*, 29 CARDOZO ARTS & ENT. L.J. 279, 323 (2011) (explaining the implications that a "memetic" account of creativity has in copyright law).

> Creativity is a process. The creative person does not "invent" ideas—they "arrive" in the brain through processes, whatever form those ideas take. Copyright law, however, is focused on incentives. . . . Much of the creative process entails borrowing from many different ideas and expressions, and copyright law focuses only on the copyrighted product at issue in any particular dispute. *Id.*

[222] *Tetris Holding v. Xio Interactive*, 863 F. Supp. 2d 394, 403 (D.N.J. 2012).

[223] See 17 U.S.C. § 408 (2012) (describing copyright registration in general).

[224] *Id.* § 408(a).

> [D]uring the subsistence of any copyright secured on or after that date, the owner of copyright or of any exclusive right in the work may obtain registration of the copyright claim by delivering to the Copyright Office the deposit specified by this section, together with the application and fee specified by sections 409 and 708. Such registration is not a condition of copyright protection.

notion that a certification process may be as ineffectual as codified law. If a company like Apple makes a reported 30% from every mobile application transaction, asking them to police themselves and possibly affect their bottom line may be an insurmountable task.[225] While Apple has changed its reporting policies and made it easier to remove material that may be infringing, copying of works has continued.[226]

If there were a process in place, how would certification work? If countries around the world have difficulty adopting a unified copyright protection system, it seems unlikely that various publishers and business could come to a unilateral agreement for video games. Considering that the video game industry is built on the principle that some copying has always been acceptable, it seems doubtful that game publishers could reach a consensus on a copyright certification process. "Copyright is designed to promote the progress of the sciences and useful arts through a temporary monopoly, for a small exclusivity window to provide a large incentive for content creation."[227] As both the aforementioned registration process and the *Dr. Mario* patent show, truly innovative game processes can already participate in various and rigorous certification processes. Furthermore, this could be a time where an extra regulatory system hampers growth. When video games were in their infancy, lack of protection may have increased the growth of the industry. "At least some of this increased protection was surely needed to promote further creativity in the video game industry,

---

[225] *See* Casillas *supra* note 117, at 168.
> The case also raises questions as to when parties such as Apple, who require developers using in-app purchasing to share 30 percent of their revenue, are liable for approving games that are blatant knock-offs. To incentivize Apple (as well as others who operate online "marketplaces") to safeguard their games, developers should include provisions in their contracts that impose liability on store operators for not providing adequate stop-measures for selling clones. *Id.*

[226] *See* Lunsford *supra* note 42, at 116–17.
> It is difficult to tell whether the Tetris Holdings and Spry Fox cases have changed anything. First, neither case reached the appellate level, so their authority will only be persuasive for the majority of courts. Second, neither case fundamentally changed or clarified the application of the rules for videogame cases. Instead, the outcomes of the modern cases could be a result of recent courts' differing applications of the tests in light of the development of legal standards for software copyright. *Id.*

[227] Derek Khanna, *Guarding Against Abuse: The Costs of Excessively Long Copyright Terms*, 23 COMMLAW CONSPECTUS 52, 92 (2014).

particularly as the home gaming market developed, but for a short time, the lack of effective protection may have accelerated the industry's development."[228]

While these could be viewed as broad generalizations, it is a very real possibility that creating a certification system could have a far more constrictive outcome than intended. A certification system could put the levers of creativity into established self-interested entities and create and perpetuate a copyright rent-seeking system.[229] There is the likelihood larger interests could be first to file for certification, and have greater resources to challenge something viewed as infringing.[230] It is important to point out that copyright law already subjects work to a low threshold, and more rules could hurt the creative process.[231]

Another reason the certification process does not make a great deal of sense is because the ramifications and litigation following the *Tetris Holding* decision have not had enough time to be tested. And occasionally they raise philosophical copyright issues.

> We sometimes expect that self-motivated authors, who write for the pure fun of it, will thrive best if copyright takes its boot off their necks. But a better picture, I think, is that there are plenty of authors who are motivated both by their desire to be creative and also by their desire not to be homeless. The extrinsic motivations of a copyright-supported business model provide an "incentive," to be sure, but that incentive

---

[228] William K. Ford, *Copy Game for High Score: The First Video Game Lawsuit*, 20 J. INTELL. PROP. L. 1, 41 (2012). "Protection also increased through the judicial decisions extending copyright protection to the audio-visual elements of games. To some extent, courts even extended protection to game mechanics in video games, despite the restriction on protecting methods and processes under 17 U.S.C. § 102(b)." *Id.* at 40-41.

[229] *See* Khanna *supra* note 227, at 92 ("If we continue to subsidize rent-seeking by the heirs of existing copyright holders, rather than consider the interests of new content creators who need a shorter copyright term, we will stifle content creation.").

[230] *See* Nicholas M. Lampros, *Leveling Pains: Clone Gaming and the Changing Dynamics of an Industry*, 28 BERKELEY TECH. L.J. 743, 774 (2013).

> Barring a dramatic plunge in legal costs or a surprising new ruling that sets a far firmer legal standard than the precedent suggests, the onus will continue to be on digital distribution platforms to develop takedown review and appeal regimes that are as robust as possible while still remaining consistent with the law. This will permit developers to at least get their rightful remedy in the marketplace, if not the courts." *Id.*

[231] Andrew Gilden, *Raw Materials and the Creative Process*, 104 GEO. L.J. 355, 401 (2016) (citing 17 U.S.C. § 302(a) (2012)).

takes the form of allowing them to indulge their intrinsic motivations to be creative.[232]

There seems to be a bit of overreaction and confusion. Some even view the ruling of the court as incorrect.[233] It is indeed true, "Games rules have never been copyrightable."[234] But the point the court was trying to make in the *Tetris Holding* decision was not that "some . . . rules . . . [could] be copyrightable."[235] The court was saying in explicit terms that "wholesale copying" was not acceptable.[236] The court went so far as to note that the copying was "troubling more than the individual similarities each considered in isolation."[237]

The notion of isolation is key because when looking at an overarching regulatory scheme, it appears the *Tetris Holding* decision is being held in isolation from other video game legal decisions. The most notable of these is *Atari v. Philips*, also known as the "Pac-Man case."[238] The similarities between *Atari* and *Tetris Holding* are striking. Both are cases where a well-known commodity in the game industry successfully brought suit against an infringer. Even though they are thirty years apart, the court applies similar doctrinal analysis in making their decisions. And the court found in *Atari* that Philips had infringed because they had copied the "total concept and feel" of *Pac-Man*.[239] While there is a distinction to be drawn between "wholesale copying" and "total look and feel" the gaming market has not been stifled by protecting creative works over the last thirty years.

---

[232] Grimmelman, *supra* note 206.

[233] Maitra, *supra* note 128, at 39 ("By filtering out only the un-copyrightable idea of the game, some game rules may found to be copyrightable. This is wrong.").

[234] *Id.* at 37.

[235] *Id.* at 39.

[236] *Tetris Holding v. Xio Interactive*, 863 F. Supp. 2d 394, 413 (D.N.J. 2012).

> I note that standing alone, these discrete elements might not amount to a finding of infringement, but here in the context of the two games having such overwhelming similarity, these copied elements do support such a finding. It is the wholesale copying of the *Tetris* look that the Court finds troubling more than the individual similarities each considered in isolation.

[237] *Id.*

[238] Atari, Inc. v. N. Am. Philips Consumer Elecs. Corp., 672 F.2d 607, 610 (7th Cir. 1982).

[239] *Id.* at 620 ("Although not 'virtually identical' to PAC-MAN, K. C. Munchkin captures the 'total concept and feel' of and is substantially similar to PAC-MAN.").

If anything, the *Tetris Holding* decision was an extension and expansion of *Atari* for a changing market. A compelling argument could be made that the court was actually acting as a market regulator. In defining the boundaries for the modern era, the court could be protecting the game market from itself.

## V.    Conclusion

There are going to be situations where the legal system will need to step in to set the rules. This is evident from *Tetris Holding*. These rules should continue to build off of the precedent that began with *Pac-Man* and was strengthened by *Tetris Holding* to work to restrict duplication and foster creativity. At the same time, it is important to not go too far. A ruling of infringement on an unfinished product in the pending Glu Mobile litigation would affirm the fear that *Tetris Holding* expanded protection.

It seems that the most fitting solution to the problems facing the mobile gaming industry is to allow the market to figure it out on its own. There are going to be situations such as *Spry Fox* where it is clear there has been infringement. In those instances, infringement claims should be filed. But there are also going to be situations like *Capcom v. Data East*, where two competing video games look similar and play similarly but are different products.[240] Overbearing copyright rules could stifle creativity especially in an industry that thrives on putting a different spin on the ideas of others. For every *Mino* or *Yeti Town*, there is a *Halo* or a *Call of Duty* that takes the established genre of game and puts a unique spin upon it. Creating a certification system would protect only those who had established a profitable game and could possibly keep innovation from reaching the market. To further expand protection could create a situation where unfinished works or abandoned projects could have significant impact on the legal system.

> We sometimes expect that self-motivated authors, who write for the pure fun of it, will thrive best if copyright takes its boot off their necks. But a better picture, I think, is that there are plenty of authors who

---

[240] See Capcom U.S.A., Inc. v. Data E. Corp., 1994 WL 1751482, at *8 (N.D. Cal. Mar. 16, 1994) ("Neither these individual features, nor their particular compilation in Street Fighter II are original to Capcom. Rather, they are better viewed as unprotectable scènes à faire, 'expressions that are "as a practical matter, indispensable or at least standard in the treatment of a given [idea]."'"). *Id.*

are motivated both by their desire to be creative and also by their desire not to be homeless. The extrinsic motivations of a copyright-supported business model provide an "incentive," to be sure, but that incentive takes the form of allowing them to indulge their intrinsic motivations to be creative.[241]

Because of the dangers of overreaction, allowing the market to police itself without creating an overarching regulatory scheme will allow the mobile game industry to thrive and sort out the competitors who enter the market solely to steal the ideas of other creators.

---

[241] Grimmelman, *supra* note 206.

# NO COPYRIGHT IN THE LAW: A BASIC PRINCIPLE, YET A CONTINUING BATTLE
### Elizabeth Scheibel[1]

## I.   INTRODUCTION

It is a long established principle that "the law"— judicial opinions, statutes, and administrative regulations—is not copyrightable. This may seem like an intuitive principle or an obvious requirement in a society committed to democracy and the rule of law: if citizens are to

---

[1] J.D. Candidate, Mitchell Hamline School of Law, 2017; M.L.I.S., St. Catherine University, 2011; B.A. English, Macalester College, 2005. The author wishes to thank Minnesota's law and special librarian communities for furthering her interest in copyright law and for supporting her librarian-to-lawyer career change. The author also wishes to thank her family, especially Nick, for his daily supply of encouragement, cooking, and romantic walks with the dogg.

participate in creating law through democratic systems, they must be informed about the law. Furthermore, due process of law dictates that those subject to the rule of law must have access to the law if they are to be held responsible for complying with it.[2]

However, the uncopyrightable nature of the law has been challenged many times in copyright infringement lawsuits. Even after many cases addressing the issue, the boundaries between what constitutes the law and is, therefore, uncopyrightable, and what is additional and, therefore, copyrightable, is not always clear. These issues are exacerbated by the history of legal publishing: various branches of the federal government and state governments have relied on private entities to publish public domain material.[3] This created, and continues to create, a clash of interests between those private entities, who desire copyright protection for their works, and the public, who need access to the law that governs them.

Currently, the state of Georgia is suing a non-profit, Public.Resource.org,[4] for copyright infringement because the organization published an annotated version of the state's code on its website.[5] Public.Resource.org is arguing that since the annotated version is the state's "official code," the entirety of that code is the law and cannot be copyrighted.[6] The issues are further complicated by a

---

[2] One scholar sees additional constitutional problems at the intersection of the government and copyright in allowing the copyrighting of works that were commissioned and funded by the government. *See generally* Andrea Simon, *A Constitutional Analysis of Copyrighting Government-Commissioned Work*, 84 COLUM. L. REV. 425 (1984).

[3] *See* Sarah Glassmeyer, *State Legal Information Census: An Analysis of Primary State Legal Information*, 23–27 (2016), http://www.sarahglassmeyer.com/StateLegalInformation/wp-content/uploads/2014/04/GlassmeyerStateLegalInformationCensusReport.pdf (surveying publication of official state codes and court reporters by private entities and noting the frequent reliance on private entities for official publications).

[4] *See About Us*, PUBLIC.RESOURCE.ORG, https://public.resource.org/about/index.html (last visited May 14, 2016); *Bylaws of Public.Resource.Org, Inc.*, PUBLIC.RESOURCE.ORG § 2.1, https://public.resource.org/public.resource.bylaws.html (last visited May 14, 2016) ("The objectives and purposes of Public.Resource.Org, Inc. shall be: to create, architect, design, implement, operate and maintain public works projects on the Internet for Educational, Charitable, and Scientific Purposes to the benefit of the general public and the public interest . . . .").

[5] Compl. at 2, Code Revision Commission v. Public.Resource.org, Inc., No. 1:15CV02594 (N.D. Ga. July 21, 2015).

[6] Answer at 24, 27, 28, Code Revision Commission v. Public.Resource.org, Inc., No. 1:15CV02594 (N.D. Ga. Sept. 9, 2015); *see also* Bill Donahue, *Nonprofit Group Says Georgia Code Can't Be Copyrighted*, LAW360 (Sept. 15, 2015, 4:56 PM),

private entity, LexisNexis (not currently a party to the lawsuit), that publishes and creates the annotations in the official code.[7]

This Note will begin by surveying the history of the principle that the law is not copyrightable by looking at copyright of statutes and judicial opinions,[8] copyright of material supplementing the text of the law,[9] and, more recently, copyright of privately developed material adopted or incorporated into law.[10] The Uniform Electronic Legal Materials Act (UELMA) will also be introduced as one way for states to move forward in providing authoritative access to the law without requiring the use of a private publisher's product.[11] Next, this Note will discuss the differing legal bases used in that history as a grounding for discussing the Public.Resource.org litigation.[12] The allegations and arguments at issue in the Public.Resource.org litigation will then be described.[13] Finally, a resolution to that litigation in favor of Public.Resource.org will be proposed, while recognizing that such an outcome is unlikely.[14]

## II.     HISTORY OF COPYRIGHT AND "THE LAW"

### A.   Copyright of Statutes and Judicial Opinions

In the United States, the text of the law has long been considered to be in the public domain. The issue first reached the Supreme Court in 1834 in *Wheaton v. Peters*.[15] Though the central issue of the case centered around who properly held the copyright in the content of reports of the Supreme Court's decisions, the Court, at the very end of the majority opinion, and after disposing of the issues presented stated, "[i]t may be proper to remark that the court are unanimously of opinion, that no reporter has or can have any copyright

---

http://www.law360.com/articles/702797/nonprofit-group-says-georgia-code-can-t-be-copyrighted.

[7] Compl. at 6, Code Revision Commission v. Public.Resource.org, Inc., No. 1:15CV02594 (N.D. Ga. July 21, 2015).

[8] *See infra* Part II.A.

[9] *See infra* Part II.B.

[10] *See infra* Part II.C.1.

[11] *See infra* Part II.C.2.

[12] *See infra* Part III.A.

[13] *See infra* Part III.B.1.

[14] *See infra* Part III.B.2.

[15] *See* Wheaton v. Peters, 33 U.S. (8 Pet.) 591 (1834).

in the written opinions delivered by this court; and that the judges thereof cannot confer on any reporter any such right."[16]

The issue was more squarely confronted by the Court in *Banks v. Manchester*.[17] A publisher, having received by contracting with the state of Ohio the exclusive right to publish reports of state court decisions, sought to prevent another from copying and publishing the decisions.[18] The Court rejected the possibility of copyright in judicial decisions:

> Judges, as is well understood, receive from the public treasury a stated annual salary, fixed by law, and can themselves have no pecuniary interest or proprietorship, as against the public at large, in the fruits of their judicial labors. This extends to whatever work they perform in their capacity as judges, and as well to the statements of cases and head notes prepared by them as such, as to the opinions and decisions themselves. The question is one of public policy, and there has always been a judicial consensus, from the time of the decision in the case of Wheaton v. Peters, 8 Pet. 591, that no copyright could under the statutes passed by Congress, be secured in the products of the labor done by judicial officers in the discharge of their judicial duties. The whole work done by the judges constitutes the authentic exposition and interpretation

---

[16] *Id.* at 668. Many later opinions and other commentators have described this as the holding of the case. *See* Veeck v. S. Bldg. Code Cong. Int'l, Inc., 293 F.3d 791, 795 (5th Cir. 2002) (introducing the *Wheaton* Court's statement on copyright of judicial opinions by saying "the Supreme Court interpreted the first federal copyright laws and unanimously held . . ."); Marvin J. Nodiff, *Copyrightability of Works of the Federal and State Governments Under the 1976 Act*, 29 ST. LOUIS L. J. 91, 99 (1984) ("In the historic case of *Wheaton* . . . , the Supreme Court held that federal court opinions are in the public domain."). However, since the Court's statement was made after disposing of the case at hand and was not essential to its decision about the necessity of following the formalities required by copyright statutes, it must be classified as dictum rather than a holding. *See* Irina Y. Dmitrieva, *State Ownership of Copyrights in Primary Law Materials*, 23 HASTINGS COMM. & ENT L.J. 81, 84 (2000) (classifying the statement on copyright of the law as dictum and noting that the Court did not cite any legal authority for its proposition). The widespread adoption of the statement as a settled legal principle after *Wheaton*, however, shows that the principle is not open to dispute, despite its misunderstood beginning as a mere aside.

[17] *See* Banks v. Manchester, 128 U.S. 244 (1888).

[18] *Id.* at 247–48.

of the law, which, binding every citizen, is free for publication to all, whether it is a declaration of unwritten law, or an interpretation of a constitution or a statute.[19]

The *Banks v. Manchester* court referred to a Massachusetts Supreme Court decision that made a similar public policy determination:

> [J]ustice requires that all should have free access to the opinions, and that it is against sound public policy to prevent this, or to suppress and keep from the earliest knowledge of the public the statutes, or the decisions and opinions of the Justices. Such opinions stand, upon principle, on substantially the same footing as the statutes enacted by the Legislature.[20]

Soon after these early cases, Congress considered various proposals and recommendations about specifically excluding both federal and state judicial opinions, laws, and similar categories of legal material from being available for copyright. However, many of these recommendations were not adopted in the Copyright Act of 1909.[21] The 1909 Act only provided that "[n]o copyright shall subsist . . . in any publication of the United States Government,"[22] therefore excluding state and local material and leaving open difficulties with the use of the word "publication."[23]

The current Copyright Act says that "[c]opyright protection under this title is not available for any work of the United States Government."[24] This retains the general principle of prohibition of

---

[19] *Id.* at 253–54 (citing Nash v. Lathrop, 142 Mass. 29, 35 (1886)). The *Banks v. Manchester* decision also emphasized that copyright could only belong to a citizen or resident of the United States, so the State did not qualify as an "author" under then-current copyright statutes. *Id.* at 253.

[20] Nash v. Lathrop, 142 Mass. 29, 35 (1886).

[21] Nodiff, *supra* note 16, at 94–95.

[22] Act of Mar. 4, 1909, ch. 320, § 7, 35 Stat. 1077 (codified at 17 U.S.C. § 7 (1946)).

[23] *See* Nodiff, *supra* note 16, at 94–95 (reviewing the legislative history of the 1909 Act and finding that "publication" was neither defined in the Act nor clarified by the legislative history).

[24] 17 U.S.C. § 105 (2012). Though the current text of § 105 effectively codifies that material such as federal statutes and judicial opinions is not copyrightable, it does not shed light on what effect that has on material added to the text of the law itself, such as annotations or page numbers.

copyright from the 1909 Act while switching to the concept of "work," instead of "publication."[25]

Despite the absence of state and local law in the federal statute excluding government works from copyright protection,[26] the common law principle that the law itself is not copyrightable is firmly established and has been since the late nineteenth century. Therefore, the principle that the words of a judicial opinion or statute are in the public domain would be safe from challenge regardless of whether a state has a statute parallel to the federal law embodied in § 105.[27]

### B.  Copyright of Material Beyond the Text of Statutes and Judicial Opinions

Although judicial decisions stating that the law is not copyrightable have been consistent with regard to the text of the law,[28] decisions about material beyond the text are more varied.[29] However, it

---

[25] See Nodiff, supra note 16, at 94–95 (contrasting the 1909 Act with the 1976 Act, which used the term "work" instead of "publication" and defined "work of the United States Government").

[26] State statutes vary greatly in addressing copyright of state government works. See generally Dmitrieva, supra note 16 (surveying state laws providing for copyright of primary law materials).

[27] As of 2000, according to one study reviewing state statutory provisions related to copyright of primary legal materials, Illinois was the only state explicitly placing its statutes in the public domain. Id. at 97. A more recent study reviewed copyright notices on websites containing such material and found that only Massachusetts specified that it claimed no copyright in the text of its case law. Glassmeyer, supra note 3, at 20. Of note to those interested in Georgia's suit against Public.Resource.org, Georgia is last in Glassmeyer's "Openness of Legal Information" rankings. Id. at 34–36; see infra Part III.B.1.

[28] One early case came to an opposite conclusion. See Gould v. Banks, 2 A. 886, 896 (Conn. 1885) ("The judges and the reporter are paid by the state; and the product of their mental labor is the property of the state . . . . The courts and their records are open to all. The reasons given by the supreme court . . . constitute no part of the record therein."). However, very soon after, another court refused to follow the decision. See State of Connecticut v. Gould, 34 F. 319, 320 (C.C.N.D.N.Y. 1888). The Connecticut court then concluded in 1892 that Gould could not be good law in light of Banks v. Manchester. See Peck v. Hooker, 23 A. 741, 742 (Conn. 1892).

[29] Compare W. Pub. Co. v. Mead Data Cent., Inc., 799 F.2d 1219, 1226-27 (8th Cir. 1986) (concluding that West's arrangement of judicial opinions is the result of considerable labor, talent, and judgment and thus meets the standard for intellectual-creation), with Matthew Bender & Co. v. W. Pub. Co., 158 F.3d 693, 699 (2d Cir. 1998) (concluding that since "internal pagination of West's case reporters does not entail even a modicum of creativity, the volume and page numbers are not original components of West's compilations and are not themselves protected by West's compilation copyright").

is generally established that copyright can subsist in elements that are original and additional to the uncopyrightable text itself, though what qualifies as original or additional has been contested.

The history of copyright in material beyond the text of the law stretches back almost as far as the history of the lack of copyright in the law. In 1851, in *Little v. Gould*, the court acknowledged that no copyright existed in the judicial opinions themselves,[30] but found that the state could copyright the volumes of court reports that included summaries of cases, headnotes, and other material.[31]

A different court, in *Davidson v. Wheelock*, reached a parallel conclusion with regard to state constitutions and statutes, noting that such materials "are open to the world. They are public records, subject to inspection by every one."[32] Yet, a compilation or digest of those records "may be so original as to entitle the author to a copyright on account of the skill and judgment displayed in the combination and analysis."[33]

Later, that same court relied on *Davidson* to arrive at the same conclusion about state court reports[34] that *Little v. Gould*[35] had. The court further expounded on the policy basis for its decision by noting its importance in a just society:

> [I]t is a maxim of universal application that every man is presumed to know the law, and it would seem inherent that freedom of access to the laws, or the official interpretation of those laws, should be co-extensive with the sweep of the maxim. Knowledge is the only just condition of obedience.[36]

As further justification, the court called attention to the democratic system of government by describing citizens as "part owner[s]" of the laws: "[e]ach citizen is a ruler,—a law-maker,—and as such has the right of access to the laws he joins in making and to any official

---

[30] Little v. Gould, 15 F. Cas. 604, 606 (C.C.N.D.N.Y. 1851).
[31] *Id.* at 612.
[32] 27 F. 61, 62 (C.C.D. Minn. 1866).
[33] *Id.*
[34] Banks & Bros. v. W. Pub. Co., 27 F. 50, 59 (C.C.D. Minn. 1886).
[35] Little v. Gould, 15 F. Cas. 604, 612 (C.C.N.D.N.Y. 1851); *see supra* notes 30–31 and accompanying text.
[36] *Banks & Bros.*, 27 F. at 57.

interpretation thereof."[37] Several other courts subsequently reiterated
the rule that although no copyright exists in statutes and judicial
opinions, copyright can exist in original compilation and annotation
materials added to those texts.[38]

Although the precise scope of the availability of copyright in
compilations of and material added to the law has been litigated many
times, the suits generally center on whether the additional material or
method of compilation was sufficiently original or creative to meet
standards of copyrightability.[39] These questions, unfortunately, do not
directly shed light on the conflicted status of an annotated code that is
also a state's official code, which is at the heart of the suit between
Georgia and Public.Resource.org.[40]

C.   Recent Issues: Laws Adopting Text Copyrighted by Private Parties
     and the Uniform Electronic Legal Materials Act

     1.   Laws Adopting Text Copyrighted by Private Parties: Veeck

---

[37] *Id.* It is interesting to notice that in this section of the opinion, the court does not
provide any legal authority for the stated principles, other than observing that "[t]he laws
of Rome were written on tablets and posted, that all might read, and all were bound to
obedience" and acknowledging that "English courts generally sustain the crown's
proprietary rights in judicial opinions." *Id.*

[38] *See* Callaghan v. Myers, 128 U.S. 617, 647–49 (1888); Howell v. Miller, 91 F. 129,
138 (6th Cir. 1898); Ex Parte Brown, 78 N.E. 553, 558 (Ind. 1906). *Harrison Co. v. Code
Revision Commission,* which is especially notable in light of the suit against
Public.Resource.org for copying Georgia's annotated code, *see infra* Part III.B, notes that
even if the state had contracted for publication of an annotated version its code, the
contracted publisher did not have an exclusive right to publish the laws since they were
public records. 260 S.E.2d 30, 34 (Ga. 1979). In a related case, the state of Georgia
argued that that it should be able to copyright its statutes so that it could insure accuracy
in any published statutes, but the court rejected this argument and noted that "anyone
citing the [unofficial version] will do so at his peril if there is any inaccuracy in that
publication or any discrepancy between [the official version] and [the unofficial version].
A person takes the same risk, of course, whenever he cites the [unofficial versions of the
United States code]; since both of these codifications are unofficial, the language in the
statutes-at-large (or the official codifications) published by the Government Printing
Office would control." Georgia v. Harrison Co., 548 F. Supp. 110, 114–15 (N.D. Ga.
1982), *vacated,* 559 F. Supp. 37 (N.D. Ga. 1983).

[39] *See generally* Deborah Tussey, *Owning the Law: Intellectual Property Rights in
Primary Law,* 9 FORDHAM INTELL. PROP. MEDIA & ENT. L.J. 173 (1998).

[40] *See infra* Part III.

What happens when the government adopts copyrighted material into law through incorporating the copyrighted text into law? This has been the question in more recent cases in the area of copyright and the content of the law.

The First Circuit Court of Appeals addressed the topic in dictum when addressing a suit of Building Officials and Code Administrators (BOCA), a private organization that creates regulations for building construction.[41] The BOCA Code was adopted in Massachusetts, and then the defendant published its own version of the State Code without recognition of BOCA's copyright.[42] The court reviewed the relevant cases[43] and found that the differing lines of reasoning used in these opinions was significant enough to describe in detail:

> BOCA's argument implies that the rule of *Wheaton v. Peters* was based on the public's property interest in work produced by legislators and judges, who are, of course, government employees. This interpretation of the cases is not without foundation; there is language in some of them that emphasizes the inconsistency of private ownership of the law with its creation under government sponsorship.
>
> But BOCA's argument overlooks another aspect of the ownership theory discussed in these cases. The cases hold that the public owns the law not just because it usually pays the salaries of those who draft legislation, but also because, in the language of *Banks v. West*, "Each citizen is a ruler,-a law-maker." The citizens are the authors of the law, and therefore its owners . . . .
>
> Along with this metaphorical concept of citizen authorship, the cases go on to emphasize the very important and practical policy that citizens must have free access to the laws which govern them. This

---

[41] Bldg. Officials & Code Adm. v. Code Tech., Inc., 628 F.2d 730 (1st Cir. 1980).
[42] *Id.* at 732.
[43] *See id.* at 733–34. Many of the cases cited by the court are discussed previously in this Note. *See supra* Parts II.A–B.

policy is, at bottom, based on the concept of due process.[44]

This detailed examination of the case law of the uncopyrightable nature of the law illustrates that, despite the consistency of the general rule of prohibition of copyright for such material, the reasoning behind the rule is not agreed upon among legal authorities.

The status of copyrighted material adopted into law was again at issue in *Veeck v. Southern Building Code Congress International, Inc.*[45] ("SBBCI"). The matter involved an individual who copied and distributed, via a free website, building codes that had been incorporated into municipal codes but were originally created by a private entity that owned the copyright in the codes.[46] After receiving a cease-and-desist letter, Veeck sought a declaratory judgment declaring that he did not infringe SBCCI's copyright.[47]

The court held that privately drafted model codes lose their copyright protection when adopted by municipal or state governments.[48] The court relied on the Supreme Court precedents in *Wheaton*[49] and *Banks v. Manchester*.[50] The court additionally relied on the merger doctrine—that the idea of the specific municipal building codes at issue can be expressed only through the precise words of the enacted code, rendering the words of the code uncopyrightable[51]—and

---

[44] *Bldg. Officials & Code Adm.*, 628 F.2d at 734 (citations omitted). The inconsistent nature of the reasoning provided by courts in this area means that the law of copyright of primary legal information is less settled and less predictable than it first appears. *See infra* Part III.A.

[45] Veeck v. S. Bldg. Code Cong. Int'l, Inc., 293 F.3d 791 (5th Cir. 2002) (en banc), *cert. denied*, 539 U.S. 969 (2003). *See generally* Shubha Ghosh, *Copyright As Privatization: The Case of Model Codes*, 78 TUL. L. REV. 653 (2004) (discussing the *Veeck* case in detail).

[46] *Veeck*, 293 F.3d at 793–94.

[47] *Id.* at 794.

[48] *Id.* at 800.

[49] *Id.* at 795, 798, 800 (citing Wheaton v. Peters, 33 U.S. (8 Pet.) 591 (1834)); *see supra* notes 15–16 and accompanying text (discussing *Wheaton*).

[50] *Veeck*, 293 F.3d at 795–800; *see supra* notes 17–19 and accompanying text (discussing *Banks v. Manchester*).

[51] *Veeck*, 293 F.3d at 801. "In some circumstances, . . . a given idea is inseparably tied to a particular expression. In such instances, rigorously protecting the expression would confer a monopoly over the idea itself, in contravention of the statutory command. To prevent that consequence, courts have invoked the merger doctrine." 4-13 Nimmer on Copyright § 13.03 (LexisAdvance, 2016). The merger doctrine is usually traced to *Baker*

on viewing the content of the codes as facts, which are uncopyrightable.[52] Finally, the court resolved apparent conflicts between precedents in different circuits by distinguishing between standards and codes, saying that when standards were found to be copyrightable, the cases involved private standards that were incorporated by reference and "were created by private groups for reasons other than incorporation into law."[53]

The future of copyright in content created by private parties and subsequently incorporated into law is uncertain; one commentator noted that there is an unresolved circuit split.[54] These cases have not brought much clarity to the field of copyrightability and the law when the official source of the law includes copyrighted material,[55] but they do suggest that courts deciding such issues need to consider policy concerns about public access to the law.[56]

2.  *The Uniform Electronic Legal Materials Act: Making Authoritative Versions of the Law Accessible and Able to be Authenticated*

---

v. *Selden*. 101 U.S. 99, 103 (1879); *see also* 1-2 Nimmer on Copyright § 2.18 (LexisAdvance, 2016) (discussing *Baker* and noting that its discussion had drawn criticism in the scholarly literature).

[52] *Veeck*, 293 F.3d at 801. The touchstone cases for the rule that facts are uncopyrightable are *Feist Publications, Inc. v. Rural Telephone Service Co.*, 499 U.S. 340, 344–45 (U.S. 1991), and *Harper & Row, Publishers, Inc. v. Nation Enterprises*, 471 U.S. 539, 556 (1985).

[53] *Veeck*, 293 F.3d at 805.

[54] Lawrence A. Cunningham, *Private Standards in Public Law: Copyright, Lawmaking and the Case of Accounting*, 104 MICH. L. REV. 291, 300–07 (2005) (discussing the BOCA suit, *Veeck*, and others, while noting the limitations of the judiciary in addressing this area).

[55] These cases will likely be important in any decisions on the merits in suits involving Public.Resource.org's copying of materials incorporating privately developed standards. *See infra* Part III.B.2.

[56] *See* Cunningham, *supra* note 54, at 297–98 (noting that the majority and dissent decisions in *Veeck* emphasized different aspects of competing policy objectives and the need for balancing of public policies in such cases); *see generally also* Nina A. Mendelson, *Private Control over Access to the Law: The Perplexing Federal Regulatory Use of Private Standards*, 112 MICH. L. REV. 737 (2014) (arguing, in the context of private standards incorporated into regulatory schemes, that access to the law needs to be better and easier for reasons beyond public policy concerns, such as that regulatory beneficiaries need notice of the contents of standards and that the public needs to be able to invoke mechanisms of accountability, including voting, contacting Congress, participating in agency procedures, and seeking judicial review).

Although the law is not copyrightable, it is sometimes only available in its official[57] form through a product that contains additional copyrightable material, such as a print volume of a court reporter[58] or state statutes[59] that includes annotations. Another hurdle to the public accessing the law is the potential for confusion about whether a particular version is official, and can be relied on as authoritative, or not.[60]

---

[57] "The word 'official' means that the text of the statutes is the legal evidence of the law in a court of law." NATIONAL CONFERENCE OF STATE LEGISLATURES, OFFICIAL VERSION OF THE STATE STATUTES/CODE (March–July 2011),
http://www.ncsl.org/documents/lsss/Official_Version_Statutes.pdf.
[58] Every volume of West's National Reporter System is an example of this. *See* THOMSON REUTERS, USING WEST'S NATIONAL REPORTER SYSTEM (2010), http://lscontent.westlaw.com/images/content/nationalreporter10.pdf.
[59] Note, for example, that both official and unofficial print versions of Minnesota's state code exist. A set of books entitled *Minnesota Statutes* is published by the Minnesota Revisor's office and is an official version. *Minnesota Statutes: Official Versions of Minnesota Statutes*, OFFICE OF THE REVISOR OF STATUTES,
https://www.revisor.mn.gov/*statutes*?view=info (last visited May 14, 2016). *Minnesota Statutes Annotated* is published by Thomson Reuters. *Minnesota Statutes Annotated*, THOMSON REUTERS, http://legalsolutions.thomsonreuters.com/law-products/Statutes/Minnesota-Statutes-Annotated-Annotated-Statute--Code-Series/p/100028621 (last visited May 14, 2016). *Minnesota Statutes Annotated* is not listed as an official version of Minnesota Statutes. *See Minnesota Statutes: Official Versions of Minnesota Statutes*, OFFICE OF THE REVISOR OF STATUTES,
https://www.revisor.mn.gov/*statutes*?view=info (last visited May 14, 2016).
[60] *See* CODE OF GEORGIA - FREE PUBLIC ACCESS, http://www.lexis-nexis.com/hottopics/gacode/Default.asp (last visited May 14, 2016). This portal to Georgia's code is entitled "Code of Georgia – Free Public Access"; it states that the "website is maintained by LexisNexis®, the publisher of the Official Code of Georgia Annotated, to provide free public access to the law." *Id.* But this language does not make it clear whether or not this online version is designated as an official version, and so lawyers needing an official version because they will use the text in legal proceedings should be wary. *See id.* This website formerly included language that specified that only the print version was authoritative, but this author was unable to locate that language; perhaps it has been removed in light of the litigation described in this Note. *See* Answer at 24, Code Revision Commission v. Public.Resource.org, Inc., No. 1:15CV02594 (N.D. Ga. Sept. 14, 2015) (referring to Exhibit F, a screenshot of a previous version of the portal's entry page); *see also infra* Part III.B.1. Once a user clicks the "I Agree" button and begins to view the material, the beginning search page refers to the material as "Official Code of Georgia," but when viewing a specific code section, the heading on the page only mentions the code's "official" status through the presence of O.C.G.A. citations, which are followed by a heading that merely says "Georgia Code." *See* CODE OF GEORGIA - FREE PUBLIC ACCESS, http://www.lexis-nexis.com/hottopics/gacode/Default.asp (last visited May 14, 2016) (noting that the search page and specific code sections not available via direct link and a user of any of these pages must begin at this cited portal and accept the Terms & Conditions). The text

The Uniform Electronic Legal Materials Act ("UELMA") is an attempt to fix these problems by requiring states that adopt such legislation to provide online versions of legal material that are as authoritative as the print versions historically relied on.[61] "The Act requires that official electronic legal material be: (1) authenticated, by providing a method to determine that it is unaltered; (2) preserved, either in electronic or print form; and (3) accessible, for use by the public on a permanent basis."[62] The authentication aspect is key; some states previously offered official versions online, but these versions were not authenticated and therefore were open to question about their accuracy.[63] The authentication aspect may seem unimportant to the lay user, but attorneys downloading copies of statutes, or receiving such downloaded copies from others, and using the documents in legal proceedings should be able to know, through the authentication process, that the text on which they are relying is accurate.[64]

---

of Georgia's code does not provide further clarity; the only provision about publishing an official code is that "[t]he Code Revision Commission shall provide for the publication of the Official Code of Georgia Annotated . . . ." O.C.G.A. § 28-9-5(a), current through the 2015 Regular Session. This is in contrast to a state like Minnesota, which is more explicit about how one knows whether a version is authoritative and can be used in legal proceedings: "Any volume of Minnesota Statutes, supplement to Minnesota Statutes, and Laws of Minnesota certified by the revisor according to section 3C.11, subdivision 1, is prima facie evidence of the statutes contained in it in all courts and proceedings." MINN. STAT. § 3C.13 (2014).

[61] *Electronic Legal Material Act: Description*, UNIFORM LAW COMMISSION, http://www.uniformlaws.org/Act.aspx?title=Electronic+Legal+Material+Act (last visited May 14, 2016).

[62] *Id.*

[63] RICHARD J. MATTHEWS & MARY A. BAISH, STATE-BY-STATE REPORT ON AUTHENTICATION OF ONLINE LEGAL RESOURCES 3 (Am. Ass'n of Law Libraries 2007)("A significant number of the state online legal resources are official but none are authenticated or afford ready authentication by standard methods. State online primary legal resources are therefore not sufficiently trustworthy."). Authenticated, and therefore trustworthy, sources are important for those engaging with the legal system; recall the warning in *Georgia v. Harrison Co.* that one citing an unofficial version "[did] so at his peril if there is any inaccuracy . . . or any discrepancy between [official and unofficial versions]." 548 F. Supp. 110, 114 (N.D. Ga. 1982) *vacated*, 559 F. Supp. 37 (N.D. Ga. 1983).

[64] *See, e.g., Document Authentication*, OFFICE OF THE REVISOR OF STATUTES, https://www.revisor.mn.gov/pubs/publish_hash.php?type=statutes&id=3E.02 (last viewed Jan. 9, 2016) (providing an example of an authentication process in which a user can upload the document she is using as her source of the law and find out whether it is an authentic copy).

UELMA has been adopted in twelve states and has been introduced in two more.[65] UELMA is quite flexible[66]: states can include or exclude certain categories of legal information,[67] there is no specific technology designated by the Act, and, though only a unit or employee of the state government can be the official publisher, states can still contract with commercial publishers to produce official versions.[68] There does not appear to have been any litigation as of yet about whether or not a state's implementation properly complies with the legislation or what ramifications a state's adoption of UELMA has on copyright issues.[69]

Depending on how a state implements UELMA,[70] it can avoid clashes between the interests of private publishers of legal information and the public with respect to the availability of official versions of the state's laws because the public does not have to use a private

---

[65] *Electronic Legal Material Act: Description*, UNIFORM LAW COMMISSION, http://www.uniformlaws.org/Act.aspx?title=Electronic+Legal+Material+Act (last visited May 14, 2016).

[66] *See Uniform Electronic Legal Material Act Summary*, UNIFORM LAW COMMISSION, http://www.uniformlaws.org/ActSummary.aspx?title=Electronic%20Legal%20Material%20Act (last visited May 14, 2016).

[67] Minnesota, for example, includes its Constitution, session laws, codified statutes, and administrative rules in its adoption of UELMA, but does not include judicial opinions. *See* MINN. STAT. 3E.02 (2014).

[68] *Uniform Electronic Legal Material Act Summary*, UNIFORM LAW COMMISSION, http://www.uniformlaws.org/ActSummary.aspx?title=Electronic%20Legal%20Material%20Act (last visited May 14, 2016).

[69] This author did not check each statute derived from UELMA in each adopting state for citing court cases. However, WestlawNext searches by this author on January 28, 2016, of all state and federal cases for the terms and phrases "UELMA," "electronic legal materials act," and "electronic legal material" did not return any relevant cases; in all searches but the last phrase, there were no cases.

[70] The argument has been made that UELMA may turn out to be ineffective and that Georgia's current online statutes could be found to meet UELMA's requirements of authentication, preservation, and accessibility. Beth Ford, Note, *Open Wide the Gates of Legal Access*, 93 OR. L. REV. 539, 562–63 (2014). However, before concluding that a state like Georgia has met the Uniform Act's requirements even without adopting it, a more detailed analysis would be required, especially on the question of whether Georgia's online code is authenticated, since authenticated is different from official, *see supra* note 63, and there are not currently any statements or functions related to authentication on the O.C.G.A. website. *See supra* note 60 (describing the information presented to a user of the O.C.G.A. online). However, the fact remains that despite the promotion of access to legal information through the creation of UELMA and despite its adoption in some states, there are still significant barriers to access to reliable legal information, even in states that have adopted UELMA. *See* GLASSMEYER, *supra* note 3, at 1, 3.

publisher's product to access version that is both official and authenticated. Georgia has not adopted UELMA[71] and continues to have a close relationship with a private entity for publication of its official code,[72] so the state has created confusion and issues for itself and users of its code by outsourcing its publishing and designating an annotated code as the official version.

III.    THE PUBLIC.RESOURCE.ORG SUIT: AN OPPORTUNITY TO SUPPORT PUBLIC ACCESS TO THE LAW

*A.    Differing Legal Bases of Uncopyrightability of the Law*

The history of copyright in the text of statutes, judicial opinions, and in material added to those texts, along with recent developments in cases like *Veeck* and in legislation like UELMA, shows that copyright of the law is still unsettled territory, even amidst general consistency about the principle that the law is uncopyrightable.

Another layer of complication is that courts discussing the uncopyrightability of the law are not entirely consistent in how they ground that principle,[73] making predicting the outcome of suits on the subject even more difficult than usual.[74]

Some courts emphasize the fact that the government is like the employee of the people, and thus the law (and sometimes government works more generally) belongs to the people under principles reminiscent of work made for hire.[75] A work made for hire exists when

---

[71] *Electronic Legal Material Act: Description*, UNIFORM LAW COMMISSION, http://www.uniformlaws.org/Act.aspx?title=Electronic+Legal+Material+Act (last visited May 14, 2016).

[72] Compl. at 7–8, Code Revision Commission v. Public.Resource.org, Inc., No. 1:15CV02594 (N.D. Ga. July 21, 2015). As discussed below, it is interesting that the state of Georgia has brought suit to protect the copyright owned by LexisNexis, a private entity. *See infra* Part III.B.1.

[73] Additionally, some of the early cases that became important precedents in this area, *see supra* Parts II.A and II.B, are lacking in any reasoning on which to base their conclusions. *See* Davidson v. Wheelock, 27 F. 61, 62 (C.C.D. Minn. 1866); Wheaton v. Peters, 33 U.S. (8 Pet.) 591 (1834).

[74] An additional consideration is the more fundamental problem, from a constitutional separation of powers perspective, of judicial branches making public policy judgments, when "public policy pronouncements are a unique prerogative of the legislative branch." Dmitrieva, *supra* note 16, at 117.

[75] *See* 17 U.S.C. § 101 ("A 'work made for hire' is—(1) a work prepared by an employee within the scope of his or her employment; or (2) a work specially ordered or commissioned for use [in specific categories of works], if the parties expressly agree in a

an employee who creates a copyrightable work does not own the copyright; instead, the employer owns it.[76] The Court in *Banks v. Manchester* calls out this idea, noting that judges are paid out of the public treasury.[77]

Other courts focus on public policy, democratic ideals of an informed populace, and due process concerns that require people to have access to the laws that govern them, while stating that the law is not copyrightable and exists in the public domain. The court in *Nash v. Lathrop* simply thought that "justice requires" such access.[78] In *Banks & Brothers v. West Publishing Co.*, the court noted the "maxim" that all are presumed to know the law, so it is only just that all have access to the law.[79] The court also called attention to each citizen's role as a "law-maker," which is the result of a democracy dependent on the participation of the public.[80]

Some courts discuss both lines of reasoning and are unclear about which is the main basis for their holdings. Even in its description of the relationship between the work product of government officials and the public, *Banks v. Manchester*, when it highlighted that the law is "binding [on] every citizen," seemed to suggest that due process principles are at play.[81] The cases dealing with privately created codes adopted into law acknowledge the varying reasonings used in the relevant precedents but do little to resolve whether one or another is superior.[82]

---

written instrument signed by them that the work shall be considered a work made for hire."); *see also* 1-5 NIMMER ON COPYRIGHT § 5.13 (LexisAdvance 2016) (summarizing the law of copyright and works of the United States government and the work made for hire concepts involved).

[76] *See* 1-5 NIMMER, *supra* note 75.

[77] Banks v. Manchester, 128 U.S. 244, 253 (1888); *see also supra* notes 17–20 and accompanying text.

[78] 142 Mass. 29, 35 (1886).

[79] 27 F. 50, 57 (C.C.D. Minn. 1886); *see also supra* notes 34 and accompanying text.

[80] *Banks & Bros. v. W. Pub. Co.*, 27 F. at 57; *see also supra* notes 37 and accompanying text. This statement could also be interpreting as conjuring work made for hire principles, with the citizen as employer and the government as employee, so it could be argued that this reasoning fits in the first category. *See supra* notes 75–76 and accompanying text (discussing the use of work made for hire-like principles in cases concerning copyright of the law).

[81] Banks v. Manchester, 128 U.S. 244, 253–54 (1888) (citing Nash v. Lathrop, 142 Mass. 29, 35 (1886)) (noting that the law is "binding on every citizen").

[82] *See* Bldg. Officials & Code Adm. v. Code Tech., Inc., 628 F.2d 730, 734 (1st Cir. 1980); Veeck v. S. Bldg. Code Cong. Int'l, Inc., 293 F.3d 791, 800–05 (5th Cir. 2002) (en

Of these differing foci of reasoning, the second, emphasizing democratic ideals and due process principles, is the better one; it upholds the central importance of having the law in the public domain in the United States and avoids possible loopholes in the work made for hire analogy. Grounding the uncopyrightability of the law in due process and democratic principles means that government units, such as state legislatures, must consider their official, authoritative versions of laws as being in the public domain.

The varied reasoning used by courts suggests that the reasoning is not important. Perhaps courts assume that the principle is so obvious and, at this point, firmly established that it is not necessary to carefully identify the legal basis for the proposition. However, the reasoning used to place the law in the public domain could have implications for whether or not certain material is determined to be in the public domain.

For example, if work made for hire principles are used,[83] and judges and legislators are considered employees, and the public are viewed as employers for works created by government officials in their official capacities, the public owns the copyright in such works. However, this reasoning could have unintended limits. A United States citizen who is not a resident or tax-payer in a particular state might not be considered as included in the public owning the copyrights to government works created by that state's judges and legislators, and that person, unlike a person who lives in that state, would be infringing on the copyright of that state if he engaged in infringing conduct.[84]

Additionally, whether or not a corporation would be included in "the public" that owns the copyrights could be another source of problems. If corporations are people for such purposes, in what state do the corporations participate in the ownership of government works? Could they claim such ownership in more than one state? Can human persons who pay taxes in several states do so? Which taxes trigger such ownership? Many benefits of governments are only given to residents or other specific members of the public; use of the law could be argued to be no different.

---

banc), *cert. denied*, 539 U.S. 969 (2003); *see also supra* notes 44, 48–53 and accompanying text (discussing reasoning in *Bldg. Officials & Code Adm.* and *Veeck*).
[83] *See supra* notes 75–76 and accompanying text.
[84] *See* Dmitrieva, *supra* note 16, at 113–14 (arguing that this "metaphorical concept of citizen authorship" is not the best model and is impractical in the United States of today).

What happens if the government, the employee of the people, did not write the law? Is the public's rightful access to the law lessened when government representatives only did the work of enacting a particular law, but did not create it? This is the issue in the BOCA and *Veeck* cases, but the answers to these questions still are not clear.[85] The public policy concern shown in these cases could be a justification for why Georgia should lose its lawsuit[86]: if the state is designating material as its official law, even if that material would otherwise be copyrightable, then it is not subject to copyright, as in *Veeck*.

All of these issues suggest that the public domain status of statutes and judicial decisions is more safely maintained by the public policy and due process reasoning used by the Court in *Nash v. Lathrop*[87] and like cases.[88] That reasoning more reliably promotes public access of the law and other government information. It also places the burden on states and other would-be copyright owners, such as publishers of legal information, to show why denying public domain status of the law and material associated with the text of the law does not offend principles of democracy and due process. The alternative is to place the burden on the public to show why particular material is of the type of material that the public has a right to have through a work made for hire relationship with the government.

B.   *Resolving Code Revision Commission v. Public.Resource.org, Inc.*

1.   *Facts and Allegations of Case.*

*Code Revision Commission v. Public.Resource.org, Inc.*[89] is an opportunity for a court to provide greater support of public access to the law and greater clarity in the reasoning underlying that policy. The suit highlights the problems and confusion that can arise when a state offers an official version of its code only through using a private publisher's products or services and designates an annotated code as its official code.

---

[85] *See supra* Part II.C.2; *see also generally* Ghosh, *supra* note 45.
[86] *See infra* Part III.B.2.
[87] Nash v. Lathrop, 142 Mass. 29, 35 (1886).
[88] *See* Banks & Bros. v. W. Pub. Co., 27 F. 50, 57 (C.C.D. Minn. 1886); *see also supra* notes 78–90 and accompanying text (discussing reasoning in *Nash* and *Banks*).
[89] No. 1:15CV02594 (N.D. Ga. filed July 21, 2015).

This is not Public.Resource.org's first time in court, or its first time in court over an alleged copyright infringement of legal materials. The organization has recently been in litigation to obtain Internal Revenue Service records and to defend against infringement actions arising out of publishing federal and state regulations online.[90]

On July 21, 2015, the Code Revision Commission, on behalf of the State of Georgia, filed suit against Public.Resource.org, claiming violations of the Copyright Act,[91] because of Public.Resource.org's "systemic, widespread and unauthorized copying and distribution of the copyrighted annotations in the Official Code of Georgia Annotated."[92]

---

[90] Public.Resource.org v. U. S. Internal Revenue Serv., 78 F. Supp. 3d 1262, 1268 (N.D. Cal. 2015) (granting summary judgment to Public.Resource.org and requiring the government to produce requested documents); Am. Educ. Research Ass'n, Inc. v. Public.Resource.org, Inc., 78 F. Supp. 3d 542, 551 (D.D.C. 2015) (striking Public.Resource.org's demand for a jury trial in suit for infringement of plaintiffs' copyright in educational and psychological testing standards incorporated into the Code of Federal Regulations and state laws; suit is ongoing); Am. Soc'y for Testing & Materials v. Public.Resource.org, Inc., 78 F. Supp. 3d 534, 542 (D.D.C. 2015) (striking Public.Resource.org's demand for a jury trial in suit for infringement of plaintiffs' copyright in safety codes and standards incorporated by state and local governments into statutes, regulations, and ordinances; suit is ongoing); *see also* Tim Cushing, *Public.Resource.Org Sued (Again) For Publication Of A Document Incorporated Into Federal Regulations [Update]*, TechDirt (May 29, 2014, 3:29 AM), https://www.techdirt.com/articles/20140526/17193727368/publicresourceorg-sued-again-publication-document-incorporated-into-federal-regulations.shtml (discussing the American Education Research Association suit and providing links to articles about other Public.Resource.org suits); Victor Li, *Who Owns the Law? Technology Reignites the War Over Just How Public Documents Should Be*, ABA J. (Jun. 2014), available at http://www.abajournal.com/magazine/article/who_owns_the_law_technology_reignites_t he_war_over_just_how_public_document (reviewing the career of Public.Resource.org founder Carl Malamud and discussing differing viewpoints on Malamud's tactics and recent litigation).

[91] Compl. at 14, Code Revision Commission v. Public.Resource.org, Inc., No. 1:15CV02594 (N.D. Ga. July 21, 2015) (claiming violations "of one or more of Sections 106, 501–503, and 505 of the Copyright Act"). The Commission had previously sent Public.Resource.org a "Cease and Desist" letter, *id.* Exhibit 4, to which Public.Resource.org responded and stated that it "respectfully reject[ed] the distinction between 'the statutory text itself' and additional materials, as both are integral part and parcel of the only Official Code of Georgia Annotated, such material constituting the official law as published by the State." *Id.* Exhibit 5.

[92] Compl. at 2, *Code Revision Commission*, No. 1:15CV02594. Note that the content provided by Public.Resource.org therefore goes beyond what is provided online for free through the Georgia legislature's portal to the O.C.G.A., which, despite often using O.C.G.A. as its title, does not provide any of the annotations, so it is the annotations that are at the center of this dispute. *See* sources cited *supra* note 60. The Complaint specifies that the Commission does not and could not assert copyright in the statutory text itself.

Specifically, the Commission alleges that Public.Resource.org has "copied at least 140 volumes/supplements containing the O.C.G.A. Copyrighted Annotations" and posted these works "on at least one of its websites."[93] Further copying was alleged through posting of the material on another website, to which Public.Resource.org indicated that it was the owner of the works, resulting in many downloads of the annotations,[94] and through distribution of USB drives containing copies of the annotations.[95] The Commission additionally alleged that Public.Resource.org has created unauthorized derivative works in a manner that "encourg[es] the creation of further [such] works."[96] The Commission is seeking injunctive relief, as well as attorneys' fees and costs.[97]

The Complaint describes Public.Resource.org and its founder, Carl Malamud, as engaged in "a larger plan designed to challenge the letter of U.S. copyright law and force government entities . . . to expend tax payer dollars in creating annotated codes and making those annotated codes easily accessible."[98]

The Commission's view of the problem is that if the annotations to its code are freely available online, the publisher, LexisNexis, will not be able to sell copies of the annotated code, causing "Georgia [to] be required to either stop publishing the annotations altogether or pay for development of the annotations using state tax dollars."[99] In this way, the Commission has framed itself as the defender of the public, who will eventually lose the annotations as a

Compl. at 8, *Code Revision Commission*, No. 1:15CV02594. The Complaint further describes the free online access that is available and states that LexisNexis is required to publish that resource by the terms of its contract with the State. *Id.*

[93] *Id.* at 9.
[94] *Id.* at 9–10.
[95] *Id.* at 12–13.
[96] *Id.* at 2, 9.
[97] *Id.* at 16–17.
[98] *Id.* at 10–11; *see also* Mike Masnick, *State Of Georgia Sues Carl Malamud For Copyright Infringement For Publishing The State's Own Laws*, TECHDIRT (Jul. 24, 2015, 6:10AM), https://www.techdirt.com/articles/20150723/17125231743/state-georgia-sues-carl-malamud-copyright-infringement-publishing-states-own-laws.shtml (complaint available for viewing). The Complaint and Exhibits also detail Malamud's previous copying of government and legal information. *Id.* at 11.
[99] Compl. at 2–3, Code Revision Commission v. Public.Resource.org, Inc., No. 1:15CV02594 (N.D. Ga. July 21, 2015).

resource if Public.Resource.org is allowed to continue its posting of annotations.[100]

The Complaint specifies that the annotations are only added in the annotated publication and are not enacted law.[101] The Complaint also details the process of creating the annotations[102] and the specifics of the contractual arrangement between the State of Georgia and LexisNexis, which include that the annotations and other original works are works made for hire and the copyright in them is owned by the Commission.[103]

Public.Resource.org's Answer admitted many of the allegations about what it had done with the annotations in the O.C.G.A. but denied that the Commission owns a valid copyright in the annotations[104] and further denied "the bizarre, defamatory, and gratuitous allegation that it has a 'strategy of terrorism.'"[105] The Answer raised ten affirmative defenses.[106] The second defense stated that the O.C.G.A. is in the public domain and not copyrightable subject matter and further reiterated Public.Resource.org's position that the State "has no copyrights in works that government entities have enacted as law" and that "[t]he O.C.G.A. including annotations, regardless of how they were authored, is the law of Georgia, and the law should be free to the public."[107] The ninth and tenth defenses directly addressed the Commission's request for an injunction by stating that there should be no injunction because of a lack of irreparable injury and because it would be against the public interest.[108]

Public.Resource.org went on to counterclaim and seek a declaratory judgment that its actions do not infringe any copyright.[109] The counterclaim outlined Mr. Malamud's contributions to public

---

[100] See id. at 2–3.
[101] Id. at 7.
[102] Id. at 6–7.
[103] Id. at 7–8. The state's ownership of the copyrights explains why the publisher is not the complaining party in this litigation, as it has been in other cases. See infra Part II.B.
[104] See generally, Answer and Counterclaims, Code Revision Commission v. Public.Resource.org, Inc., No. 1:15--2594 (N.D. Ga. Sept. 14, 2015).
[105] Id. at 7.
[106] Id. at 10–11.
[107] Id. at 10.
[108] Id. at 11.
[109] Id. at 12.

access to government information,[110] as well as the non-profit contributions of Public.Resource.org.[111]

The counterclaim also describes language in the O.C.G.A's annotations that warned against using a different, unofficial version of Georgia's statutes.[112] Public.Resource.org then describes the restrictive conditions of using the online version of the O.C.G.A. and again calls attention to its unofficial status,[113] including providing an exhibit showing the website portal to the O.C.G.A. with language specifying that the print version is the authoritative version.[114]

Public.Resource.org further outlines a view of the law that relies on authorship by the people and requires public availability under principles of the rule of law generally, the lack of a defense of ignorance of the law, and the Constitution's protections of people reading and communicating the law.[115] Public.Resource.org argues that Georgia has incorporated the annotations and other material beyond the legislatively enacted text by incorporating that material in its official version of the Code, and thus use of that material by others "is lawful through the doctrine of merger."[116] Additionally, Public.Resource.org claims that "[e]ven if copyright law protected authorship by private parties after it is incorporated into law, . . . [its] use of the complete O.C.G.A. is fair use."[117]

The Commission answered the counterclaim[118] and filed an Amended Complaint; the only substantive difference from the first Complaint is that, at allegation 18, the Commission alleged that Public.Resource.org has "copied at least 52 different volumes/supplements containing the 2015 O.C.G.A. Copyrighted

---

[110] *Id.* at 14–18.
[111] *Id.* at 19–21.
[112] *Id.* at 22–23.
[113] *Id.* at 23–24.
[114] *Id.* at 24 (referring to Exhibit F, a screenshot of a previous version of the portal's entry page); *see also supra* note 60.
[115] *Id.* at 25–26.
[116] *Id.* at 26–27; *see also supra* note 51 (discussing the merger doctrine).
[117] *Id.* at 27. "[T]he fair use of a copyrighted work . . . for purposes such as criticism, comment, news reporting, teaching, . . . scholarship, or research, is not an infringement of copyright. In determining whether the use made of a work in any particular case is a fair use" four factors will be considered. 17 U.S.C. § 107.
[118] Answer to Affirmative Defenses and Counterclaim, Code Revision Commission v. Public.Resource.org, Inc., No. 1:15-cv-2594 (N.D. Ga. Oct. 8, 2015).

Annotations" since the initial filing of the suit.[119] Public.Resource.org has filed an Answer to the Amended Complaint incorporating a response to the new allegation that mirrors its previous assertions of having done the copying alleged but denying that the material at issue was protected by copyright.[120]

There has been no substantive filings beyond the pleadings; as of this writing, the parties had begun discovery in the midst of filing the amended pleadings.[121]

### 2.   How the Case Should Be Decided

As of March 23, 2016, the parties in *Code Revision Commission v. Public.Resource.org, Inc.* have not yet filed any motions that would resolve any of the claims, so it is currently unknown exactly how they will frame their arguments and what legal authorities they will rely on.[122]

It seems likely that the Commission will largely rely on cases that distinguish between the text of the law and supplemental material and specify that the former is not copyrightable but the latter is.[123] Narrowly focusing on and following the cases that hold supplemental material copyrightable[124] has an appealing simplicity and would avoid sending states that have arrangements like Georgia's[125] scrambling to

---

[119] Amended Complaint, Code Revision Commission v. Public.Resource.org, Inc., No. 1:15CV02594 (N.D. Ga. Oct. 8, 2015).

[120] Answer to Amended Complaint and Counterclaim, Code Revision Commission v. Public.Resource.org, Inc., No. 1:15CV02594 (N.D. Ga. Oct. 22, 2015).

[121] *See* Code Revision Commission v. Public.Resource.org, Inc., No. 1:15CV02594 (N.D. Ga.) (including docket entry 12, Joint Preliminary Report and Discovery Plan; entry 13, a Scheduling Order for discovery to end on March 18, 2016; entries 14 and 15, Certificates of Service of initial disclosures by each party; and entries 20 through 25, Certificates of Service by both parties of responses and objections to interrogatories and requests for production of documents).

[122] *See* Code Revision Commission v. Public.Resource.org, Inc., No. 1:15CV02594 (N.D. Ga.).

[123] *See supra* Part II.B.

[124] *See supra* Part II.B.

[125] For example, it appears that South Dakota also uses a private publisher for its official version of its print code. *See South Dakota Codified Laws*, LEGALSOLUTIONS.THOMSONREUTERS.COM, http://legalsolutions.thomsonreuters.com/law-products/Primary-Law-Materials-CasesC-Codes-/South-Dakota-Codified-Laws-Annotated-Statute--Code-Series/p/100001432 (last visited May 14, 2016) (specifying that the books are published "under an exclusive contract with the South Dakota Code Commission"). South Dakota does publish its

address the implications of needing to provide versions beyond what they currently provide and the implications of having contractual obligations with private publishers that are irreconcilable with the court's holding.

In countering the Commission's precedent-based argument, Public.Resource.org would likely be successful if it analogized this litigation to cases holding that material adopted into a code, even if privately created and otherwise copyrightable, is not copyrightable.[126]

The most difficult part of the Commission's argument will be carefully defining the meaning of the term "official" in light of Georgia's code publication arrangements and addressing the implications of the State of Georgia having designated an annotated version as its official version.

To highlight the importance of the meaning of "official" and to offer its own appealingly simple conclusion, Public.Resource.org will likely argue that designating a version of a legal code as "official" encompasses the entirety of that version, thus putting it into the public domain. Further, Public.Resource.org may try to draw attention to the uncomfortable position that the Commission is inescapably supporting: that the onus is on a reader of the O.C.G.A. to differentiate between which bits of text are official and uncopyrightable and which are not official and are copyrightable. This position gives a bad taste in a country where the law is not copyrightable, which may cause a judge or jury to be very hesitant to accept the Commission's position.

Yet, from a broader perspective of anticipating similar issues in the future, Public.Resource.org would benefit more from concentrating on convincing a judge or jury to take a broader view of the case and focus on the reasoning behind the uncopyrightability of the law. This could be a difficult path if the judge is not receptive to public policy arguments, but Public.Resource.org may have an easier time

---

statutes online, but it is unclear from the website whether or not it is an official version. *See Codified Laws*, SOUTH DAKOTA LEGISLATURE LEGISLATIVE RESEARCH COUNCIL, http://legis.sd.gov/statutes/Codified_Laws/ (last visited May 14, 2016). Chapter 2-16, "Codes and Compilations," of South Dakota Codified Laws does not appear to provide for the online publication of its code. *See* S.D. CODIFIED LAWS §§ 2-16-3 *et seq.* (West, WestlawNext through 2015 Regular Session). *See also Statutes/Code: Publisher and Frequency of Printing*, NATIONAL CONFERENCE OF STATE LEGISLATURES (Jul. 2011), http://www.ncsl.org/documents/lsss/Publisher_Printed_Statutes.pdf (listing publishers of each state's printed code: legislature, state, revisor, Lexis/Nexis, and/or Thompson [sic] Reuters (West)).

[126] *See supra* Part II.B.1.

bringing in such arguments because arguments about public policy and democratic ideals have previously influenced decisions about copyright and the law.[127]

Even a judge not otherwise responsive to public policy arguments could reach a result that takes the various public policy concerns into account because the BOCA case and *Veeck* both discussed and placed significant importance in these arguments. Although those cases are not in the same federal appellate circuit as Georgia,[128] they have persuasive value both as cases decided in federal appellate courts and as issues that involved the intersection of copyright of material created by a private entity and copyright of the law.

Public.Resource.org should additionally attack the Commission's description of the way it and the public will be harmed if Public.Resource.org is allowed to continue; the Commission's pleading that it needs to prevail because otherwise it will have to stop publishing annotations or spend taxpayer money to do so is strange when the annotations are not freely available to the public anyway. Though details of the contract between the State of Georgia and LexisNexis have not been publicly disclosed in the litigation, it seems that LexisNexis is already recouping the costs of creating the annotations and other supplemental material by selling print and online copies of the (actually annotated, unlike the free online version) O.C.G.A.; even if LexisNexis doesn't retain ownership of that material under the contract, it is still profiting from producing it.

The necessity that the Commission is claiming becomes more dubious in light of the publishing practices of some other states. Consider Minnesota, where a private publisher creates and sells an annotated version of the statutes[129] while the State publishes an official version both in print[130] and online,[131] without any copyrighted material

[127] *See supra* Part III.A.
[128] Georgia is in the 11th Circuit. *Court Role and Structure*, UNITED STATES COURTS, http://www.uscourts.gov/about-federal-courts/court-role-and-structure (last visited May 14, 2016).
[129] *Minnesota Statutes Annotated*, LEGALSOLUTIONS.THOMSONREUTERS.COM, http://legalsolutions.thomsonreuters.com/law-products/Statutes/Minnesota-Statutes-Annotated-Annotated-Statute--Code-Series/p/100028621 (last visited May 14, 2016) (stating the retail cost as $8,323.00).
[130] *Statutes-2014 Full Set*, MINNESOTA'S BOOKSTORE, http://www.comm.media.state.mn.us/bookstore/mnbookstore.asp?page=viewbook&BookID=81734&stocknum=14347&CatId=280 (last visited May 14, 2016) (stating the retail cost as $255). The State of Minnesota specifies that this is one of two official versions. *About Statutes*, OFFICE OF THE REVISOR

confusingly mixed in. Either way, the public does not have free access to the annotations, but in the case of Minnesota, the public does have access to an official version.

Despite the various arguments available to Public.Resource.org, it seems likely that, should the litigation proceed to judgment, the Commission will prevail and the matter will result in a decision with a narrow scope based on applying cases that hold supplemental material copyrightable.[132] Public.Resource.org has demanded a jury trial,[133] and it is possible that public policy arguments about what ordinary citizens should be able to expect when seeking legal information might resonate with a jury, but if the judge thinks that the law compels a resolution in the Commission's favor, jury-friendly arguments may not be enough. A judge, even if sympathetic to public policy arguments and larger implications of democratic and constitutional principles, may find the thrust of precedent inescapable and may prefer to leave the policy determinations to appellate courts and legislatures.

Even if the matter is resolved in Public.Resource.org's favor, it would remain to be seen whether the court would use reasoning that focuses on the idea of governments as creating works made for hire, with the people as the owner of the law, or on broader democratic ideals of an informed populace and due process requiring that people have access to the laws that govern them. The latter would be the better reasoning because it would be based on foundational democratic and constitutional principles and it would not leave the uncopyrightability of the law open to new creative attacks.[134] This case should be seen not as a run-of-the-mill copyright infringement case but as an important challenge to the scope of the principle of the people as the source of government and law.

---

OF STATUTES, https://www.revisor.leg.state.mn.us/statutes/?view=info (last visited May 14, 2016).

[131] *2015 Minnesota Statutes*, OFFICE OF THE REVISOR OF STATUTES, https://www.revisor.leg.state.mn.us/statutes/ (last visited May 14, 2016). The State of Minnesota specifies that this is one of two official versions. *About Statutes*, OFFICE OF THE REVISOR OF STATUTES, https://www.revisor.leg.state.mn.us/statutes/?view=info (last visited May 14, 2016).

[132] *See supra* Part II.B.

[133] Answer at 1, Code Revision Commission v. Public.Resource.org, Inc., No. 1:15CV02594 (N.D. Ga. Sept. 14, 2015).

[134] *See supra* Part III.B.2.

In addition, a finding for Public.Resource.org could push states like Georgia[135] to change publishing practices in ways that would avoid suits like this in the future. Until Georgia creates an official, authenticated version of its code that is accessible to the public, preferably online pursuant to a UELMA-based law, it cannot claim that the annotated code at issue in this case is protected by copyright. As the official version of the state's code, it is in the public domain, even though it contains additional material that might *otherwise* be copyrightable. Georgia is not complying with the due process and democratic public policy concerns underlying the principle of the law as in the public domain. This is an unnecessary situation in today's world, where websites are commonplace and some states have shown that it's possible to provide this information without relying on private publishers who have competing interests.[136]

## IV.    CONCLUSION

It is generally settled that the law is not subject to copyright, and yet, even in a time of proliferation of governmental and legal material online, provided directly by governmental bodies, copyright is used by governments and private entities to restrict access to the law. This is an access-to-justice issue that can be solved with little fuss; many state governments have already done so by adopting UELMA and putting official, authenticated primary law online. This means that an organization like Public.Resource.org would have no reason to copy the material, and if it did copy the material, it would not be subject to an infringement action.

The Public.Resource.org case illustrates the ongoing issues in this area. The case ought to come out in favor of Public.Resource.org because the public policy principles of democracy and due process behind exclusion of the law from copyright protection are extremely important, and the State of Georgia is pushing against such policies by continuing to publish its official code as it does. However, it seems

---

[135] *See generally* GLASSMEYER, *supra* note 3 (surveying the state of access to state primary legal material).
[136] *See supra* note 59 (describing the availability of official and unofficial Minnesota statutes in print), 130–31 (describing the availability of official Minnesota legal information in print and online, without the involvement of a private entity); *see also*, GLASSMEYER, *supra* note 3, at 6 (finding that most, yet not all, of the reviewed online versions of the law were unofficial).

likely that the court will follow precedents holding that annotations to
primary legal material are copyrightable and so find that
Public.Resource.org is infringing by copying and distributing them.
Such a decision would be to the detriment of the public, which needs to
have reliable access to accurate versions of the laws that govern it. To
have otherwise flies in the face of ideals of democracy and due process.

www.ingramcontent.com/pod-product-compliance
Lightning Source LLC
Chambersburg PA
CBHW031049180526
45163CB00002BA/753